— 150 —
TEA HOUSES
YOU NEED
TO VISIT BEFORE
— YOU DIE —

By Léa Teuscher

Lannoo

*The first cup kisses away my thirst,
and my loneliness is quelled by the second.
The third gives insight worthy of ancient scrolls,
and the fourth exiles my troubles.
My body becomes lighter with the fifth,
and the sixth sends word from immortals.
But the seventh – oh the seventh cup –
if I drink you, a wind will hurry my wings
toward the sacred island.*

— Lu Tong (795–835 AD), translated by Christopher Nelson

From the intensely smoky Chinese lapsang souchong to Japanese genmaicha dotted with popped brown rice, from ice-cold American sweet tea to the time-consuming but deliciously foamy West African *ataya*, the world of tea is truly full of wonders. It might have been overshadowed in recent years by the popularity of a certain beverage made from roasted beans (We will avoid using the 'C-word' wherever possible in this book), but tea is still the world's most-consumed beverage after water, and tea-drinking traditions remain strong and are even thriving, with a new generation discovering the beauty of bright-green matcha and fragrant masala chai. In this book, I hope to show you what's brewing, whether it's in a cool café in Istanbul, a historic tea plantation in Darjeeling, an elegant hotel in London or a beautiful Kyoto *ochaya*. Every country has unique teas and different ways of savouring them, whether they are true teas made from the leaves of *Camellia sinensis* or from other plants such as rooibos and yerba maté, and I hope to celebrate as many of them as possible within these pages. I can't decide which one I prefer myself: as a teetotal Londoner, I start my day with a strong cup of Yorkshire Tea and a dash of milk, but I like nothing more than a cold jasmine or lemon iced tea on a hot day, an Earl Grey on a rainy afternoon or a calming verbena in the evening. All in all, I'd say that with an average of about five a day, this book has been fuelled by at least 500 cups of tea. I wish for you to enjoy many more, and discover your new favourite teas and unique blends along the way.

OVERVIEW

ASIA

ANJI
01 **LATITUDE AT BANYAN TREE ANJI** — P.10

BALI
02 **WOODS BALI** — P.12

BANGKOK
03 **SINDHORN KEMPINSKI HOTEL BANGKOK** — P.13
04 **KSANA MATCHA** — P.16

BEIJING
05 **AMAN SUMMER PALACE** — P.17
06 **LAO SHE TEAHOUSE** — P.18
07 **MANDARIN ORIENTAL QIANMEN BEIJING** — P.19

BISEI
08 **STARGAZING TEA HOUSES** — P.22

BUKHARA
09 **SILK ROAD TEA HOUSE** — P.23

CHENGDU
10 **HEMING TEAHOUSE** — P.24

CHIANG MAI
11 **ARAKSA TEA GARDEN** — P.25
12 **MONSOON TEA WAT KET** — P.27

DARJEELING
13 **GLENBURN TEA ESTATE** — P.28

DELHI
14 **THE TEA ROOM FROM BLOSSOM KOCHHAR** — P.29

GOA
15 **CAFE TEA TRUNK** — P.31

HANGZHOU
16 **FOUR SEASONS HOTEL HANGZHOU AT WEST LAKE** — P.32

HANOI
17 **THƯỞNG TRÀ** — P.33

HATTON
18 **CEYLON TEA TRAILS** — P.34

HONG KONG
19 **GREEN GINKO TEA** — P.39
20 **MINGCHA TEA HOUSE** — P.40
21 **TELL CAMELLIA** — P.41

JEJU
22 **OSULLOC TEA MUSEUM** — P.42

KAGOSHIMA
23 **SENGAN-EN MATCHA CAFÉ (SARYO)** — P.43

KANDY
24 **MADULKELLE TEA & ECO LODGE** — P.44

KANGRA
25 **WAH TEA ESTATE** — P.47

KATHMANDU
26 **TEA BAR BY NEPAL TEA COLLECTIVE** — P.48

KUALA LUMPUR
27 **SHAMAN TEAROOM** — P.49

KYOTO
28 **IPPODO TEA** — P.50
29 **THE SHINMONZEN** — P.51

MUMBAI
30 **RAJU KI CHAI** — P.54

MUNNAR
31 **WINDERMERE ESTATE** — P.55

NAOSHIMA
32 **GLASS TEA HOUSE 'MONDRIAN'** — P.56

SEOUL
33 **T.NOMAD** — P.57

SHANGHAI
34 **T9 PREMIUM TEA** — P.59
35 **WAN LING TEA HOUSE** — P.60

SINGAPORE
36 **TEA CHAPTER** — P.62

TAIPEI
37 **CHING SHIN FU CHUAN** — P.64
38 **YAOYUE TEAHOUSE** — P.65

OVERVIEW

	TOKYO	
39	**JUGETSUDO GINZA KABUKIZA**	P.67
40	**SOCHA**	P.68
	XIAMEN	
41	**BASAO TEA**	P.70
	YANGON	
42	**RANGOON TEA HOUSE**	P.73

EUROPE

	AMSTERDAM	
43	**MOYCHAY**	P.74
	ANTWERP	
44	**PINK VELVET**	P.79
	ATHENS	
45	**TO TSAI**	P.80
	BARCELONA	
46	**ČAJ CHAI**	P.81
	BATH	
47	**THE PUMP ROOM**	P.82
	BERLIN	
48	**GARDENS OF THE WORLD**	P.83
49	**PAPER & TEA**	P.84
50	**TADSHIKISCHE TEESTUBE**	P.86
	BRIGHTON	
51	**LEMAN TEA ROOM**	P.87
	COPENHAGEN	
52	**A.C. PERCH'S THEHANDEL**	P.88
	DUBLIN	
53	**WALL & KEOUGH**	P.91
	EDINBURGH	
54	**ROYAL DECK TEAROOM**	P.92
	GENEVA	
55	**PAGES & SIPS**	P.93
	GLASGOW	
56	**MACKINTOSH AT THE WILLOW**	P.94
	HARROGATE	
57	**BETTYS**	P.95

	HELSINKI	
58	**THÉHUONE**	P.96
	ISTANBUL	
59	**CHA'YA MODA**	P.99
60	**DEM MODA**	P.101
61	**MELEZ TEA LAB**	P.102
62	**TARIHI ÇINARALTI**	P.105
	LEICESTER	
63	**CHAIIWALA FOSSE PARK**	P.106
	LIZARD	
64	**HOUSEL BAY HOTEL**	P.108
	LONDON	
65	**CLARIDGE'S**	P.109
66	**FORTNUM & MASON**	P.110
67	**PETERSHAM NURSERIES TEAHOUSE**	P.111
68	**POSTCARD TEAS**	P.113
69	**THE GALLERY AT SKETCH**	P.114
70	**PALM COURT AT THE LANGHAM**	P.118
71	**TING AT THE SHARD**	P.119
72	**TWININGS – THE STRAND**	P.122
	LYON	
73	**LE LUMINARIUM**	P.123
	MADRID	
74	**TEAPOTS**	P.124
	NORDEN	
75	**OSTFRIESISCHES TEEMUSEUM**	P.125
	OSLO	
76	**TO SØSTRE**	P.126
	PARIS	
77	**BETJEMAN & BARTON'S TEA BAR**	P.127
78	**BONTEMPS 'LE JARDIN SECRET'**	P.128
79	**LE NÉLIE**	P.130
80	**MARIAGE FRÈRES**	P.131
81	**YAM'TCHA**	P.134
	PRAGUE	
82	**DOBRÁ ČAJOVNA**	P.135

OVERVIEW

	RIGA	
83	**TĒJO TEA HOUSE**	P.136
	SÃO MIGUEL	
84	**CHALET DA TIA MERCÊS**	P.138
	STOCKHOLM	
85	**CAFÉ SVENSKT TENN**	P.139
	STRASBOURG	
86	**LE THÉ DES MUSES**	P.140
	TOULOUSE	
87	**DU CÔTÉ DE CHEZ SWANN**	P.143
	VIENNA	
88	**HAAS&HAAS**	P.144
	WARSAW	
89	**SAME FUSY**	P.145
	ZÜRICH	
90	**CONFISERIE SPRÜNGLI**	P.147

THE AMERICAS

	ATLANTA	
91	**JUST ADD HONEY**	P.149
	BOGOTÁ	
92	**TEMPLO TÉ**	P.150
	BOSTON	
93	**ABIGAIL'S TEA ROOM & TERRACE**	P.151
	BOULDER	
94	**BOULDER DUSHANBE TEAHOUSE**	P.152
	BRASÍLIA	
95	**CASA DE CHÁ**	P.154
	BUENOS AIRES	
96	**MATEA AROMAS Y SABORES**	P.157
	CHICAGO	
97	**RUSSIAN TEA TIME**	P.158
	DALLAS	
98	**THE FRENCH ROOM AT THE ADOLPHUS**	P.160
	GAIMÁN	
99	**TY GWYN**	P.164
	LAKE LOUISE	
100	**LAKE AGNES TEA HOUSE**	P.165
	LOS ANGELES	
101	**STEEP LA**	P.167
102	**TEA AT SHILOH**	P.168
	MEXICO CITY	
103	**CASA TASSEL**	P.170
	MIAMI	
104	**JOJO TEA**	P.172
	MONTRÉAL	
105	**CARDINAL**	P.173
106	**LA BRUME DANS MES LUNETTES**	P.175
	NEW ORLEANS	
107	**BOTTOM OF THE CUP TEA ROOM**	P.176
	NEW YORK	
108	**BELLOCQ TEA ATELIER**	P.179
109	**CHA-AN TEAHOUSE**	P.182
110	**HARNEY & SONS**	P.185
111	**TÉ COMPANY**	P.186
	PASADENA	
112	**CALLISTO TEA HOUSE**	P.190
	PHILADELPHIA	
113	**THE RANDOM TEA ROOM**	P.191
	PORTLAND	
114	**SMITH TEAMAKER**	P.192
	RIO DE JANEIRO	
115	**COPACABANA BEACH**	P.193
	SAN FRANCISCO	
116	**IMPERIAL TEA COURT**	P.194
117	**JAPANESE TEA GARDEN**	P.196
	SAN JUAN CAPISTRANO	
118	**THE TEA HOUSE ON LOS RIOS**	P.197
	SANTIAGO	
119	**LA TETERÍA**	P.201

OVERVIEW

	TAMPA	
120	**TEBELLA TEA COMPANY**	P.202
	TUCSON	
121	**SEVEN CUPS FINE CHINESE TEAS**	P.206
	VALPARAÍSO	
122	**SKI PORTILLO**	P.207
	VANCOUVER	
123	**THE SECRET GARDEN TEA COMPANY**	P.210

AFRICA AND THE MIDDLE EAST

	ABIDJAN	
124	**AFRICAFÉ**	P.212
	AGAFAY DESERT	
125	**INARA CAMP**	P.213
	AL BUSTAN	
126	**THE ATRIUM TEA LOUNGE AT AL BUSTAN PALACE**	P.214
	AMMAN	
127	**RUMI CAFE**	P.215
	ASWAN	
128	**SOFITEL LEGEND OLD CATARACT HOTEL**	P.216
	BOIS CHÉRI	
129	**DOMAINE DE BOIS CHÉRI**	P.217
	CAIRO	
130	**EL-FISHAWY CAFÉ**	P.218
	CAPE TOWN	
131	**MOUNT NELSON, A BELMOND HOTEL**	P.219
	CITRUSDAL	
132	**CARMIÉN TEA SHOP AT DE TOL FARM DELI**	P.220
	DUBAI	
133	**TANIA'S TEAHOUSE**	P.221

	LIMURU	
134	**KIAMBETHU TEA FARM**	P.223
	MARRAKESH	
135	**CAFÉ GUERRAB**	P.226
136	**LE MENZEH AT LA MAMOUNIA**	P.227
	NAIROBI	
137	**MUTHAIGA TEA COMPANY**	P.228
	TANGIER	
138	**CAFÉ HAFA**	P.229
	THYOLO	
139	**HUNTINGDON HOUSE**	P.230
	TOUBAKOUTA	
140	**LES PALÉTUVIERS**	P.233
	UMHLANGA	
141	**THE PALM COURT AT THE OYSTER BOX**	P.236

OCEANIA

	AUCKLAND	
142	**CHAPTER BOOK & TEA SHOP**	P.238
	HAMILTON	
143	**ZEALONG TEA ROOM**	P.239
	MELBOURNE	
144	**OXI TEA ROOM**	P.242
145	**THE TEA ROOMS 1892**	P.243
	PERTH	
146	**CAPE ARID ROOMS**	P.245
	SYDNEY	
147	**G&TEA AT THE STAR**	P.246
148	**GUNNERS' BARRACKS**	P.248
149	**STRANGERS' RESTAURANT**	P.250
150	**WHITE RABBIT GALLERY TEA HOUSE**	P.251

ASIA　　　　　　　　　ANJI

01　LATITUDE AT BANYAN TREE ANJI

Baimu Nong, Baishuiwan Village, Tianhuangping, Anji, Huzhou, Zhejiang, China

TO VISIT BEFORE YOU DIE BECAUSE

Savour a cup of rare Anji white tea from a rooftop lounge offering views of Zhejiang's tea gardens and bamboo forests.

Located near Lingfeng Mountain, Banyan Tree Anji is about an hour's drive from Hangzhou, famous for its West Lake and its Longjing, or 'dragon well', tea. A popular weekend retreat, it's a peaceful space from which to explore the region, which is known for its amazing teas, including Anji white tea. Rich in amino acids, the tea takes its name from the jade-white colour of its leaves during the cold season and is among the rarest and most expensive teas in China. The resort runs tea-picking tours, including visits to the picturesque Huangdu Village and its lush surroundings, which encompass 16.7 hectares of tea gardens, where both Anji white and Longjing teas are grown. The best spot to enjoy a cup of tea is the hotel's Latitude rooftop lounge, which offers stunning views of the mountainous landscape. Its menu features jasmine, Keemun, *da hong pao* and *bi luo chun* teas, while the afternoon tea is seasonal. In the colder months, the menu includes a selection of fruit, such as persimmons, which you can grill at your table.

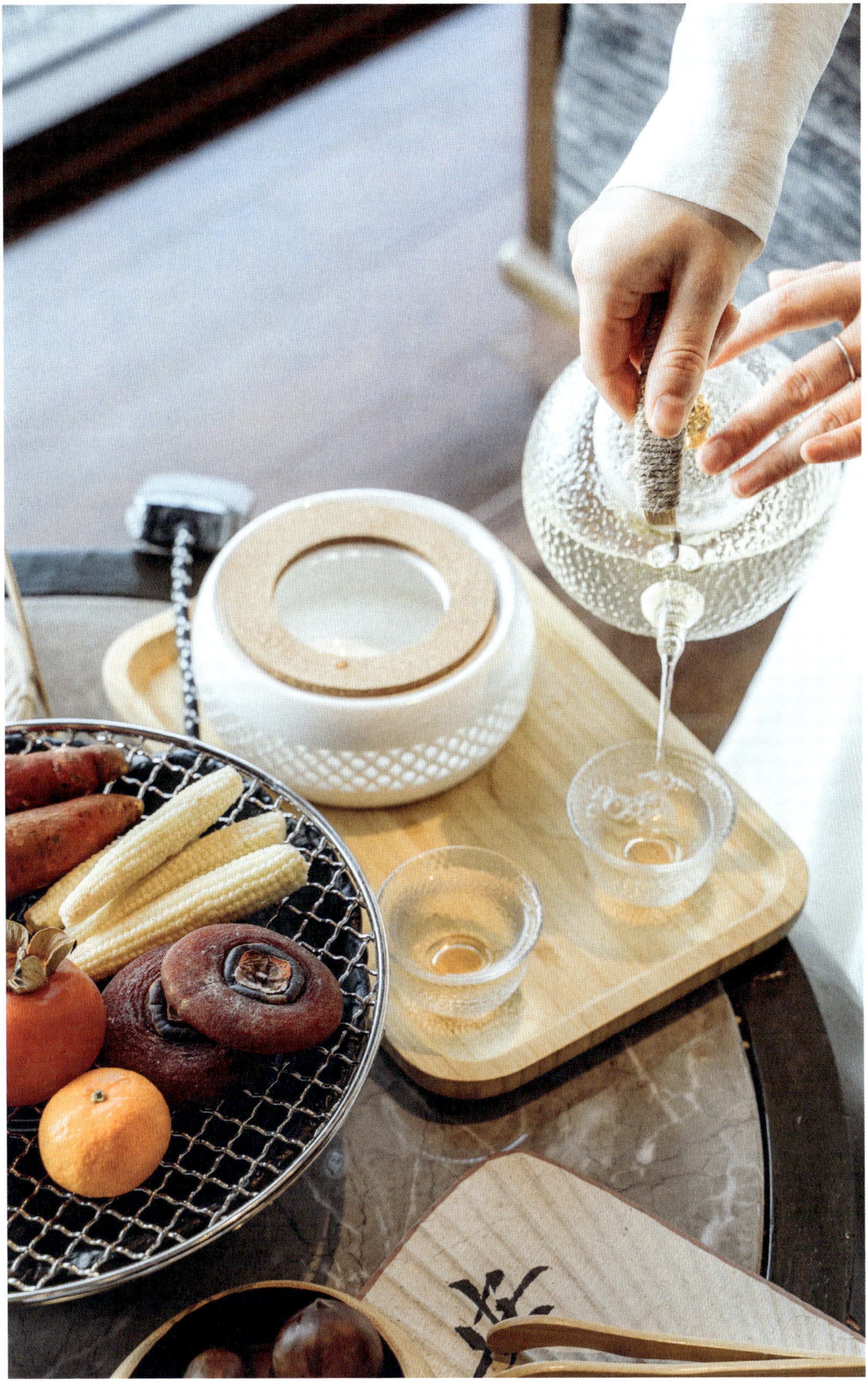

ASIA   BALI

02 WOODS BALI

Jalan Dalem Lingsir No. 8, Pererenan, Kecamatan Mengwi, Kabupaten Badung, Bali, 80351, Indonesia

TO VISIT BEFORE YOU DIE BECAUSE

Enjoy Bali's lush vegetation, healing infusions and delicious dishes at this laid-back spot on the island's western coast.

This greenery-filled restaurant was built around existing trees using reclaimed wood, and the team's love for nature extends to celebrating the power of plants through an unusual tea library. 'We tried to create a warm, cosy décor in the most natural way we could,' explains owner Joshua Criado, whose passion for tea and desire to do something original led him to offer a large selection of medicinal infusions. The bestselling Pandan Panacea, a cooling mix of pandan, pineapple and mint (good for digestion and high in vitamin C), is joined on the menu by the likes of ginseng flower and lotus leaf tea, as well as blends such as the anti-inflammatory Moringa Melody, with lemongrass and globe amaranth flower. Add to this popular jazz nights and a menu featuring *matcha* waffles with green tea jelly, or a seafood platter served on an afternoon tea stand, and you have the perfect place to hang out after a day spent at the beach or exploring Bali's temples and highlands.

ASIA BANGKOK

03 SINDHORN KEMPINSKI HOTEL BANGKOK

80 Soi Ton Son, Lumphini, Pathum Wan, Bangkok, 10330, Thailand

TO VISIT BEFORE YOU DIE BECAUSE

Enjoy a spectacular afternoon tea served on a miniature tree in this greenhouse-inspired tea lounge.

Located close to Bangkok's Lumphini Park and 'green corridor', the Kempinski Hotel is surrounded by lush vegetation. Its lobby, by P49 Deesign, is home to a tea lounge that brings the outdoors in, with ferns, orchids and birds of paradise dotted around a light-filled, double-height space opening onto the garden. Dark rattan furniture is arranged under a vaulted concrete ceiling next to an ornate glass pavilion, and it's all pretty spectacular – but wait until you see the afternoon tea. Seasonal offerings include the Verdant Afternoon Tea, served surrounded by a dry ice mist in eco-friendly containers hanging from a miniature salapee tree. Treats include scones, salmon with pickled onions on toast and salted caramel tacos, while the Tea Master's Selection features four rare teas, from a Sri Sindhorn Assam green tea to a loose-leaf silver needle white tea. You can also try the national drink, Thai iced milk tea. Ronnefeldt teas, such as Peach Blossom *sencha* and organic Pandanus black tea, as well as chrysanthemum infusions, complete the menu.

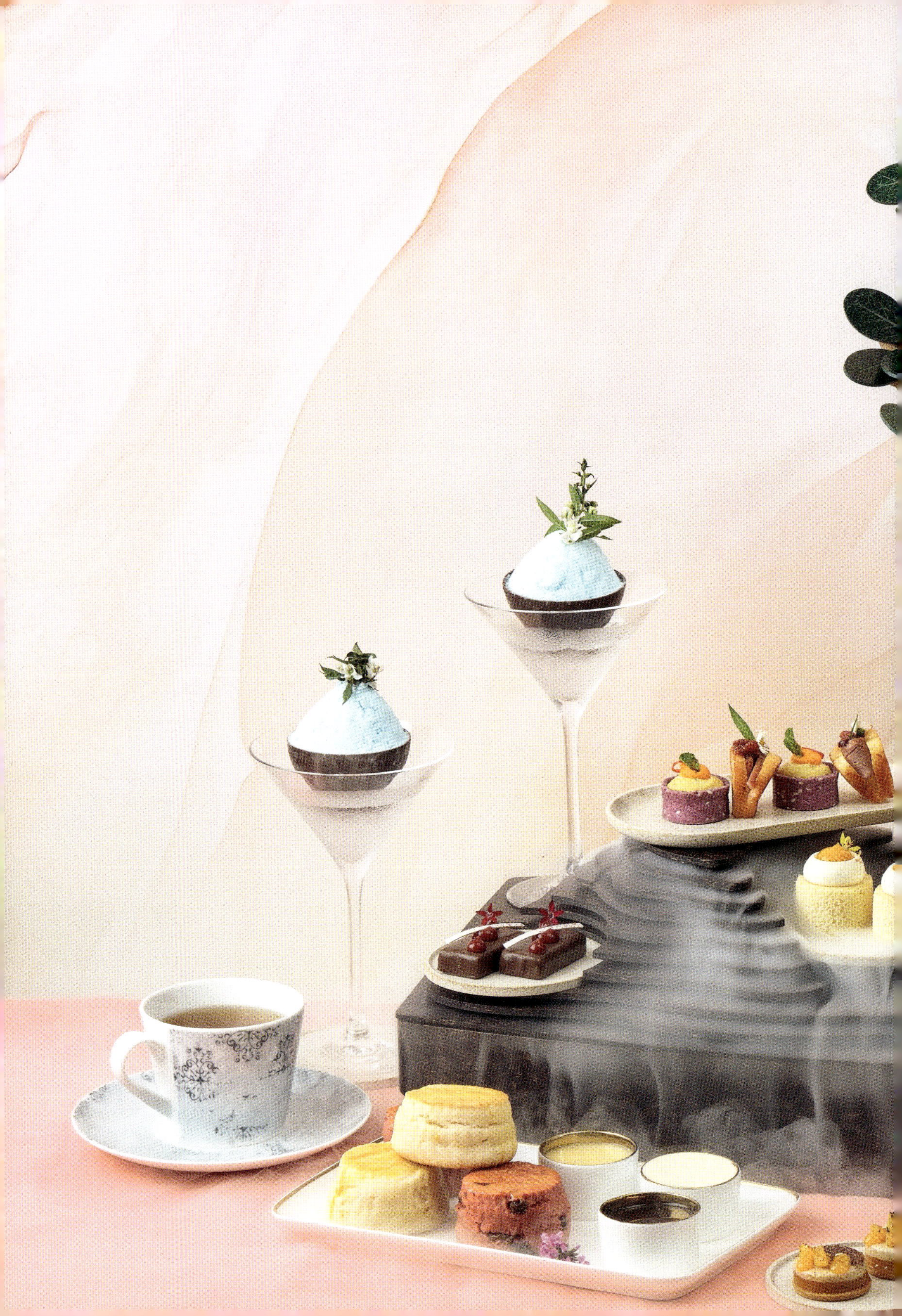

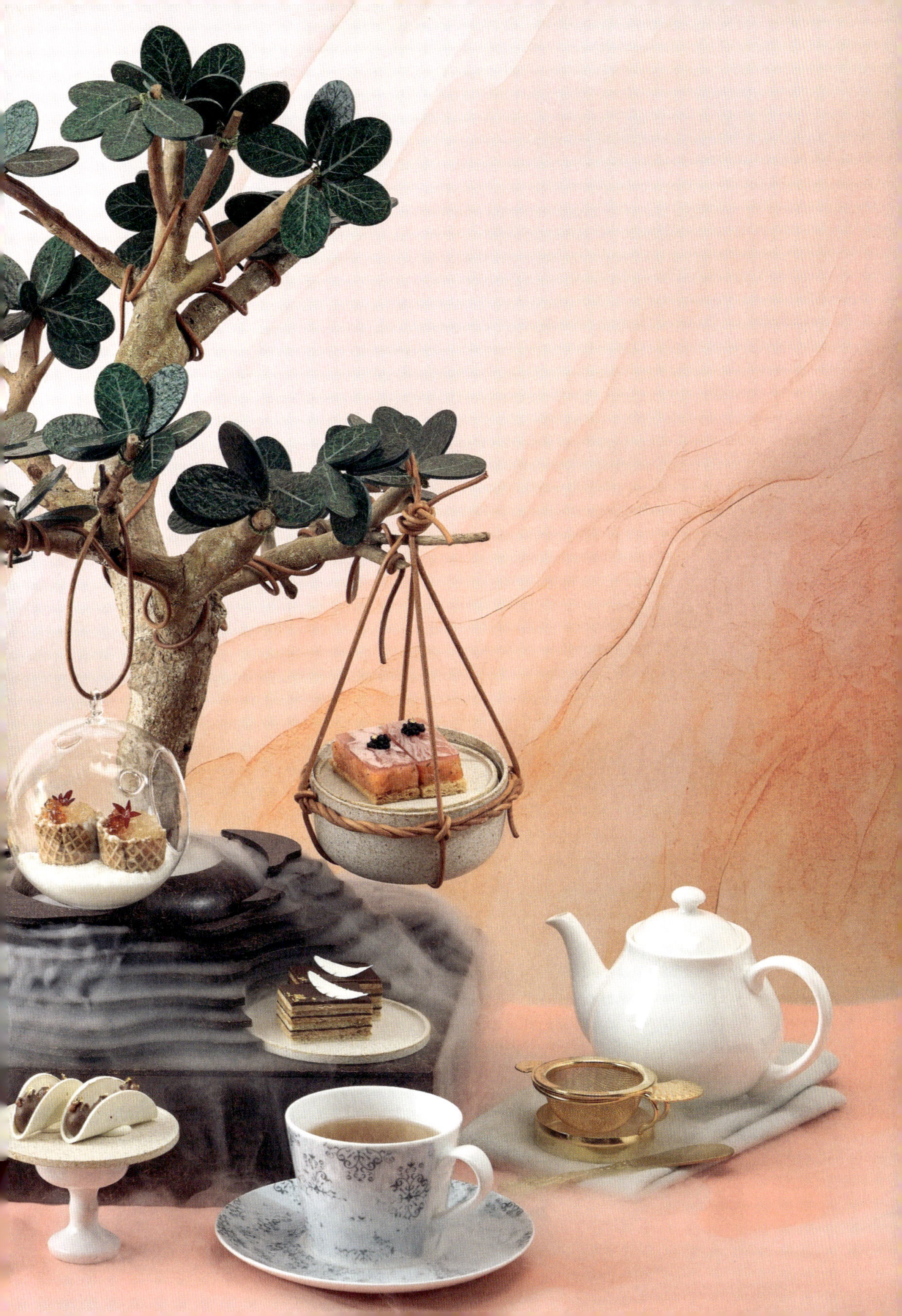

ASIA   BANGKOK

04   KSANA MATCHA

One City Centre building, 548 Phloen Chit Road, Lumphini, Pathum Wan, Bangkok, Thailand

---

TO VISIT BEFORE YOU DIE BECAUSE

This cave-like specialist matcha tea room offers a unique haven of tranquillity away from chaotic central Bangkok.

Thai tea – black tea mixed with condensed milk – sets itself apart from other South Asian milk teas with its bright-orange colour. But here at Ksana Matcha in cosmopolitan Pathum Wan, it's another tea with a bold hue that is the star of the show: matcha. Seen 'as a medium for fostering mindfulness, with its roots deeply intertwined with monk meditation', the powdered green tea is served here on simple wooden tables in a cocooning white cave designed by local practice JUTI architects. Ksana Matcha works closely with Japanese heritage farms in Uji and collaborates with cutting-edge tea estates in Shizuoka to source the finest-quality matcha and select only the finest tea leaves. Its four teas are Coastal Breeze, with umami flavours that evoke the fresh serenity of a coastal morning; Silenced Highland, with nutty and malty notes; Bitter Rainforest, which is bold and intense; and Smoky Peaks, a *hōjicha* with a hint of hickory. Also on the menu are traditional Japanese *wagashi* sweets, such as yuzu and yokan jelly.

ASIA BEIJING

05 AMAN SUMMER PALACE

1 Gongmenqian Street, Summer Palace, Haidian Qu, Beijing Shi, 100091, China

---

TO VISIT BEFORE YOU DIE BECAUSE

This is an afternoon tea fit for an empress, served in the stunning UNESCO-listed surroundings of Beijing's Summer Palace.

Drinking tea in China is a daily activity, fuelled by refilling flasks throughout the day (there are even free hot water taps in train stations) or buying a cold bottle of jasmine tea from the local shop. But here at Aman Summer Palace, tea drinking is elevated to something completely out of the ordinary. Just steps away from the Summer Palace's East Gate, in a tranquil courtyard with a lotus pond filled with koi and surrounded by ancient willow trees, you can enjoy a luxurious afternoon tea while admiring the colourful pavilions that once welcomed the Empress Dowager Cixi's guests. Facing the Summer Palace's Grand Theatre, the Reflection Pavilion offers treats such as seasonal fruit tarts and cream-filled éclairs, as well as matcha *mochi* cake and savouries such as crab focaccia. Fine teas include souchong and the famous Xihu Longjing tea. Speaking of which, there is also a beautiful Aman hotel in Hangzhou, Amanfayun, surrounded by the city's famed Longjing tea plantations.

aman.com +86 1 059 879 999

ASIA　　　　　　　　　　　　　BEIJING

06　LAO SHE TEAHOUSE

3 Qianmen West Street, Xuanwu District, Beijing, China

TO VISIT
BEFORE YOU DIE
BECAUSE

Experience tea drinking Beijing-style, with a full programme of entertainment, at one of the city's landmark teahouses.

For many Westerners, the word 'teahouse' inspires thoughts of a zen space with hushed conversations. But for Beijingers, it's a whole different story. In the Chinese capital, teahouses are a place for people to gossip, play mahjong and discuss politics while enjoying tea and perhaps even a kung fu show or a comedy act. These are lively places with huge dining rooms, and the most famous one of them all is the Lao She Teahouse, named after the writer Lao She's well-known play *Teahouse*. Skip the second-floor Si Heo Teahouse and its private tea pavilions, and instead go for a musical afternoon or evening performance in the main halls. The ticket includes tea (served in a traditional cup with a lid, by waiters in traditional *qipao* and Tang jackets), and there are snacks such as sunflower seeds, pistachios and *zilaibai* mooncakes. Another option is to enjoy the famously cheap 'big bowl' of jasmine oolong, served at the entrance during the day – a remnant of how the drink was sold at roadside stands at the turn of the 20th century.

laosheteahouse.com

ASIA — BEIJING

07 MANDARIN ORIENTAL QIANMEN BEIJING

No. 1, Caochang Alley 10, Dongcheng District, Beijing, 100005, China

TO VISIT BEFORE YOU DIE BECAUSE

Reconnect with your inner self in the tranquil surroundings of this courtyard haven in the heart of the bustling Chinese capital.

Ever since the first century, when Shennong recorded the stimulating properties of the tea as giving 'joy to the body and sparkle to the eyes', tea has been part of healing and calming rituals. Here at the Mandarin Oriental Qianmen Beijing, next to the Temple of Heaven, it forms part of the hotel's spa offering. After enjoying the spa treatment or personalised healing classes, guests are welcomed into the peaceful Tea House, which offers space for inner contemplation and refined tea ceremonies. An aesthetic, meditative ritual, the Chinese *gong fu cha* ('making tea the right way') involves precise gestures and specific teaware, as well as meticulous attention to the details, from prewarming the vessels to enjoying many rounds of the same tea, each brew slightly different from the others. You could also simply visit the serene courtyard of the hotel's Maple Lounge, and enjoy the finest traditionally served Chinese and Oriental teas, alongside an exquisite afternoon tea featuring Amur caviar, smoked pepper steak, black sesame jasmine mousse and oolong osmanthus profiteroles.

mandarinoriental.com/beijing/qianmen +86 1 085 928 888

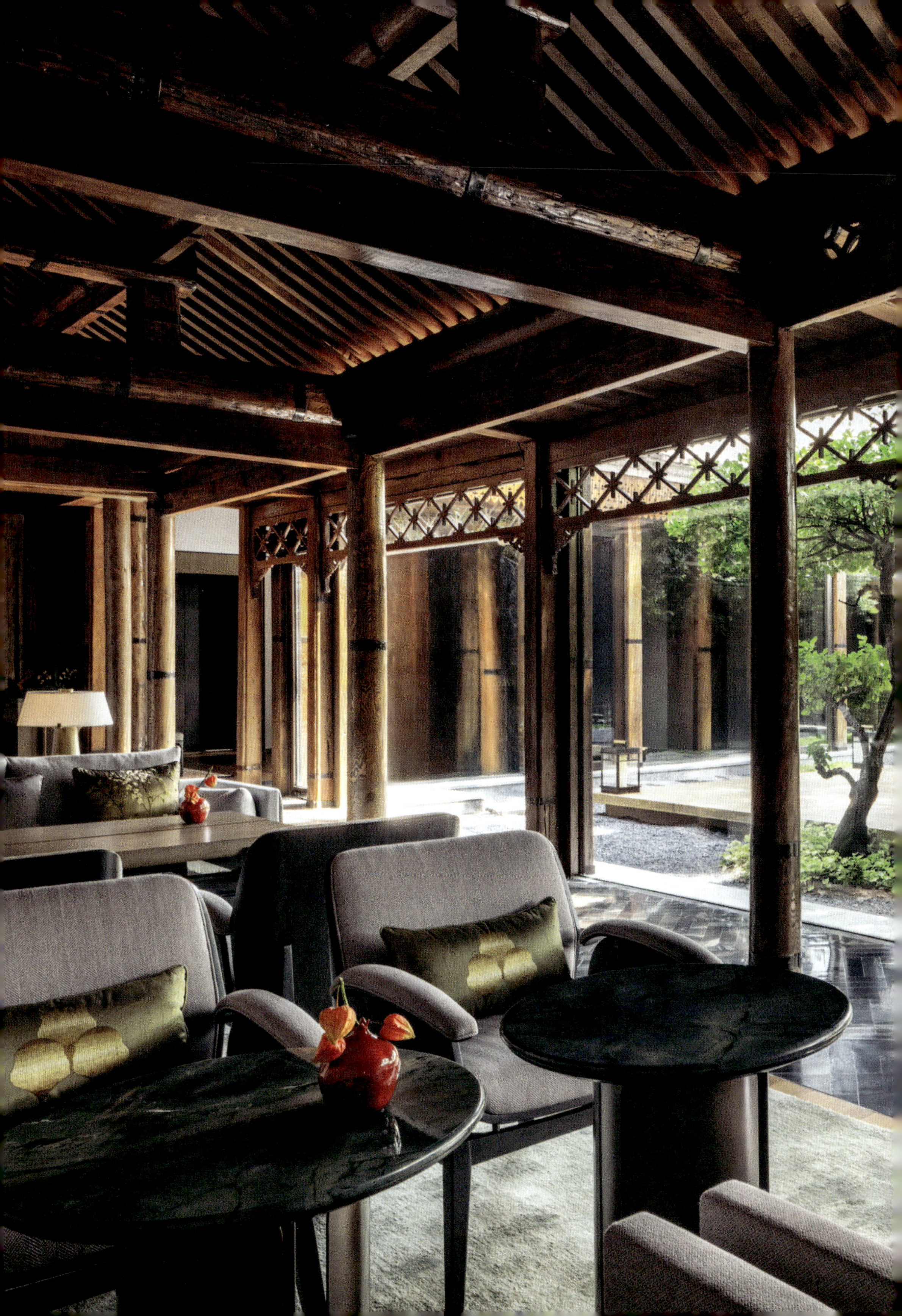

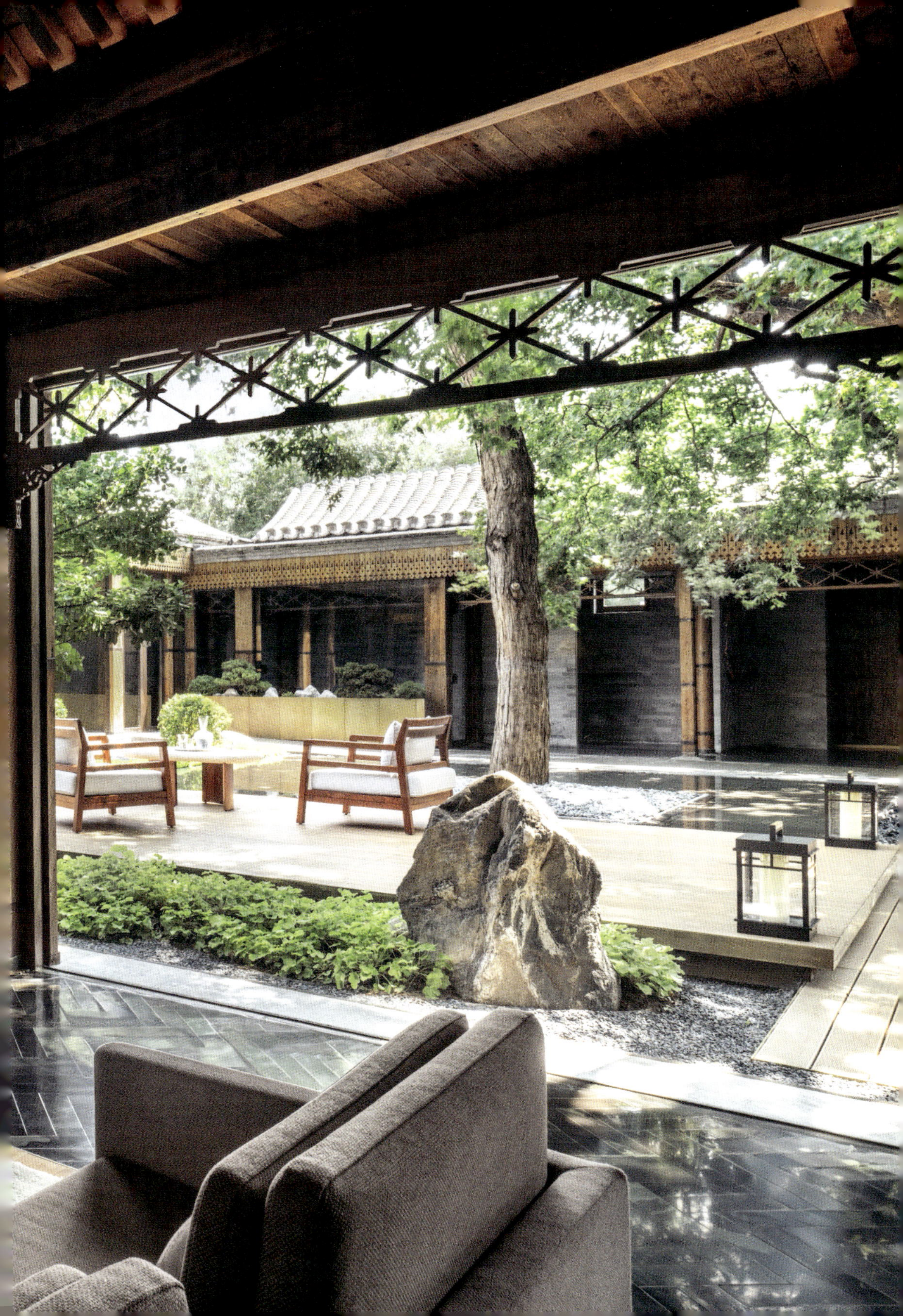

08 STARGAZING TEA HOUSES

Biseichō Miyama, 5007 Biseichō Miyama, Ibara, Okayama 714-1406, Japan

TO VISIT BEFORE YOU DIE BECAUSE

Wonder at the beauty of the Milky Way with a cup of green tea at this constellation of contemporary teahouses.

The small town of Bisei on Honshu island was the first certified International Dark Sky Community in all of Asia – fittingly, since its name means 'beautiful stars'. It is also said to be the birthplace of Eisai, a Buddhist priest credited with introducing green tea to Japan. Combining these two strands are a cluster of geometric teahouses, designed by Moriyuki Ochiai Architects for local cultural organisation ir.bisei. Located near the Bisei Astronomical Observatory, the project comprises 16 tea rooms that aim to 'connect people to the stars and nature'. Painted in bold colours, each pod is pierced with polygonal openings from which to observe the surrounding rolling hills and starry sky. 'Mirrors placed on the exterior walls also reflect the ever-changing environment, like the water surface of rice paddies scattered across Bisei,' explain the architects. The galaxy of tea rooms is used for events throughout the year, as well as the local astronomy and tea ceremony clubs. When visiting, make sure to try *mimasaka bancha*, a local sun-dried tea with a flavour similar to hōjicha.

ASIA BUKHARA

09 SILK ROAD TEA HOUSE

Khakikat Street, Bukhara, Bukhara Region, Uzbekistan

TO VISIT BEFORE YOU DIE BECAUSE

Try spiced teas and local sweets at this family-owned *choyxona*, near the domed bazaars of old Bukhara.

The Silk Road brought tea, silk and spices to Europe but was in fact a series of many different paths taken by merchants to bring luxury goods from the East to their markets in the West. One of these paths was the Northeastern Tea Road weaving through central Asia, a region still famous today for its welcoming teahouses. Take a break from the hot busy streets of old Bukhara in one of them, the Silk Road Tea House. Built of local pale bricks and decked with ornate carpets and colourful textiles, it features intricately carved wooden furniture as well as interesting house teas. Uzbekistan's national drink is plain green tea, but here you can try spiced teas (the founder is also a spice trader, whose family has been in the trade for over 600 years) such as the Spice & Herbs tea, with cardamom, cinnamon, cloves, star anise, mint, oregano and bergamot. Served in the country's celebrated blue-and-white Pahta porcelain tableware, all come with free refills and are served with Eastern sweets such as sesame and almond bites.

ASIA   CHENGDU

10   HEMING TEAHOUSE

Renmin Park, 12 Shaocheng Road, Chengdu, Sichuan, China

TO VISIT BEFORE YOU DIE BECAUSE

This Chengdu landmark is the only teahouse in this book where you can drink tea AND get your ears professionally cleaned.

Chengdu is said to have more teahouses than anywhere in China, and the Sichuan province is home to some of the oldest in the country. In the heart of the city, you will find the People's Park, where locals come to relax, play mahjong and… drink tea. At the lakeside teahouse, you can sip on *zhu ye qing* from nearby Mount Emei, *mao feng* light green tea or jasmine tea. Tea is served by waiters wielding teapots with extra-long spouts into porcelain cups with lids, with a flask of boiling water for top-ups. While away the afternoon by snacking on roasted watermelon seeds, or try the local tradition of ear cleaning. Dating from the Song dynasty, the practice is an elaborate ritual involving an array of specialised tools (those brave enough to try it say it is oddly satisfying). Next door is Zhongshuijiao, where you can try the city's famed pork dumpling in chilli oil. And for a more upscale experience – without the ear cleaning – try the Michelin-starred Mi Xun Teahouse, next to Daci Temple.

ASIA — CHIANG MAI

11 ARAKSA TEA GARDEN

87 Moo 1, Ban Chang, Mae Taeng District, Chiang Mai, 50150, Thailand

TO VISIT BEFORE YOU DIE BECAUSE

Try award-winning teas at the elegant teahouse of a certified organic boutique tea producer in mountainous northern Thailand.

Just an hour's drive from the city of Chiang Mai, on the foothills of Ban Chang forest, the Araksa Tea Garden is a little slice of green paradise. Covering an area of 111 acres, the plantation is one of the oldest in Thailand, and the first in the country to be certified USDA and EU organic for both farm and factory. Left untouched for 15 years, it was revived in 2014 and has garnered multiple prizes for its teas since. Join a tour to walk through the lush tea garden, learn about tea-growing processes and view the factory before enjoying a cup of tea with a traditional Thai snack at the teahouse. Among Araksa's award-winning teas are the Arun white tea, a 100% silver tips tea with fresh and delicate honey notes; Bluefly Tea, with lemongrass and butterfly pea flower; and Araksa Thai Tea, served iced and with milk, of course. The café also serves pad Thai and a spicy chicken salad with fried Araksa tea leaves. Araksa has another tea room in central Bangkok.

araksatea.com — +66 888 097 047

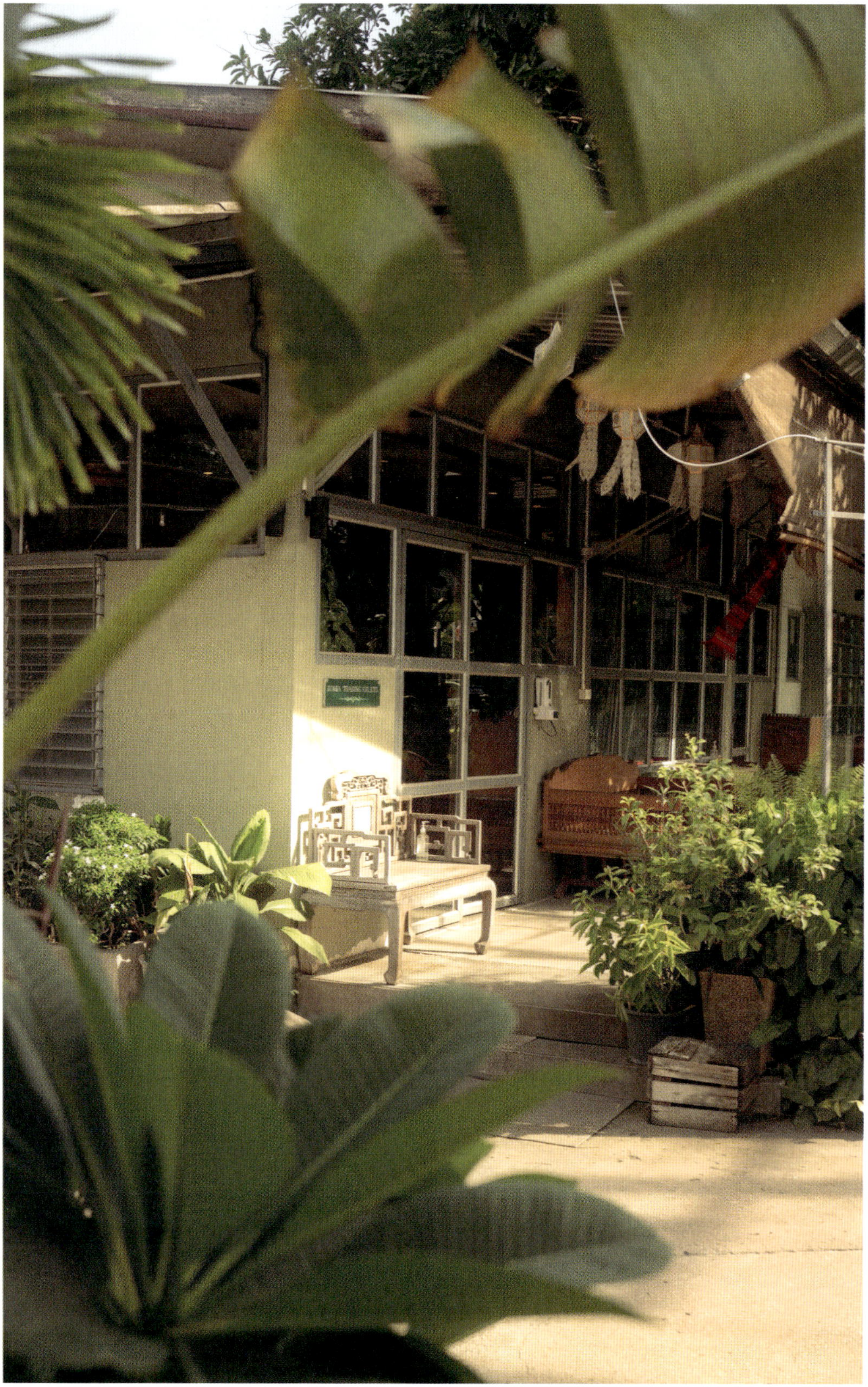

ASIA   CHIANG MAI

12 MONSOON TEA WAT KET

328/3 Charoenrat Road, Wat Ket, Chiang Mai, 50200, Thailand

TO VISIT BEFORE YOU DIE BECAUSE

Choose from over 100 types of tea, all helping to protect the forested mountains of northern Thailand, at this charming Chiang Mai teahouse.

Kenneth Rimdahl founded Monsoon Tea over 12 years ago, after travelling to northern Thailand to source ceramic teapots. There, he discovered delicacies such as fermented tea leaves, and learned that tea here had historically been used for eating rather than drinking. Realising that the endemic tea plant was growing in complete harmony with the rest of the forest, he focused his efforts on forest-friendly tea, grown without pesticides, irrigation or fertilisers. You can taste the result at the company's teahouse, just outside of the old town. Protecting nature and providing locals with a sustainable income, the beautifully packaged range includes blends inspired by local landmarks, such as the Doi Suthep temple, a green tea with strawberry, jasmine, rose, lavender and lotus. The rarest, most exclusive teas are the Jungle Teas, made with completely wild tea and requiring a four-hour trek into the jungle. You can book tea-tasting sessions or come for a bite to eat – the menu includes Lahu fresh tea leaf salad with pork and fried chicken with tea leaf paste.

monsoontea.co.th   +66 53 106 802

ASIA   DARJEELING

13   GLENBURN TEA ESTATE

Near Singritan, Darjeeling, Kambal Tea Garden,
West Bengal, 734101, India

TO VISIT BEFORE YOU DIE BECAUSE

Sip on the Champagne of Indian tea, either at the remote Glenburn Tea Estate in Darjeeling or at the Glenburn Penthouse, a boutique hotel in central Kolkata.

With the mighty Kanchenjunga mountain as a backdrop, the Glenburn Tea Estate near Darjeeling, in the Eastern Himalayas, was started by a Scottish tea company in 1859, before passing into the hands of the tea-planting Prakash family. Now the estate's beautifully renovated bungalow welcomes tourists and offers walking tours of the tea fields and the factory, as well as tasting sessions showcasing Glenburn's range of black, green, oolong and white teas. You can meet the tea pickers and have lunch in a bamboo grove by a sparkling river, before heading back for homemade cakes such as madeleines and a taste of the house's signature tea leaf pakoras – the 'two and a bud' leaf from the tea bush, delicately fried in light tempura batter. Glenburn also has a boutique hotel in Kolkata, which boasts stunning views of the city's sights; more of the estate's fine teas, such as the first-flush White Moonshine; and afternoon treats such as cardamom shortbread.

glenburnteaestate.com   +91 3 322 885 630

ASIA — DELHI

14 THE TEA ROOM FROM BLOSSOM KOCHHAR

No. 1, Hauz Khas Village, Deer Park, Hauz Khas, New Delhi, Delhi, 110016, India

TO VISIT BEFORE YOU DIE BECAUSE

Located in a trendy enclave in south Delhi, the city's first organic café serves great teas and treats in a cosy atmosphere.

Located next to the ruins of a 13th-century fortress, a large city park and a reservoir, Hauz Khas Village is known for its eclectic mix of art galleries, boutiques and vintage shops. On one of its leafy corners, you will find this organic café set up by aromatherapist Blossom Kochhar, just next to her company's Earth to Bottle Coco Store. Surrounded by greenery, the cute tea room is in the perfect location for a company that prides itself on 'being green and derived from nature'. On the menu is a variety of teas, including the bestselling jasmine, lavender and rose white teas; infusions such as lemongrass and hibiscus; and masala chai. There is also a good choice of teas from the great estates of Darjeeling and the Nilgiris. Snacks on offer include crêpes and old-fashioned pancakes, but the main events are the afternoon tea, with cookies and sandwiches; and the cream tea with scones.

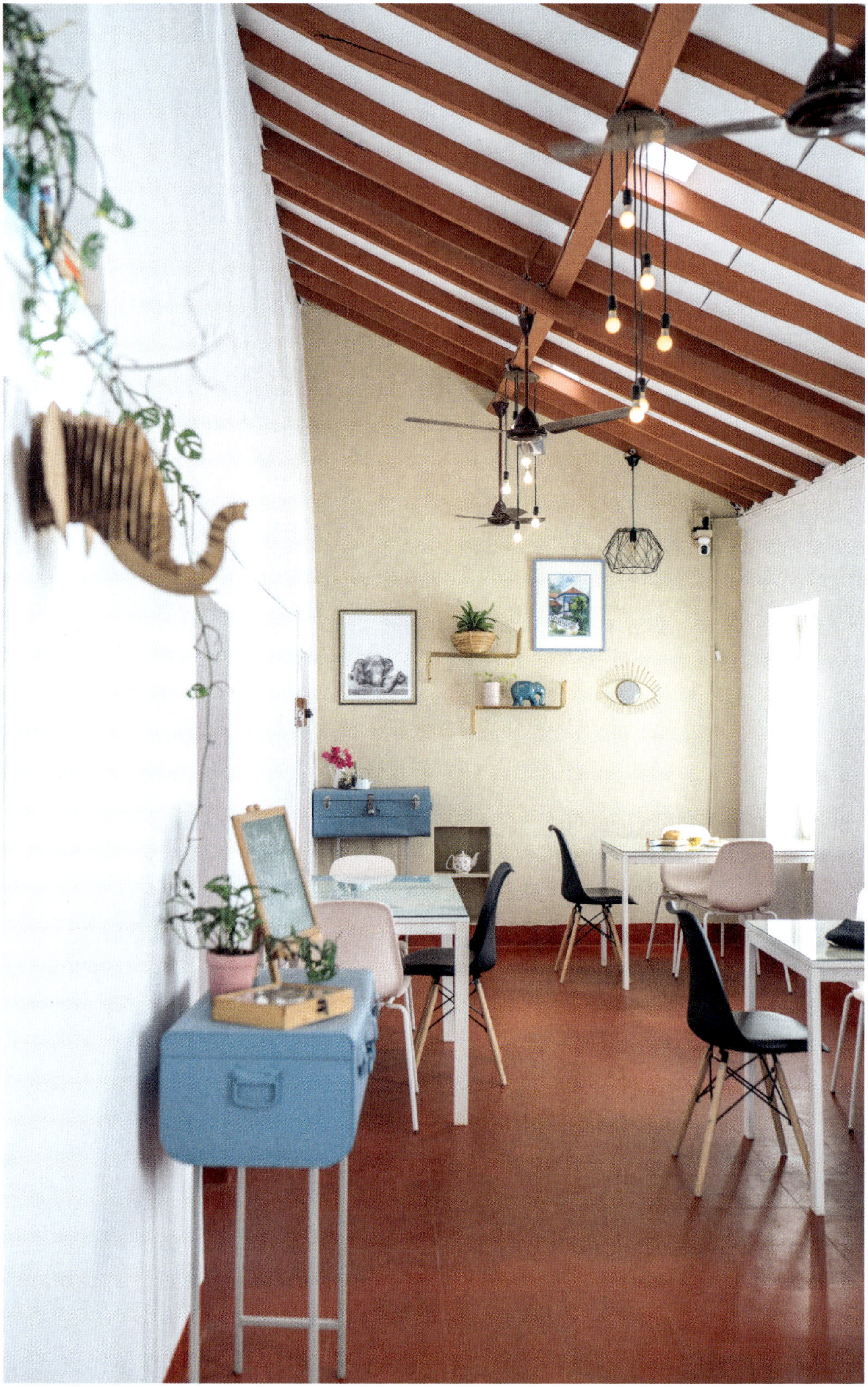

ASIA GOA

15 CAFE TEA TRUNK

162 St. Sebastian Chapel Road, Fontainhas, Altinho, Panaji, Goa, 403001, India

TO VISIT BEFORE YOU DIE BECAUSE

Sample great house blends and a Portuguese high tea at this sunny yellow teahouse in a historic district of Goa.

Cafe Tea Trunk is housed in a century-old building, hidden behind the St. Sebastian Chapel in Goa's quaint Fontainhas district. It is part of a brand founded in 2013 by tea sommelier Snigdha Manchanda, who grew up collecting rare teas from all over the world, storing them in her father's vintage trunk. She's turned her childhood passion into a high-quality label, with big plans to change the status quo in India, where around 90% of the country's quality tea gets exported, repackaged and sold back in Indian supermarkets. At this lovely café, you can taste some of the blends she has spent years researching, including the bestselling Marigold Green Tea, infused with marigold and lemongrass, and Saffron Kahwa Green Tea, a blend of saffron, rose, almonds and cardamom. You can also order a Goan-Portuguese high tea, which celebrates Goa's multicultural heritage with dishes such as prawn *rissóis* and *bolo de laranja* (orange cake). Manchanda also leads tea workshops, including a tea-blending basics masterclass, where you can make a personalised gift for the tea lover in your life.

ASIA HANGZHOU

16 FOUR SEASONS HOTEL HANGZHOU AT WEST LAKE

5 Lingyin Road, Xihu District, Hangzhou, Zhejiang, 310013, China

TO VISIT
BEFORE YOU DIE
BECAUSE

Board a traditional wooden boat and enjoy a cup of famous Longjing tea on the way to this lakeside hotel in beautiful Hangzhou.

The best way to arrive at the Four Seasons West Lake hotel is a boat ride on the city's famous lake, the subject of hundreds of Chinese poems since the Tang dynasty. You'll pass lakeside pavilions and water lilies while sipping on a cup of Longjing tea, also known as 'dragon well'. It's the region's most famous export and at the top of the list of China's 10 most famous teas. 'Tea is drunk to forget the din of the world,' as scholar Tian Yiheng once wrote, so you will be all relaxed when arriving at the hotel. Surrounded by landscaped gardens with a bamboo forest, ponds and secluded glades, it's the perfect base to explore the Longjing tea plantations just up the road. Book a tour to go tea picking, or explore the little teahouses and eateries dotted in the area, before heading back to the hotel's Michelin-starred restaurant. Chef Wang Yong makes the most of local ingredients, with dishes including a Longjing tea crème brûlée. Come in March and April for the freshest teas.

fourseasons.com/hangzhou +86 57 188 298 888

ASIA HANOI

17 THƯỞNG TRÀ

2 Tông Đản Phòng 301, Tập Thể, Hanoi, 100000, Vietnam

TO VISIT BEFORE YOU DIE BECAUSE

A little urban oasis in central Hanoi, this tea room serves over a hundred different teas in a unique, atmospheric setting.

Hidden away on the third floor of an old apartment building on Hanoi's Tong Dan Street, this wonderful teahouse was founded in 2010 by tea artisan Nguyễn Việt Bắc. On its menu are over a hundred teas, including the finest Vietnamese teas. With the team's expert guidance, you can choose one of them depending 'on your preference, your health or even the weather'. Sit on the little plant-filled balcony to take in the view of scooters and cyclos whizzing by on the leafy street, and sample teas such as gentle Luc Tea or earthy Hoang Son Mao Phong. 'The Vietnamese teas you should try at our teahouse,' says owner Linh Lê Ngọc, 'are Bach Hac, a very popular green tea from Tân Cương, Thái Nguyên, that everyone drinks in Vietnam; thousand-year-old Shan Tuyet teas, found only in the Tay Con Linh mountains; and oolong teas, a speciality of the Bảo Lộc region.' The tea room also offers high-quality teas from China, Japan and Europe, and runs workshops and tea experiences.

facebook.com/thuongtra +84 888 222 991

ASIA   HATTON

18 CEYLON TEA TRAILS

Norwood Estate Bogawantalawa, Hatton, Sri Lanka

TO VISIT
BEFORE YOU DIE
BECAUSE

Drink in the freshest tea and stunning landscapes at these tea planters' bungalows in Sri Lanka's Central Highlands UNESCO World Heritage Site.

Conceived by the Fernando family, founder of local tea producer Dilmah, and part of Relais & Châteaux, this resort comprises historic tea planters' bungalows perched at an altitude of 1,250 metres in Sri Lanka's Central Highlands. Spread out across Dunkeld Estate, each has a swimming pool and offers either lakeside or tea estate views, as well as access to the historic tea-making facilities. A tour will take you around the factory, explaining what went into creating the perfect cup of Ceylon tea in 1867. Apparently, it involved 'equal parts science, art, sleight of hand, and a spot of luck – and not much has changed since.' There are no set menus, as meals are curated around guests' preferences, but there is a signature culinary experience: a tea-infused dinner celebrating the different flavour profiles of the teas grown in various regions of Sri Lanka. Dishes include Earl Grey-cured fresh salmon, Moroccan Mint tea-crusted lamb cutlet, and vanilla panna cotta with hibiscus tea sauce.

resplendentceylon.com/teatrails   +94 117 745 730

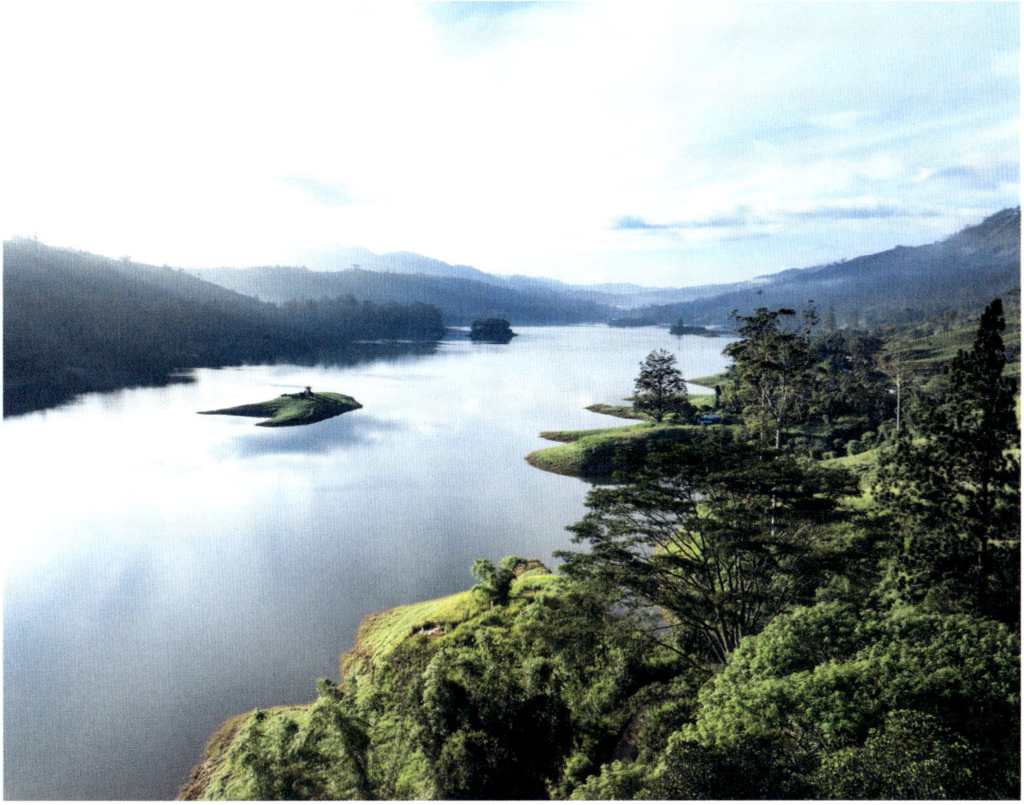

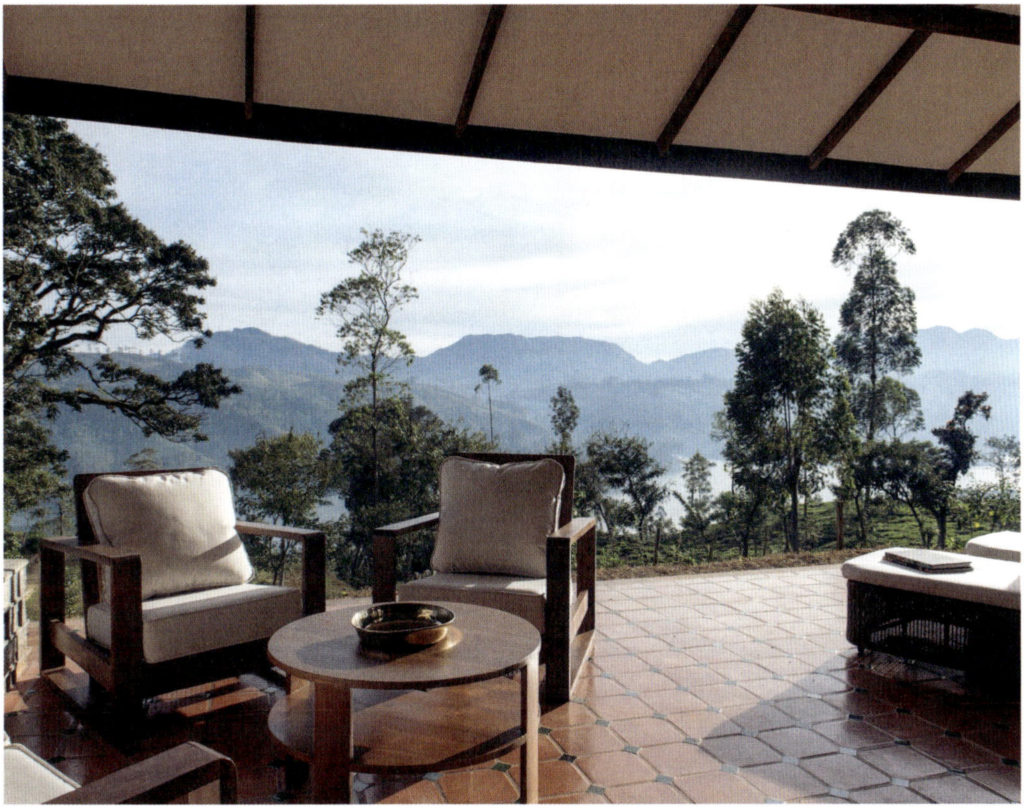

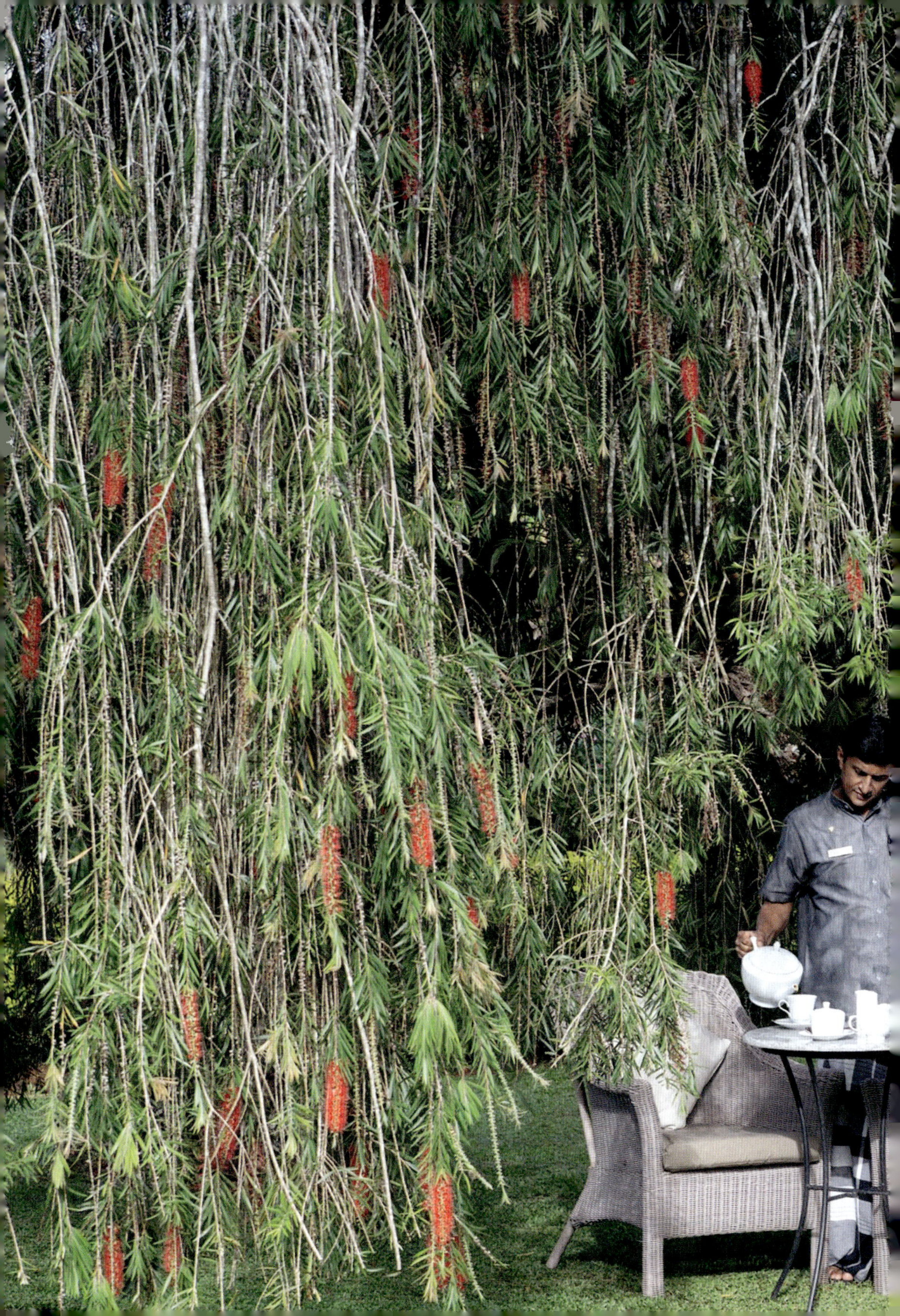

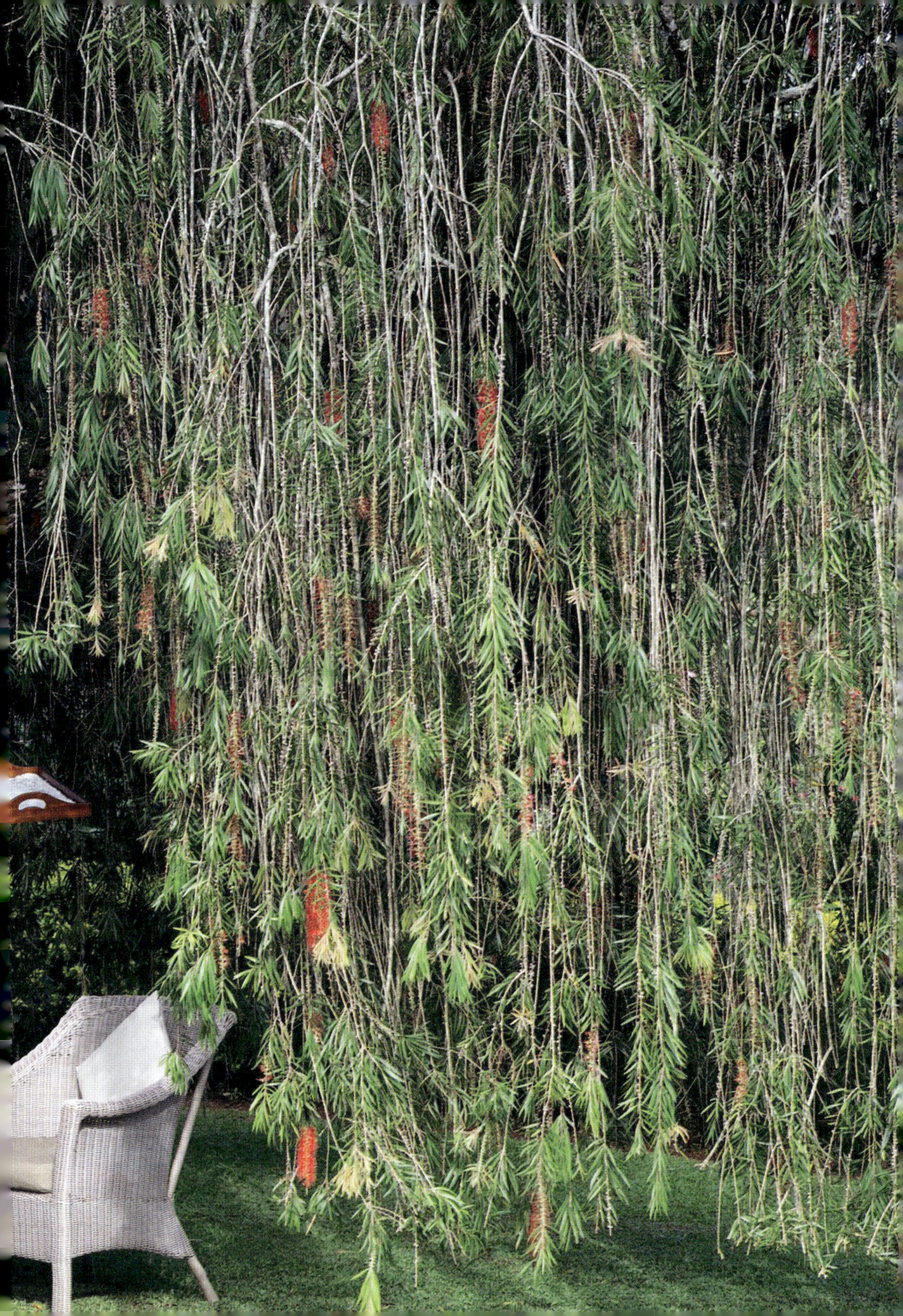

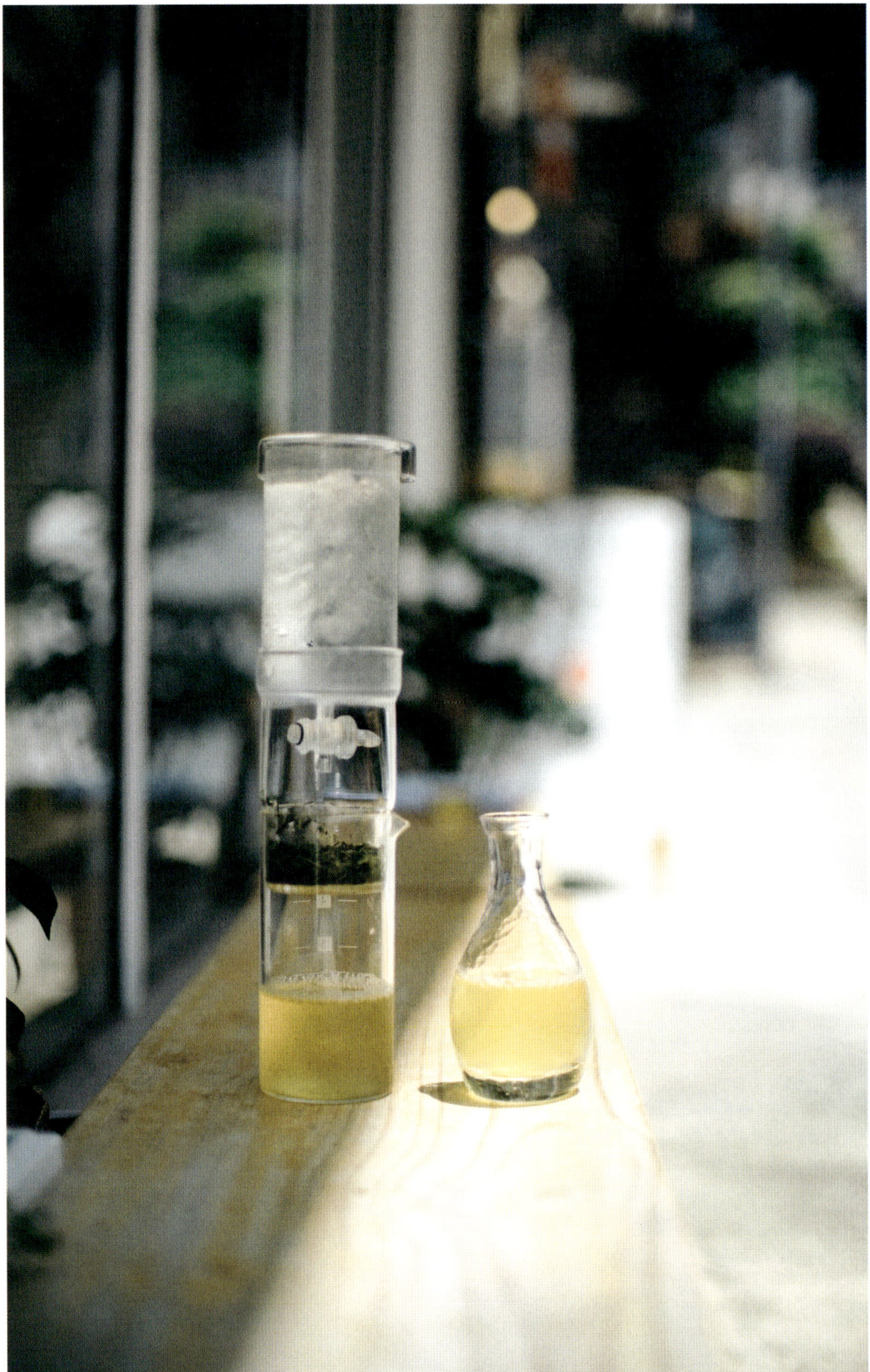

ASIA   HONG KONG

19   GREEN GINKGO TEA

Shop 110, Pacific Place, 88 Queensway, Admiralty, Hong Kong, China

TO VISIT BEFORE YOU DIE BECAUSE

Try a yuenyeung tea coffee or fine oolong at this elegant little tea bar, before heading to the city's Museum of Tea Ware

Revamped by Thomas Heatherwick in 2005, Pacific Place is one of Hong Kong's finest and shiniest shopping malls. Among its luxury shops you will find this small tea bar, specialising in fine teas from China and Japan. Established in 2017, it is popular for its high-quality drinks, including a bestselling matcha made with coconut water, Okinawa Lime green tea, Peach Phoenix oolong and mulberry leaf tea. Make sure to try the tea coffee, called *yuenyeung* or yin-yang in Hong Kong, made with Yunnan coffee beans mixed with roasted *shuisin* oolong tea. Chinese teas are sourced from regions such as Sichuan, Canton and Fujian, while small bites include cookies, a signature matcha ice-cream and Hoshino matcha chocolate. Green Ginkgo Tea also offers 'Teascovery' workshops, a tea subscription service and bespoke blends. If you fancy a stroll, take your drink to the lovely Hong Kong Park next door. The gardens are home to Flagstaff House, the Museum of Tea Ware, where the permanent exhibition traces the history of Chinese tea drinking through stunning vessels and utensils.

greenginkgotea.com   +852 64 086 348

ASIA HONG KONG

20 MINGCHA TEA HOUSE

Unit B2, 15/F, Block B, Fortune Factory Building,
40 Lee Chung Street, Chai Wan, Hong Kong, China

TO VISIT BEFORE YOU DIE BECAUSE

Known for its Jasmine Blossoms flowering tea, this award-winning tea shop and tasting room is a must-try when in Hong Kong.

Run by designer turned entrepreneur Vivian Mak, MingCha was established in 1999 with the aim of creating a friendly environment for people to understand tea. The award-winning tea brand, shop and tasting room has garnered praise for its unique and fun approach to workshops, as well as its patented Jasmine Blossoms Tea. Dubbed 'the only blooming tea that tastes as good as it looks', it is scented with fresh jasmine flowers. Each tea ball is made with green tea buds and young leaves, air-dried lily and thousand day red flowers and is delicious hot or cold. It's such a joy to watch the tea balls unfurl in hot water, with the floral scent rising from the teapot. Other firm favourites include White Peony Supreme white tea, Tanyang Golden Rim black tea (the original English Breakfast tea) and Teguanyin Classic oolong tea. There's a series of workshops to choose from, including one for children, whose curiosity and sensitivity make them the perfect tea tasters. A range of beautiful tea gifts completes the offering.

mingcha.com +852 25 202 116

ASIA HONG KONG

21 TELL CAMELLIA

LG/F, H Code, 45 Pottinger Street, Hong Kong, China

TO VISIT BEFORE YOU DIE BECAUSE

Staffed by passionate bartenders, this Hong Kong bar fuses tea and cocktail culture to dizzying effect.

At first sight, Tell Camellia looks like your standard hip bar, with a moody atmosphere and elaborate cocktails. But the clue is in the name, the tea leaf wallpaper and the matcha whisk-inspired lighting. This place is all about tea, and how to use its fragrant leaves to create inspiring cocktails – or 'teatails', as the friendly team would say. Opened in 2019 by award-winning mixologist Gagan Gurung, the basement bar found instant recognition for its menu full of original drinks, often featuring tea-infused spirits, such as a Ceylon tea gin and a *pu-erh* tea whisky. A customer favourite is the Fat Fat High, which blends the aromatic notes of jasmine and matcha tea with the rich, savoury essence of duck fat and tequila, topped with a dusting of bee pollen and a garnish of amaranth. Also popular is the Not Negroni, featuring 'the rich and earthy notes of hōjicha tea, perfectly balanced by the bittersweet kick of Campari', as well as vermouth, fig leaf and gin.

@tellcamellia

ASIA JEJU

22 OSULLOC TEA MUSEUM

15 Sinhwayeoksa-ro, Andeok-myeon, Seogwipo-si, Jeju-do, South Korea

TO VISIT BEFORE YOU DIE BECAUSE

Set on a tea farm on the volcanic island of Jeju, this stylish tea room serves award-winning Korean teas.

South Korea's Jeju Island is a popular tourist destination, and one of its top sights is this beautiful organic tea farm and museum by Osulloc. The Korean brand started growing tea here in only 1979, after painstakingly transforming the rocky land into tea fields, but it has since won a string of prestigious prizes for its teas, thanks to the area's unique climate, with clouds and fog creating a natural shading effect and improving the colour of the leaves. Among its award-winning teas are Illohyang, a first-flush green tea handpicked in early April, and Sejac, the brand's signature green tea. You can try them at the museum's teahouse, which also serves blended teas, such as Samdayeon Jeju Tangerine, and lots of pretty tea-flavoured treats, such as matcha tiramisu and Jeju green tea cheesecake. Make sure to visit Tea Stone, an experience space where you can take classes as well as see a tea master at work. Osulloc also has teahouses in Seoul, including a flagship location in the Bukchon district.

us.osulloc.com/osulloc-tea-museum +82 647 945 312

ASIA KAGOSHIMA

23 SENGAN-EN MATCHA CAFÉ (SARYO)

9700-1 Yoshino-chō, Kagoshima, 892-0871, Japan

TO VISIT BEFORE YOU DIE BECAUSE

Located on the southwestern tip of Japan, this matcha café serves the region's finest green tea and confectionery.

A samurai's rural retreat surrounded by classic Japanese gardens, Sengan-en Saryo has been in the hands of the Shimadzu family for over 350 years and boasts stunning views of Sakurajima volcano. It is located in Kagoshima, a subtropical region known for its fine green teas, and for being the country's second-largest tea producer. After a tour of the house and grounds, visitors can stop for lunch at the contemporary matcha café, which overlooks a quiet garden. Here, guests are served the finest Kirishima matcha, along with a sweet of their choice: sweet potato; *karukan* (a steamed sweet bun made from grated yam and rice flour); or the house's speciality, a yuzu, gingko nut and mushroom sweet based on the family crest and named Flying Dragon Head. Bestselling desserts include an affogato made by pouring strong matcha over vanilla ice cream and *saryokuma* (polar bear of the teahouse), a cute take on the region's famed *shirokuma* shaved-ice treat. There is also a restaurant and a mochi shop, where you can try the sweet treat loved by the samurai of Satsuma.

sengan en.jp +81 992 471 551

ASIA   KANDY

24   MADULKELLE TEA & ECO LODGE

Madulkelle, Kandy, Sri Lanka

TO VISIT BEFORE YOU DIE BECAUSE

Stay in a tent on an actual tea field in the heart of Sri Lanka, and wake up to a nice cuppa and stunning views of the surrounding mountains.

Despite the bumpy road that leads from Kandy to Madulkelle Tea & Eco Lodge, this place is definitely worth the drive. You will be sleeping in a beautifully appointed tented room, pitched right in the middle of a working tea field that is part of a 25-acre estate dating back to the 1860s. Located 1,000 metres above sea level, the solar-powered resort offers views of the Knuckles Mountain Range, so called because of its shape, which is similar to a clenched fist. After visiting local tea-making facilities – Kandy tea is known for its robust flavour and bright, slightly coppery tone – you can take a dip in the pool and enjoy a local iced black tea with lime, or a tea-based cocktail such as the Camble Cooler. Meals are prepared with care using produce grown in the lodge's own organic garden (which can also be explored), while traditional Sri Lankan rice and curry is served with pol sambol. High tea comes with home-baked cakes, while activities such as yoga, hikes and visiting the nearby waterfalls complete the picture.

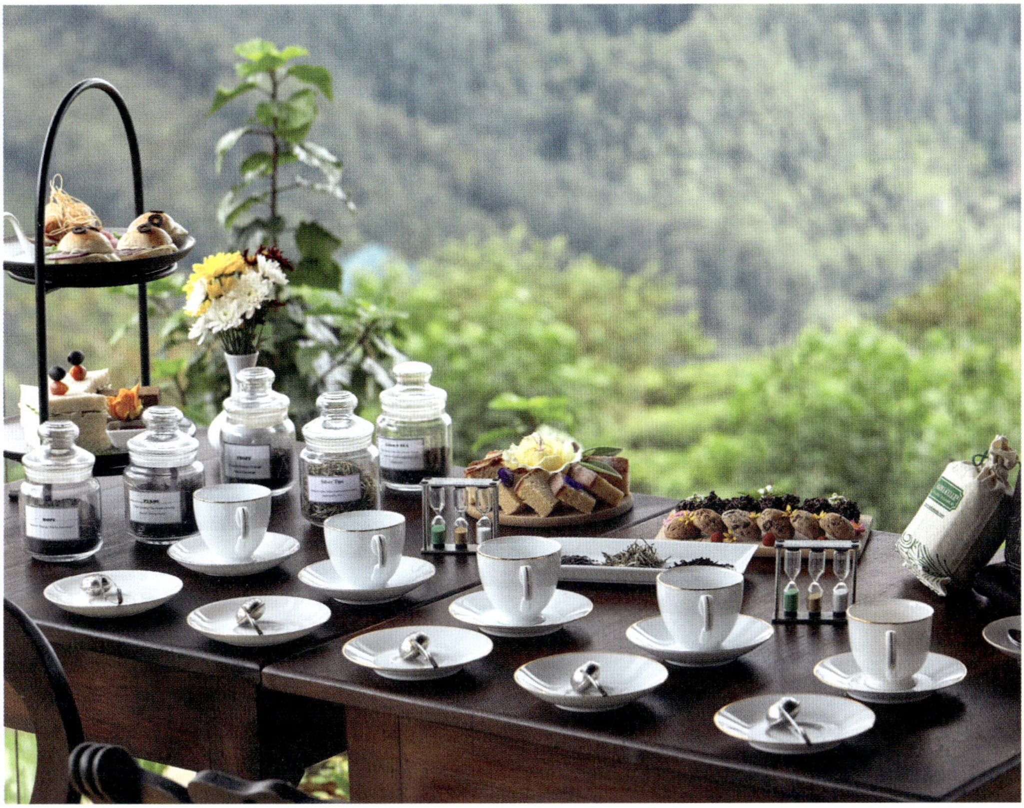

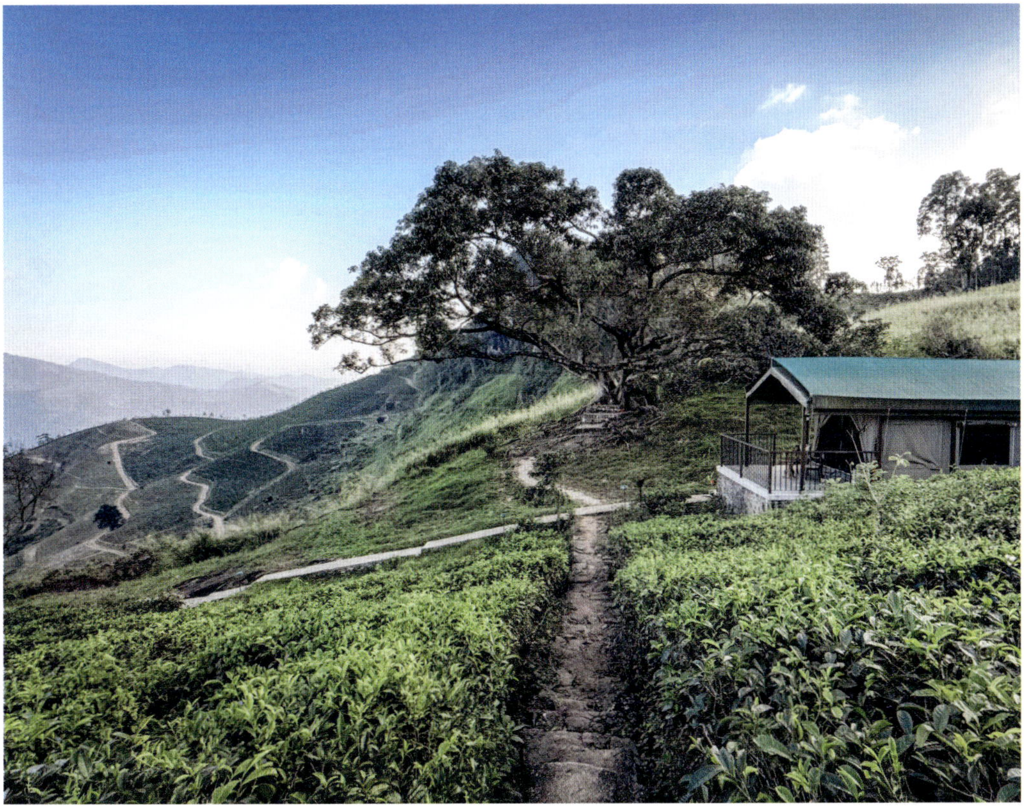

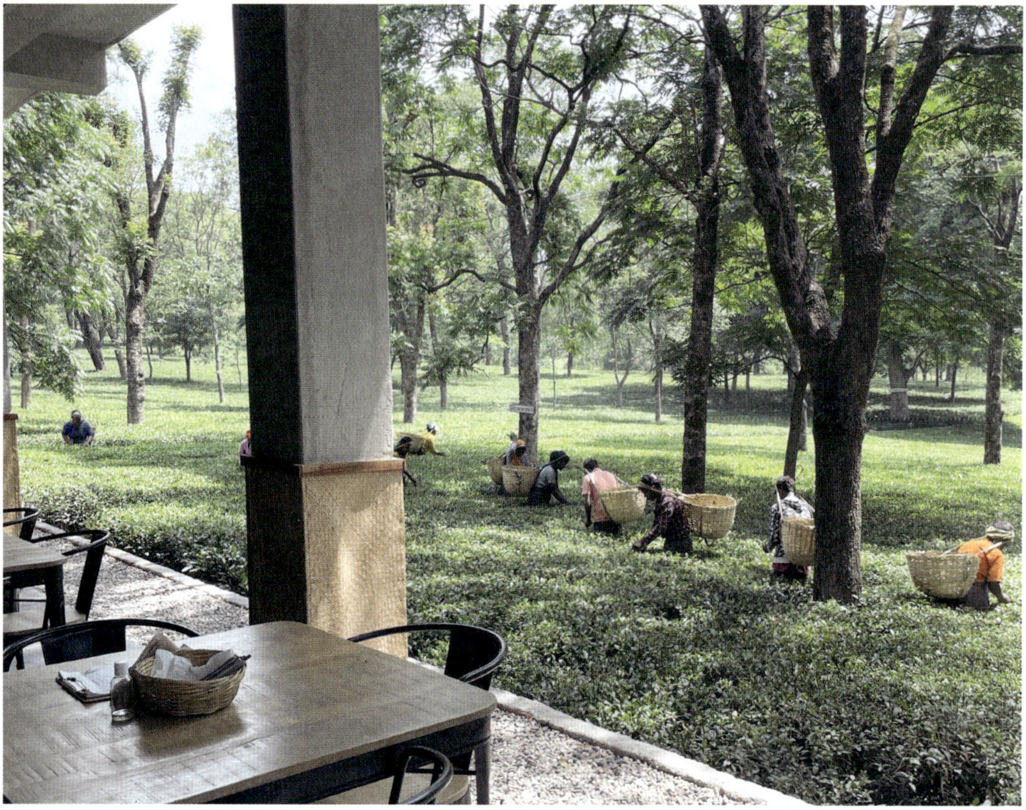

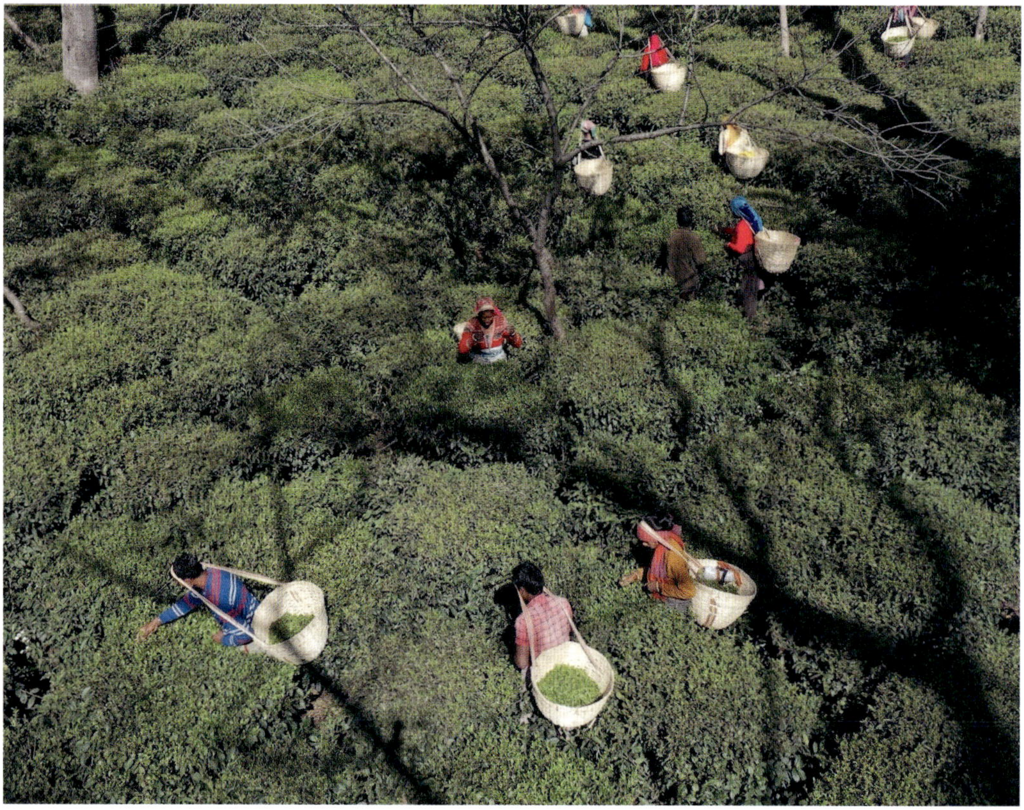

ASIA　　　　　　　　　　　　　　　　KANGRA

25　WAH TEA ESTATE

Panchrukhi Road, Patti, Deogran, Palampur, Himachal Pradesh, 176061, India

TO VISIT BEFORE YOU DIE BECAUSE

This lively tea room and café opens directly onto the tea fields of the Kangra Valley's largest manufacturing tea estate.

Surrounded by snow-capped mountains, this beautiful estate in Palampur certainly has the wow factor – in fact, its name means 'wow' in Urdu, and it comes from one of its past proprietors, the son of the Nawab of Wah in Pakistan. Today, it's looked after by members of the third and fourth generations of the Prakash family, Deepak and Surya. Guests can take a walk amidst the rolling bushes, take part in an in-depth tea estate and factory tour, and enjoy tasting over 25 varieties of tea. The estate's organic teas include the bestselling white peony tea, rose tea and Kashmiri *kahwa* tea, which can be enjoyed on a terrace with benches that hang directly over the tea gardens. There's also plenty of delicious dishes to sample. 'After our visit to the UK, we could not resist adding scones to the menu. They have become one of our specialities, especially since you don't find scones in India easily,' says Surya. 'We also serve kangri dham, a full serving of different curries and rice and rotis unique to this region.'

wahtea.com　　　　　　　　　　　　+91 9 831 017 629

ASIA KATHMANDU

26 TEA BAR BY NEPAL TEA COLLECTIVE

Kathmandu Guest House, Thamel, Saat Ghumti, Kathmandu, 44600, Nepal

TO VISIT BEFORE YOU DIE BECAUSE

Discover Nepal's finest organic teas at this tea bar in the bustling centre of Kathmandu, thanks to its team of expert 'tearistas'.

Founded by Nishchal Banskota in 2016, the Nepal Tea Collective aims to put the spotlight on the Himalayan country's finest organic teas. Located in the capital's central Thamel district, its tea bar is the place to let the friendly staff guide you through a choice of tea flights. Bestselling teas include White Champagne, made from white Prakash tea and served as a cold brew in Champagne glasses, and Kathmandu Cosmos, a masala chai made from black tea from the Kanchanjangha Tea Estate. In the evenings, you can listen to folk musicians playing instrumental songs and sip on a cup of award-winning Kumari Gold, a black tea with caramel, baked fruit and honey flavours. The company also runs immersive holidays in Nepal's Tea Gardens. Guided by the passionate founders, these include visits to four family farms and factories; sessions where you can learn to pluck, craft and taste your own tea; cookery workshops; a stay in a sky dome; and unlimited cups of premium Nepali tea throughout the trip.

nepalteacollective.com +977 9 802 807 667

ASIA   KUALA LUMPUR

27 SHAMAN TEAROOM

Multiple locations, Kuala Lumpur, Malaysia

TO VISIT BEFORE YOU DIE BECAUSE

Follow this artists' collective online to find out where next to catch their intriguing mix of contemporary art, tea and sound.

Malaysia is famous for its *teh tarik*, a frothy, sweet milk tea, and some say the best one to be found is at Mansion Tea Stall in Kuala Lumpur. But thanks to artists' collective Shaman Tearoom, led by Aiwei Foo and Kent Lee, the capital is also home to a series of very unusual ways to enjoy tea. The pair focuses on the integration of art, tea, sound and sensory experiences, and their work has been exhibited in museums and tea rooms all over Asia. Their Tea & Frequency series, for example, centres on tea and sound, 'aiming to align us with our immediate surroundings through mindfulness', and is guided by a tea ceremony, accompanied by a minimal soundscape, healing ambient music and vocal toning. Shaman Tearoom also runs live performances, which typically incorporate music composition, acoustic instruments, spoken word, and vocal improvisation with a digital audio workstation (DAW), culminating in a tea ceremony.

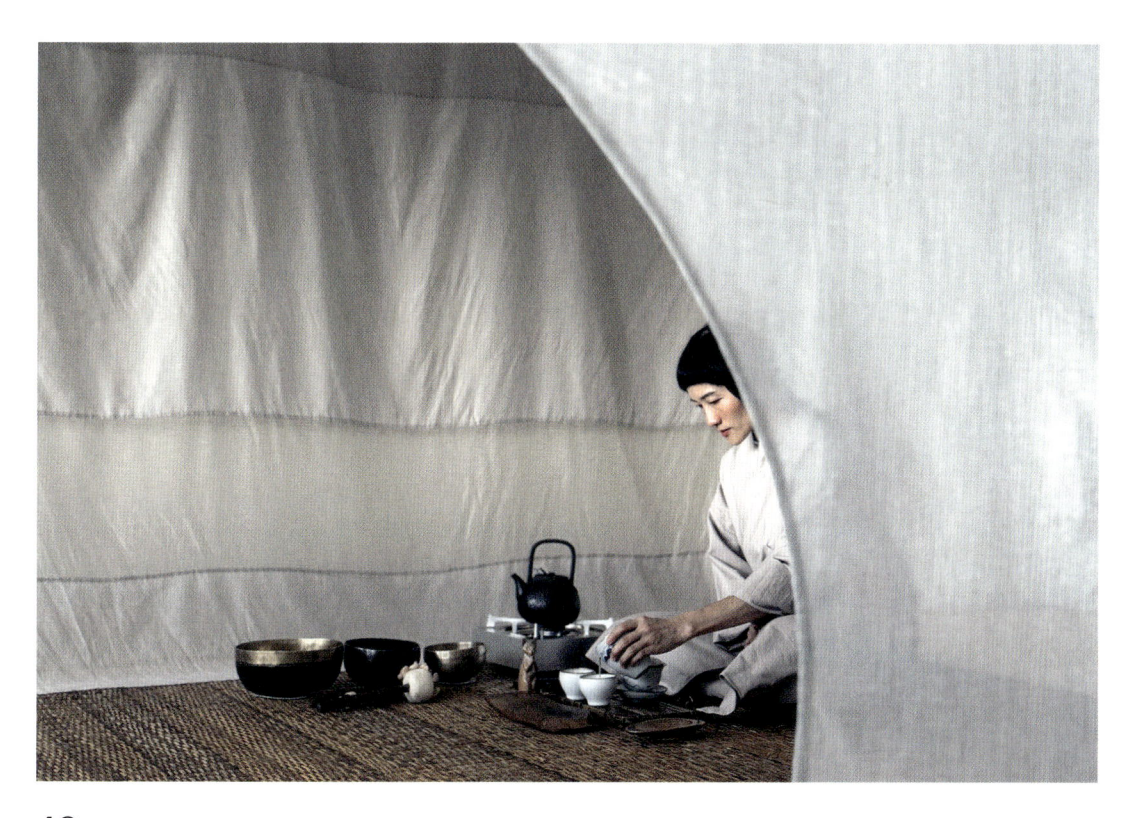

@shamantearoom

ASIA　　　　　　　　　　　　KYOTO

28　IPPODO TEA

52 Tokiwagi-cho, Nakagyo-ku, Kyoto, 604-0915, Japan

TO VISIT BEFORE YOU DIE BECAUSE

This historic teahouse in central Kyoto is the place to sample a great variety of high-quality green teas and pretty sweets.

Just south of Kyoto's Imperial Palace is a two-storey building that houses the boutique and tea room of the illustrious family-run tea company Ippodo, founded in 1717 as Omiya, and named Ippodo in 1846 by Prince Yamashina, who loved their teas. Admire the old storefront, pass through the *noren* curtains and you will find a large shop counter with tea jars and a washi menu hanging above it. To the right is the tea room, which comprises three seating areas, while upstairs are rooms for workshops and classes. If you would like to learn how to prepare the tea, let the staff know when ordering, and they will guide you through the process. The traditional method involves whisking the matcha and hot water in a bowl before topping it up with more water and pouring it into a cup. The menu features teas exclusive to the store, from a Kitano-no-Mukashi matcha to a Premium Select sencha. You can have delicious sweets with the tea, too – they are sourced from Kyoto's famous confectioners and include local favourites such as *yatsuhashi* (cinnamon cookies).

ippodo-tea.co.jp

ASIA   KYOTO

29 THE SHINMONZEN

235 Nishino-cho, Shinmonzen-dori, Higashiyama-ku, Kyoto, 605 0088, Japan

---

TO VISIT BEFORE YOU DIE BECAUSE

Sample some of Ogata's unique tea blends and exquisite pastries at The Shinmonzen, a hotel designed by Tadao Ando in the centre of Kyoto.

Undoubtedly one of Japan's most beautiful hotels, The Shinmonzen is located along the Shirakawa River in Gion. It was designed by leading Japanese architect Tadao Ando to embody 'a fusion of the past, the present, and the future'. Its afternoon tea, curated by executive chef Koji Tachikake and pastry executive chef Hana Yoon, features seasonal pastries, such as crab cream croquette sandwiches and a signature Tahitian vanilla millefeuille, and is served on a bespoke stand by Shinichiro Ogata and locally made ceramic dishes. The hotel is also home to a gorgeous Ogata boutique, designed by the perfectly named studio Simplicity. There, you will be able to discover its 10 unique blends, as well as a selection of sweets and tea utensils. From Ka (sencha, yuzu and *kuromoji*) to Ho (barley, corn and black soybeans), it encompasses all major tea styles. You can sample some of them with your afternoon tea, as well as an Earl Grey from T-Break; a black tea from Nuwara Eliya, the highest-altitude tea-producing region in Sri Lanka, and a cold-brew sencha by Ryosen.

theshinmonzen.com   +81 755 336 553

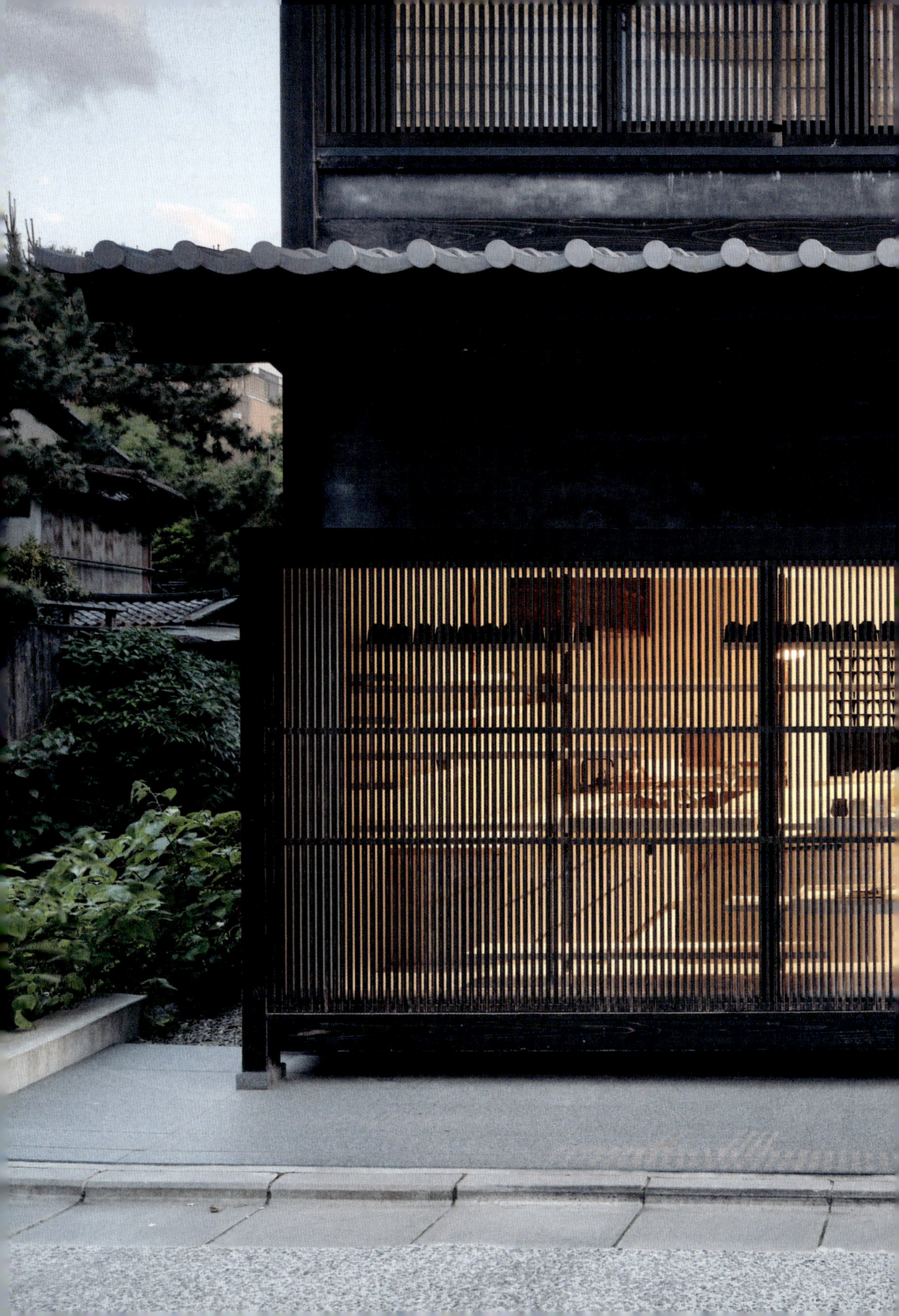

茶

OGATA

ASIA   MUMBAI

30   RAJU KI CHAI

Shop no. 4, Kamer Building, Cawasji Patel Road, next to Akbarallys Furniture, Kala Ghoda, Fort, Mumbai, Maharashtra, 400001, India

---

TO VISIT BEFORE YOU DIE BECAUSE

Choose from dozens of varieties of spiced tea at this bright new take on India's traditional chai street stalls.

Established by Dev and Sameer Sanghvi in 2017, Raju Ki Chai is an update on the ubiquitous *chai ki tapri*, the strategically placed street stalls/meeting places where Mumbaikars come for hot tea and sometimes heated discussions on everything from the latest movie to politics. The Sanghvis' take on the concept is bright and super clean, offering the added bonus of delicious snacks. Masala chai here is served in *mitti kulhad* clay cups, the traditional vessels still handmade on a potter's wheel and once forgotten in favour of glasses and paper or plastic cups. Tea comes in many varieties: there's a house special – 'a warm hug in a *kulhad*', Jain chai with fresh ginger, cardamom tea and even a chocolate chai. Healthy versions (without milk) include a simple lemon tea and variations on Ayurvedic teas such as *kali* and *hari* chai. Delicious food ranges from *bun maska*, a Parsi soft bun filled with butter and cream, to the famous Mumbai street sandwich, filled with chutney, veggies, cheese and spices, as well as Maggi instant noodles, another popular street snack here.

@rajukichai

ASIA MUNNAR

31 WINDERMERE ESTATE

Pothamedu, Munnar, Idukki District, Kerala, 685612, India

TO VISIT
BEFORE YOU DIE
BECAUSE

Surrounded by Kerala's tea plantations, this magical place offers local teas, homemade infusions and stunning views.

The Windermere Estate is actually a cardamom and coffee plantation, but there's plenty of tea to drink here, too: it is located in Kerala's Western Ghats mountains, which are dotted with tea plantations established in the late 19th century. The hilltop Windermere Estate is the best place to take in the rolling hills and cloudy valleys before heading on a guided trek through the tea gardens, perhaps to Kolukkumalai, one of the highest-altitude tea estates in India. There's also the hill resort of Munnar, or the charming local tea museum and factory to explore. Book ahead, and you can round off your tea experience with a tea tasting at Windermere itself. The hotel's lovely garden gazebo is the place for a cup of freshly brewed tea, served from a traditional samovar, or homemade infusions. These are offered along with savoury and sweet bites, changing with the seasons and the produce on offer. There is no menu here, the idea being for the chefs to take you on a culinary journey, making the best of local ingredients – including tea.

windermeremunnar.com +91 4 865 230 512

ASIA NAOSHIMA

32 GLASS TEA HOUSE 'MONDRIAN'

Benesse Art Site Naoshima, 3418 Tsumuura, Naoshima, Kagawa, 761-3110, Japan

TO VISIT BEFORE YOU DIE BECAUSE

Enjoy a cup of green tea and a Japanese sweet while taking in the work of leading artist Hiroshi Sugimoto, including his minimalist *Glass Tea House 'Mondrian'*.

Located on a cluster of islands on Japan's Seto Inland Sea, Benesse Art Site Naoshima is a mecca for art lovers, with sculptures and contemporary architecture complementing the site's natural beauty. Famously, this is where Yayoi Kusama's polka-dotted pumpkin awaits visitors on the jetty, but for our purposes, the most interesting exhibit here is found at Hiroshi Sugimoto Gallery, dedicated to the work of the Japanese photographer turned architect. In the museum lounge, you can sit around the *Three Divine Trees* table Sugimoto created out of 4,000-year-old tree trunks and enjoy a cup of green tea and a sweet while admiring Sugimoto's *Glass Tea House 'Mondrian'*. Created for the Venice Architecture Biennale in 2014, the installation is a 2.5-metre glass cube that hovers above a reflective pool. It expresses the meticulous care that goes into a tea ceremony, which Sugimoto believes encompasses all of the individual arts of the Western world: sculpture (the porcelain bowl), music (the sound of the water on the boil) and architecture (the tea ceremony arbour).

benesse-artsite.jp

ASIA — SEOUL

33 T.NOMAD

2F, 414-83 Mangwon-dong, Mapo-gu, Seoul, South Korea

TO VISIT BEFORE YOU DIE BECAUSE

This Japanese-inspired tea room offers its own blend of floral tea and handmade ceramics in a tranquil setting.

There isn't as strong of a tea-drinking culture in Seoul as in neighbouring capitals; in fact, South Korea is known as the only East Asian country that prefers coffee to tea (although many Koreans drink barley, green tea or cassia seed tea at home). Bucking the trend is T.nomad, located near Mangwon Market. Like many of the city's most interesting places, it is hidden on the second floor of a building. Here, you will find handmade pottery pieces, a peaceful atmosphere and the signature Nomad Tea. 'This premium tea is named after our café,' explains T.nomad's Youngmin Moon. 'It is blended with flowers grown in pesticide-free fields in Yeosu, Jeolla province. Thanks to its floral scent, it is loved by many customers.' Another favourite is hōjicha, slowly roasted to give it its special earthy aroma, and of course matcha, which is served with a chasen so customers can try the whisking process themselves. Sweet treats range from Korean rice cake to matcha cheesecake.

T9 PREMIUM
T9 COLORFUL COLLECTION
GOLD EARL GREY BLACK TEA
金色伯爵红茶
T9 PREMIUM TEA

ASIA　　　　　　　　　　　　　　SHANGHAI

34　T9 PREMIUM TEA

Sixth Floor, Grand Gateway 66, 1 Hongqiao Lu, Shanghai, China

---

TO VISIT BEFORE YOU DIE BECAUSE

Follow the locals to enjoy the beautifully packaged, high-quality teas of this boutique tea brand in one of Shanghai's high-end malls.

Shanghai's most famous teahouse is the historic Huxinting Teahouse in Yuyuan Garden. A city centre landmark set on a lake, with giant skyscrapers as a backdrop, it is quite a symbol of modern China. Take a look at it in the early morning to avoid the crowds; but then, for an actual cup of tea, follow the Shanghainese to a T9 tea room in one of Shanghai's luxury shopping malls, Grand Gateway. China's first boutique tea brand, T9 Premium Tea was founded in Shanghai in 2016 as an online tea supplier before opening its own teahouses. Known for its chic vintage-style packaging, the popular outfit offers a selection of 50 different teas, from classic Chinese *dong ding* oolong to herbal fruit teas and high-quality teas from India. Signature drinks include the Earl Grey tea latte and the Shanghai Magnolia, while sweet treats range from pistachio cake to colourful macarons. (For a more traditional shopping experience, you could also visit Tianshan Tea City, where you'll find every Chinese tea under the sun.)

ASIA SHANGHAI

35 WAN LING TEA HOUSE

Room 101, Building 16, 735 Julu Road, Shanghai, China

TO VISIT BEFORE YOU DIE BECAUSE

Part of a family-run tea company, this beautiful teahouse on a historic tree-lined street is the place to learn all about Chinese tea.

Open by appointment only, Wan Ling Tea House is the tea room of an eponymous online retailer specialising in directly sourced artisan teas and teaware. Located a short walk from Jing'an Temple and surrounded by the leafy streets of Shanghai's former French Concession, it is a quiet and peaceful space to explore the world of Chinese tea. It was set up by husband-and-wife team Wan Ling and James Grayland, who source authentic, single-estate loose-leaf teas, mostly from Wan Ling's native Fujian and Yunnan. Through a series of classes, Chinese tea ceremony demonstrations and workshops (in both English and Chinese, designed to suit all levels and interests), you can learn about Minnan oolongs, such as *lao cong mei zhan* and the famous *Tieguanyin*. The latter, a light jade-style oolong, comes from a high-altitude plantation rediscovered about five years ago, where the tea bushes are now many metres tall and require a combination of climbing or ladders to harvest.

wanlingteahouse.co.uk/pages/shanghai-tea-house

+44 7 881 621 330

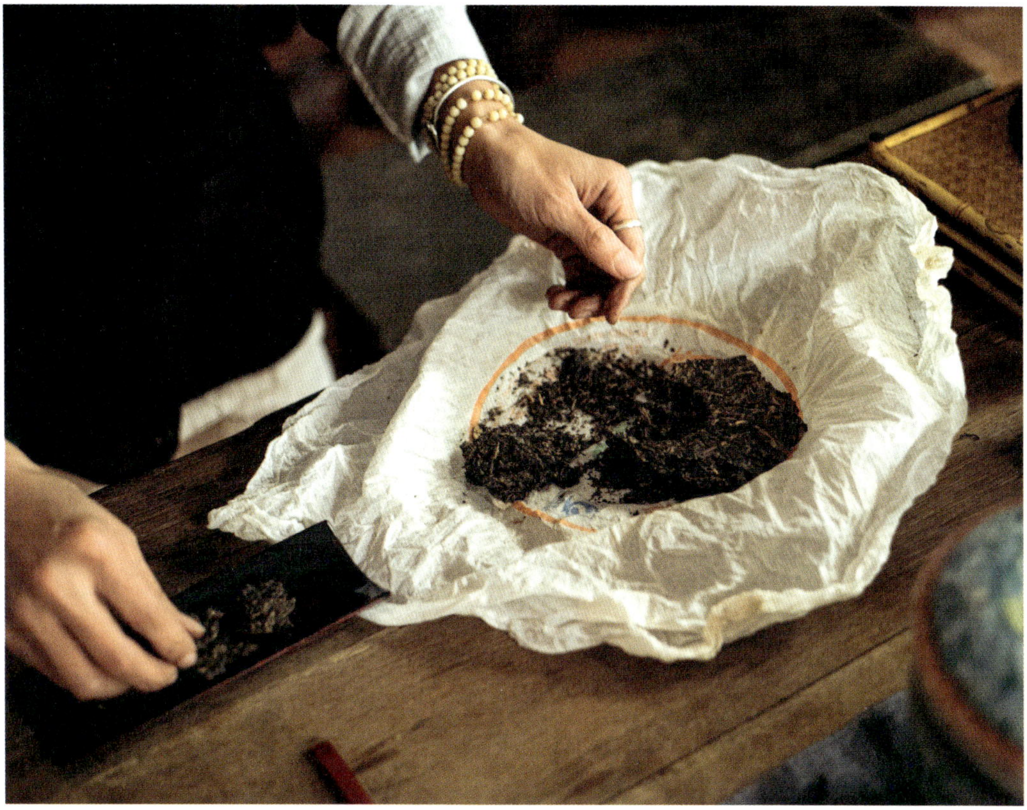

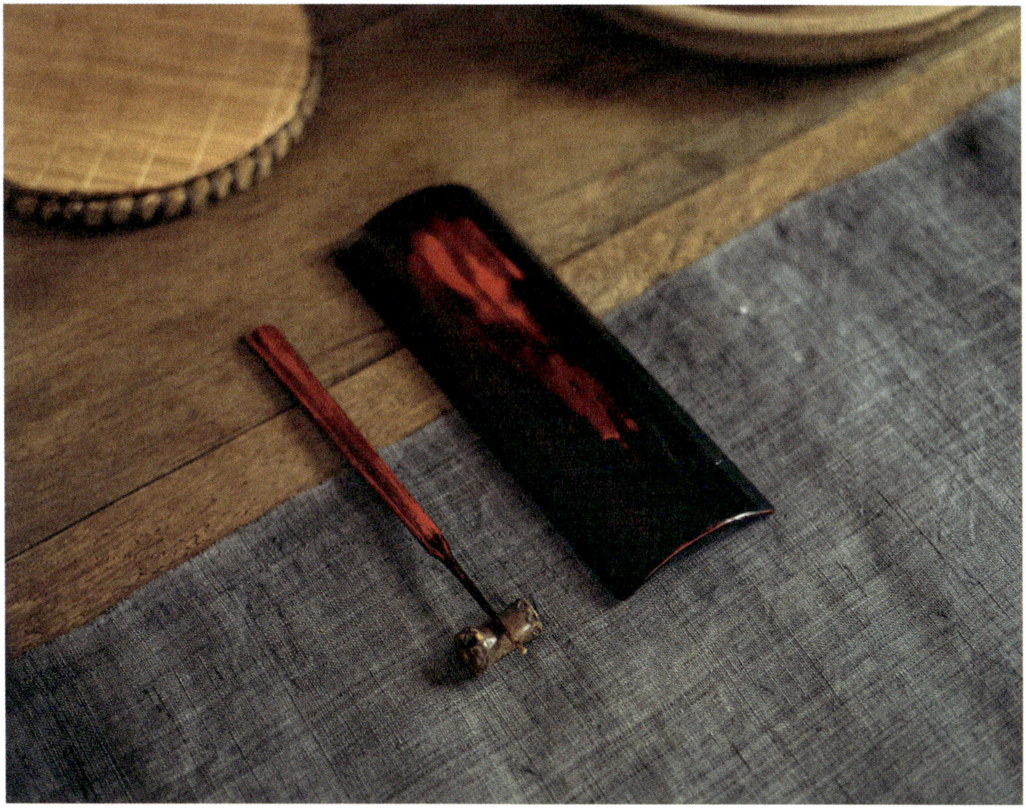

ASIA　　　　　　　　　　　　　　SINGAPORE

36　TEA CHAPTER

9 Neil Road, Singapore, 088808

TO VISIT BEFORE YOU DIE BECAUSE

A little bubble of calm in Chinatown, this teahouse has a mission to share the beauty of traditional Chinese tea.

Tea Chapter was established in 1989 by a group of Chinese tea enthusiasts in a three-storey shophouse in the heart of Chinatown. Step inside to marvel at the building's original features, experience a fine selection of handpicked tea and learn about the art and history of tea, thanks to Tea Chapter's knowledgeable staff. The brand's signature tea is the Imperial Golden Cassia, a famous light oolong tea from Fujian with a light, flowery osmanthus-like aroma, while its bestselling snack is the tea-braised egg. It is made specially in-house by simmering hard-boiled eggs for at least eight hours in a special braising liquid made of tea leaves, herbs and spices. What sets it apart from other teahouses is its peaceful ambience, with a boutique on the first floor and three different styles of tea lounge – Korean, Oriental and Japanese. Relax with traditional classical Chinese music and enjoy a cup of tea with a mini bao platter or a plate of freshly baked cookies. You can also book two different types of tea appreciation workshops, both including tea sampling and snacks.

teachapter.com　　　　　　　　　　+65 62 261 175

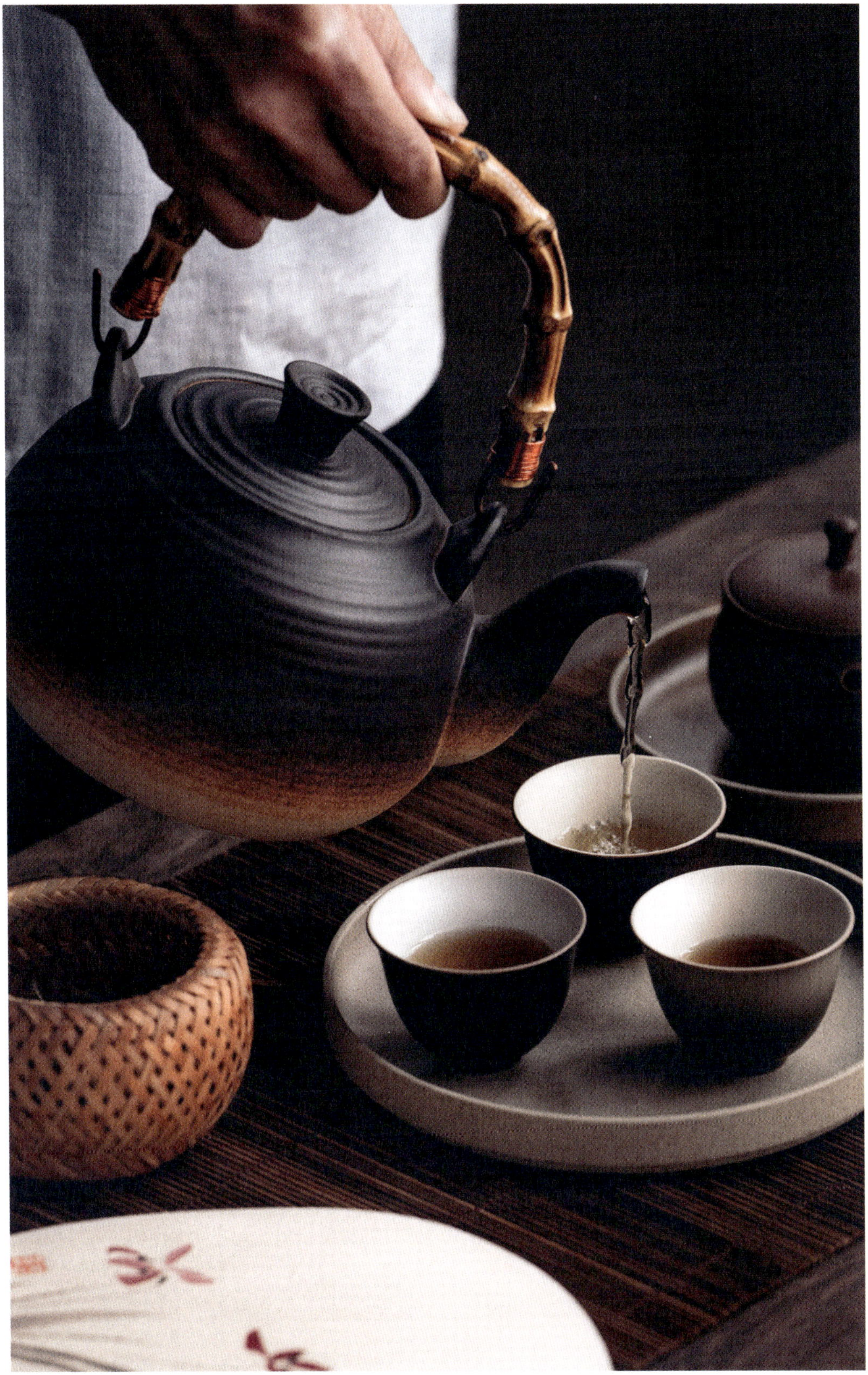

ASIA TAIPEI

37 CHING SHIN FU CHUAN

Multiple locations, Taipei, Taiwan

TO VISIT BEFORE YOU DIE BECAUSE

Taiwan's national drink, bubble tea, has taken the world by storm, so enjoy a classic pearl milk tea while walking around the capital city.

Bubble tea is said to have been invented in 1987 in Taichung, Taiwan. Since then, the tall cups of ice milk tea and tapioca pearls have taken over the country, then the world, (although abroad, people are quick to forget that it is a tea-based drink and go for fruit juices instead). The drink's popularity means that in Taipei, there is literally a bubble tea shop on every corner, and about a million tea chains to choose from, each with its own signature drink. As a result, the urban environment has been turned into a vast tea room, since you can take your giant plastic-sealed drink with you and enjoy it on the move, on a public bench or in a park. Every Taiwanese has their personal favourite tea station, but Ching Shin Fu Chuan, with its smiling heart logo, is a sure bet. One of the oldest chain stores in Taiwan, it uses premium-quality tea leaves and fresh ingredients, and its milk tea with pearls and melon oolong tea have become classics.

ASIA   TAIPEI

38 YAOYUE TEAHOUSE

No. 6, Lane 40, Section 3, Zhinan Road, Wenshan District, Taipei City, 116, Taiwan

TO VISIT BEFORE YOU DIE BECAUSE

Sip tea and watch the sun set from this 24-hour teahouse up on the hills above Taipei, a lush area known for its tea-growing history.

The best way to reach this charming teahouse on the outskirts of the Taiwanese capital is to take the Maokong Gondola and walk for about 30 minutes (although a bus can take you there too). There are many hiking paths and teahouses in the scenic Wenshan District, which used to be the country's largest tea-growing region and still produces some fine Tieguanyin oolongs and *baozhongs*. In fact, the walk will take you past Taipei Tea Promotion Center, where you can sample some local teas for free. YaoYue means 'inviting the moon', and the place is open day and night, 24/7, all year round. There is seating inside, in a restored tea farmhouse, and outside, on sheltered terraces. When ordering tea, you will be given a single, unlimited pot of water (charged per the number of customers in your party), and a choice between around 20 different high-quality teas. The tea house also offers a selection of traditional Chinese snacks.

yytea.com.tw   +886 229 392 025

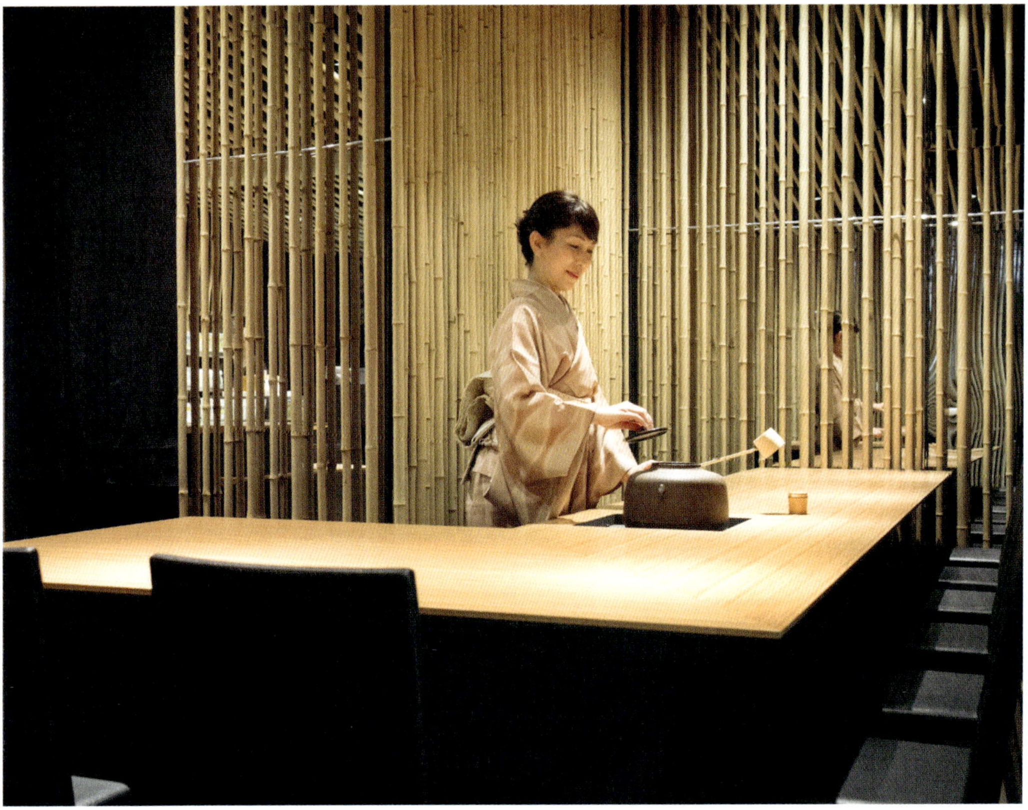

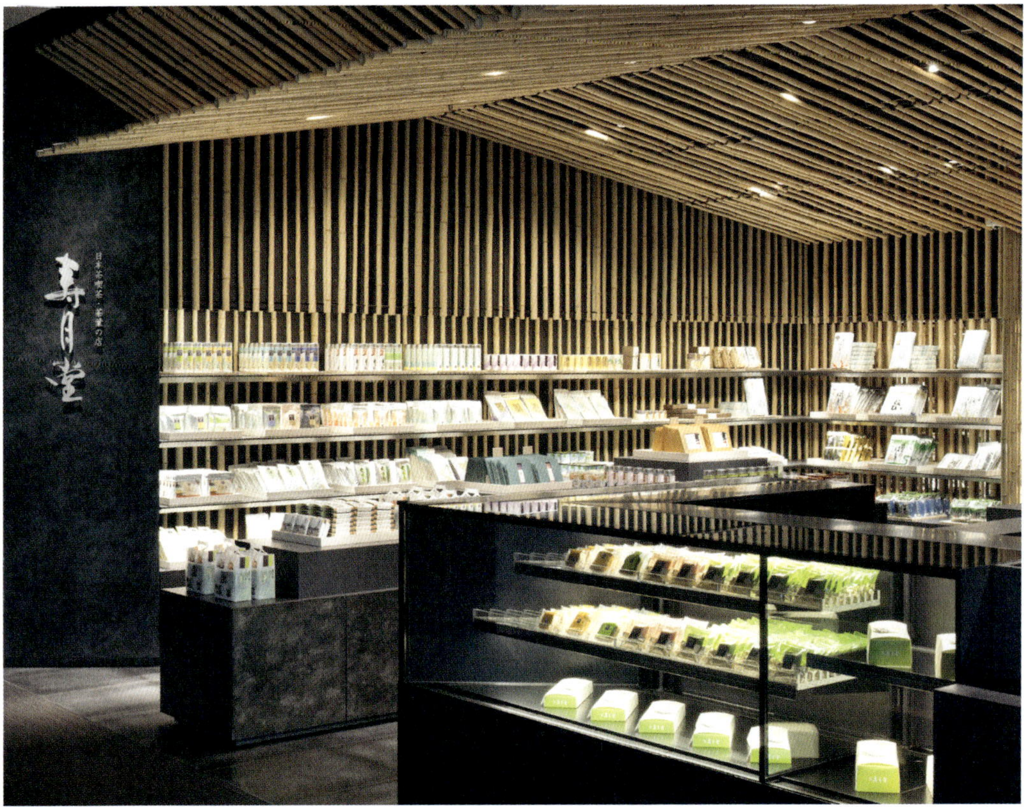
寿月堂

ASIA　　　　　　　　　　　TOKYO

39　JUGETSUDO GINZA KABUKIZA

Kabukiza Tower 5F, 4 Chome-12-15, Ginza, Chūō-ku, Tokyo, 104-0061, Japan

TO VISIT BEFORE YOU DIE BECAUSE

Sample rare gyokuro tea at leading tea company Jugetsudo's tea shop and bar, designed by Kengo Kuma.

Perched on the fifth floor of Tokyo's Kabukiza Tower, this stunning tea house was designed by leading Japanese architect Kengo Kuma. Lined with bamboo, its geometric ceiling evokes the folds of an origami creation and leads the eye to the windows framing the rooftop garden. It's a unique space for a unique brand, started by the historic seaweed company Maruyama Nori, founded in 1854. Jugetsudo selects its matcha tea leaves in the highlands of Shizuoka, near Mount Fuji, where the unique climate and fertile soil create sought-after tea-growing conditions. Its collection includes a *gyokuro* made by covering the tea leaves for two weeks before harvesting; and a range of senchas, genmaichas and hōjichas. You can pair these with sweets including matcha Mont Blanc cake, matcha cheesecake or raspberry millefeuille. The company also has an equally beautiful shop in Tsukiji (inspired by the traditional bamboo umbrella used during outdoor tea ceremonies) and another in Paris.

maruyamanori.com　　　　　+81 362 787 626

ASIA TOKYO

40 SOCHA

2 Chome-33-9, Nezu, Bunkyo City, Tokyo, 113-0031, Japan

TO VISIT BEFORE YOU DIE BECAUSE

This beautifully crafted little tea room serves fine green teas and sweet treats from the Yamanashi region in the heart of Japan.

One of the fascinating things about Tokyo is the jumble of small houses, all with different personalities, that line its charming residential streets. It is on one of these streets in the Nezu neighbourhood, near Tokyo's National Museum, that you will find this tiny tea room. It was set up by Sobokuya, a construction company from Yamanashi, and highlights two of the country's key assets: beautiful craft and tea. Taking centre stage is a table made from a single slab of Zelkova wood, supported by stones once used as the base of an ancient well; surrounding it are chairs made of tatami mats and hand-finished dirt walls. It's an intimate and relaxed spot, where, after being shown how to make freshly whisked matcha, guests are welcome to refill their teapots as much as they want. On the menu are carefully selected teas such as bō hōjicha, a roasted stem tea dating from the Edo period. They can be paired with a signature ice cream with hōjicha jelly, amazake castella cake or matcha pudding.

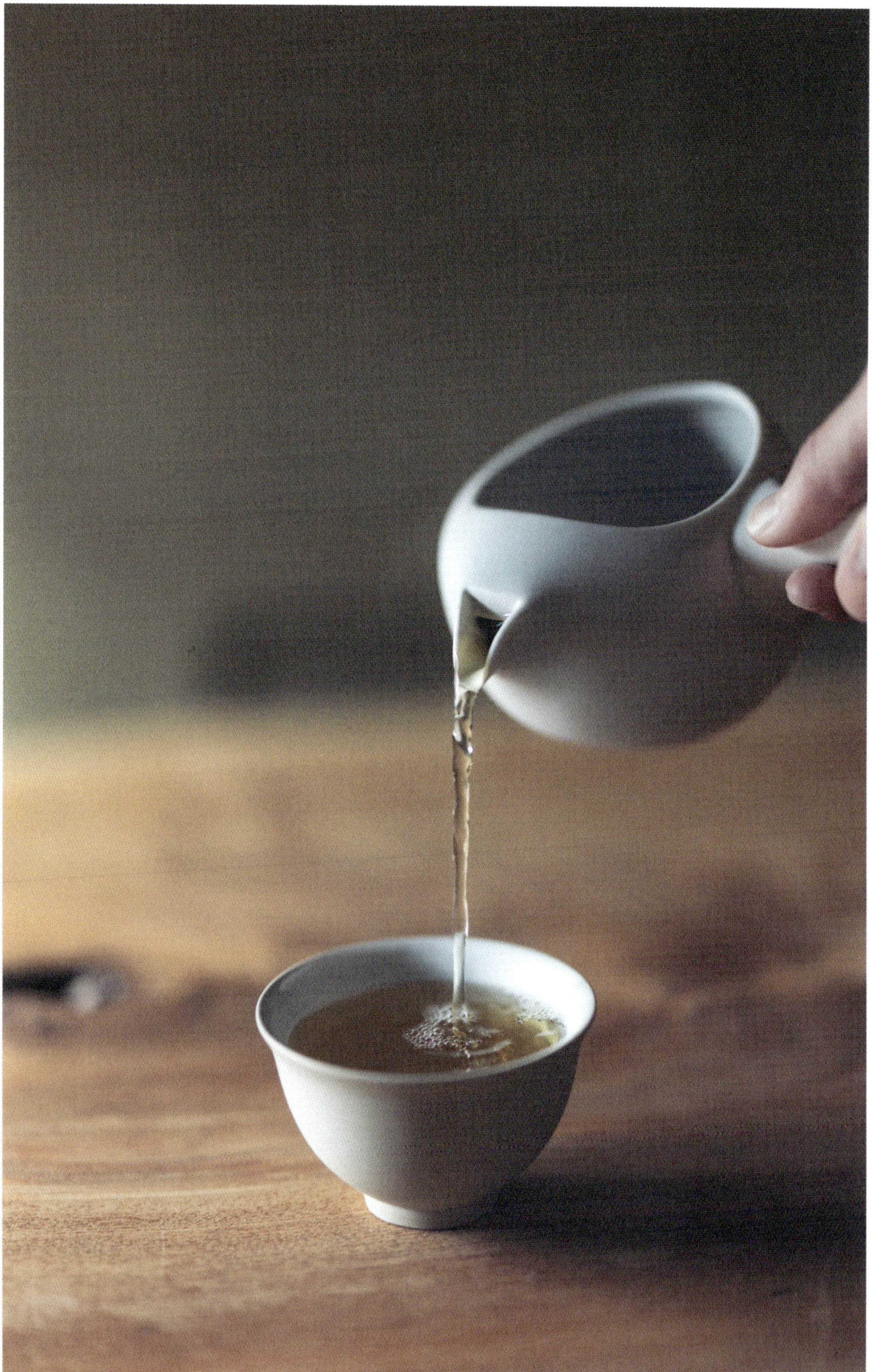

41 BASAO TEA

No. 8-5, Jianye Road, Siming District, Xiamen, China

TO VISIT BEFORE YOU DIE BECAUSE

Take a moment to breathe in this beautiful zen-like space combining the beauty of fine tea and minimalist architecture.

Established in 2011 in Xiamen, Basao Tea is named after a Japanese zen monk who became famous for travelling around Kyoto selling tea, and once wrote: 'Having learned the ways of silence, within the noise of urban life, I take life as it comes to me, and everywhere I am is true.' Fittingly, the brand's flagship store in Xiamen is a stunning pared-back space, aiming to help visitors enjoy quiet contemplation and the calming sounds of tea being prepared, poured and enjoyed. Designed by Norm Architects, the tea room is an oasis of calm lined with oak cabinets and shelves. Sit at the large stone tea counter to take part in a Chinese gong fu tea ceremony, or learn about classic Japanese matcha preparation or more contemporary ways of tea making, like Basao's nitrogen-infused cold brews. The tea sommeliers can also guide you through the company's collection, which ranges from hand-rolled Nepali tip to Hangzhou's Longjing, or 'dragon well' tea. Basao also has branches in Shanghai and Hong Kong, as well as a mobile tea bar.

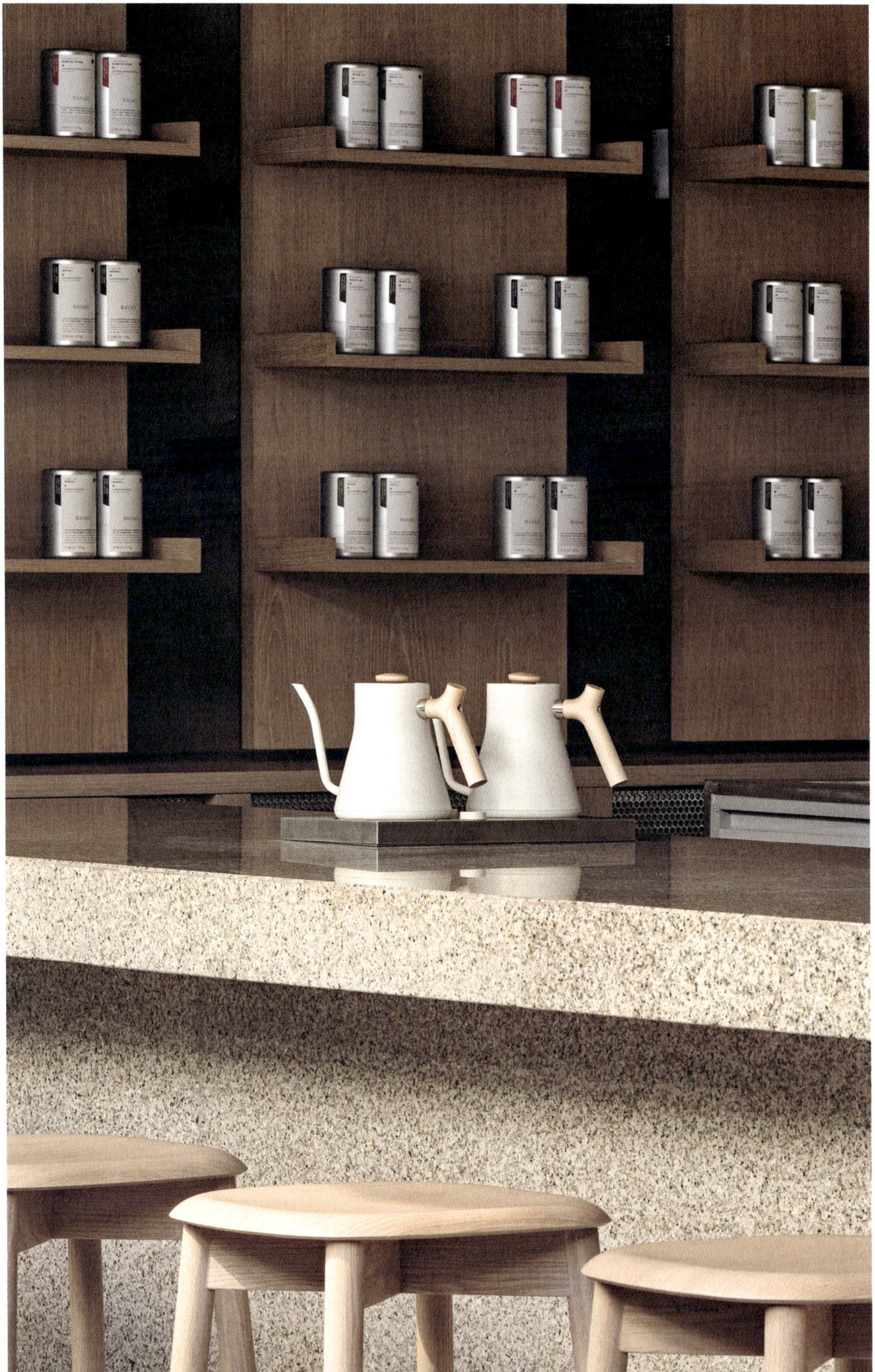

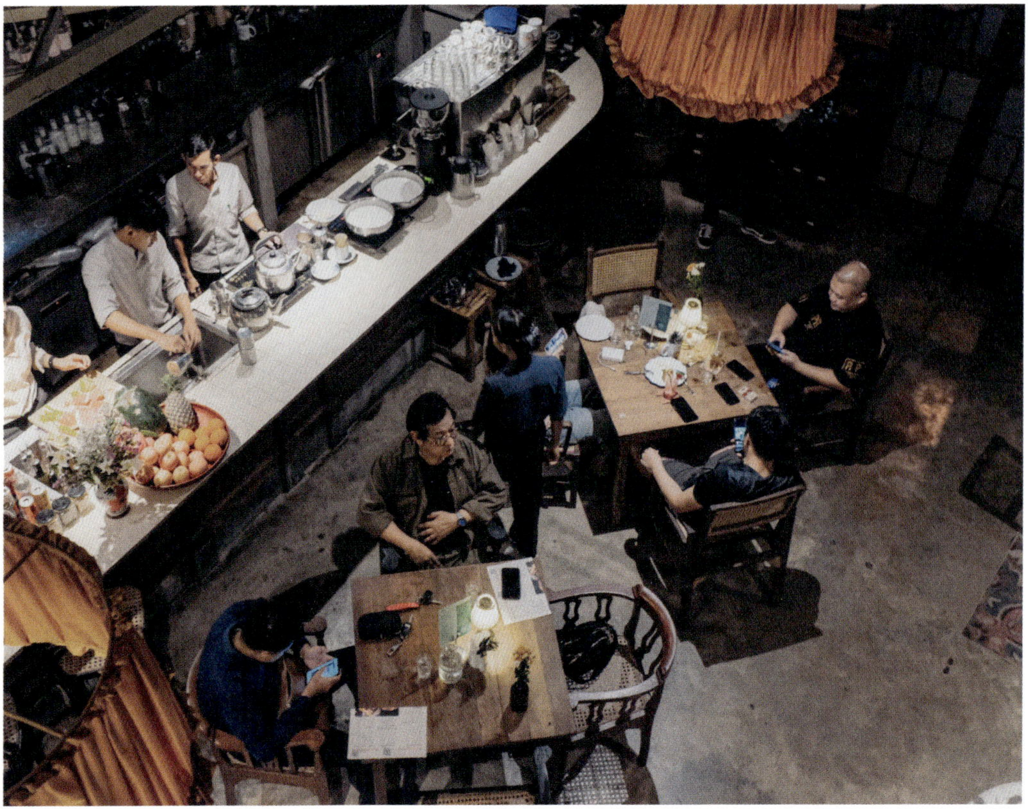

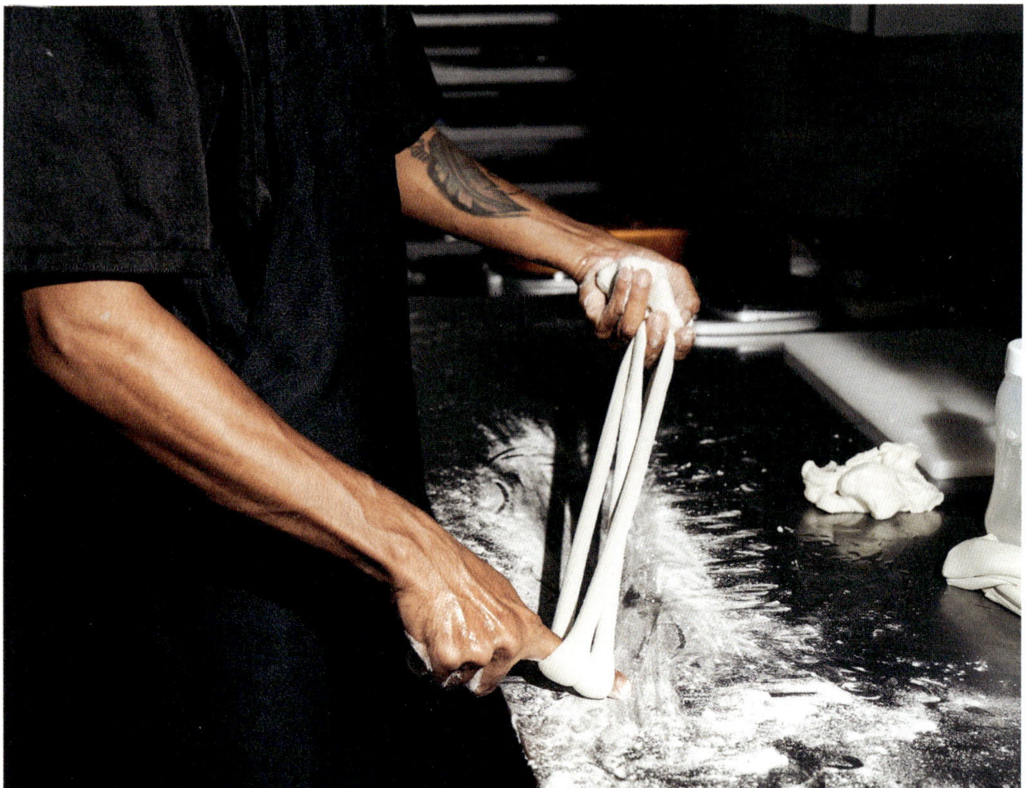

ASIA YANGON

42 RANGOONTEA HOUSE

36 Inya Myaing Road, Golden Valley, Bahan, Yangon, Myanmar

TO VISIT BEFORE YOU DIE BECAUSE

Try a milk tea and a pickled tea leaf salad at this modern Burmese teahouse, which puts the spotlight on the country's culinary diversity.

This elegant teahouse is a celebration of Myanmar's renowned tea shops, simple little cafés serving Burmese tea and snacks. Although the décor here is much grander, with high ceilings, beautiful woodworking and a long vintage bar, the place retains an authentic feel thanks to its staff and menu, which reflect the country's cultural melting pot. Make sure to try the pork marinated in tea leaves and the pickled tea leaves salad, Myanmar's national dish, along with mohinga, a fish noodle soup. The house speciality is *si lone* tea, a milk tea with cream that is said to be addictive (there is even a durian fruit version), while intriguing drinks include Singapore tea (with an espresso shot) and a cold brew made with coconut water. But the main event is of course *lahpet yay*, or Burmese pulled tea. There are 16 different versions, each featuring slightly different ratios of black tea, condensed milk and steamed milk, each with its own name. The place is so popular it has opened a new outpost in Bangkok.

rangoonteahouse.com

EUROPE — AMSTERDAM

43 MOYCHAY

Rozengracht 92H, 1016 NH Amsterdam, Netherlands

TO VISIT BEFORE YOU DIE BECAUSE

Try unique teas from around the world at this beautifully designed, expert-led tea room in the heart of Amsterdam.

This speciality tea shop and tea room was founded by Amsterdam-based tea expert Sergey Shevelev, who has dedicated his life to exploring the world of tea. The founder of the Moychay tea company and the author of a book on Chinese tea, he has travelled extensively to tea-producing regions to source sustainable loose-leaf teas directly from the farmers. Unsurprisingly, his tea room offers 250 premium teas from 13 different countries, including rare and exotic varieties difficult to find elsewhere. Bestselling teas include GABA oolongs from Lugu and Alishan Shou Gong, premium-grade culinary matcha and Menghai *shu cha* pu-erh – all come with interesting background stories, which the friendly team will share with you. There are two different seating areas: a cosy lounge downstairs and a serene Asian tea room upstairs. The experimental tea bar specialises in tea-infused mocktails, such as a latte with CBD, blue matcha and lavender and a yerba *maté* with lemon syrup, ginger and turmeric. Also available are thousands of authentic teaware items.

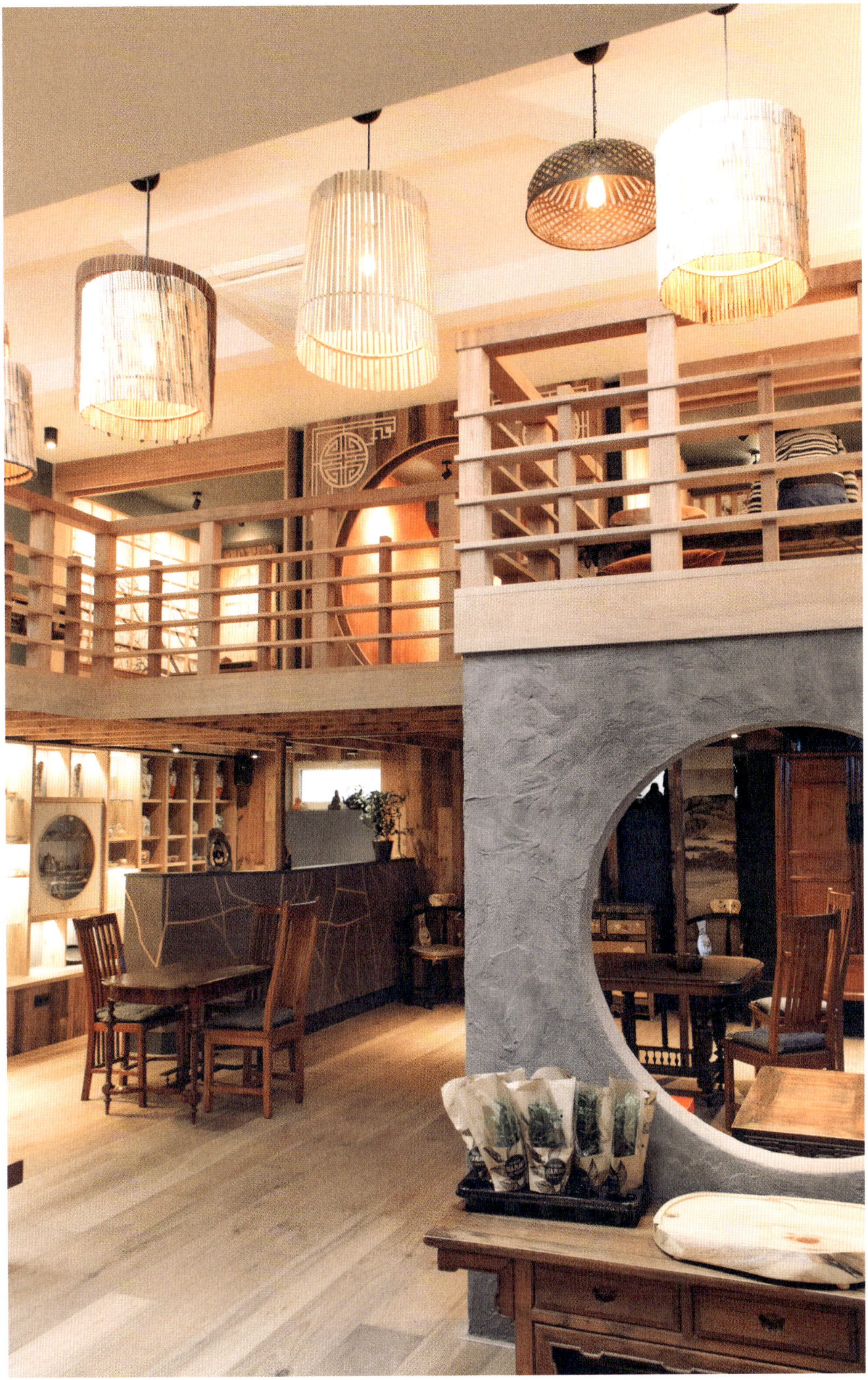

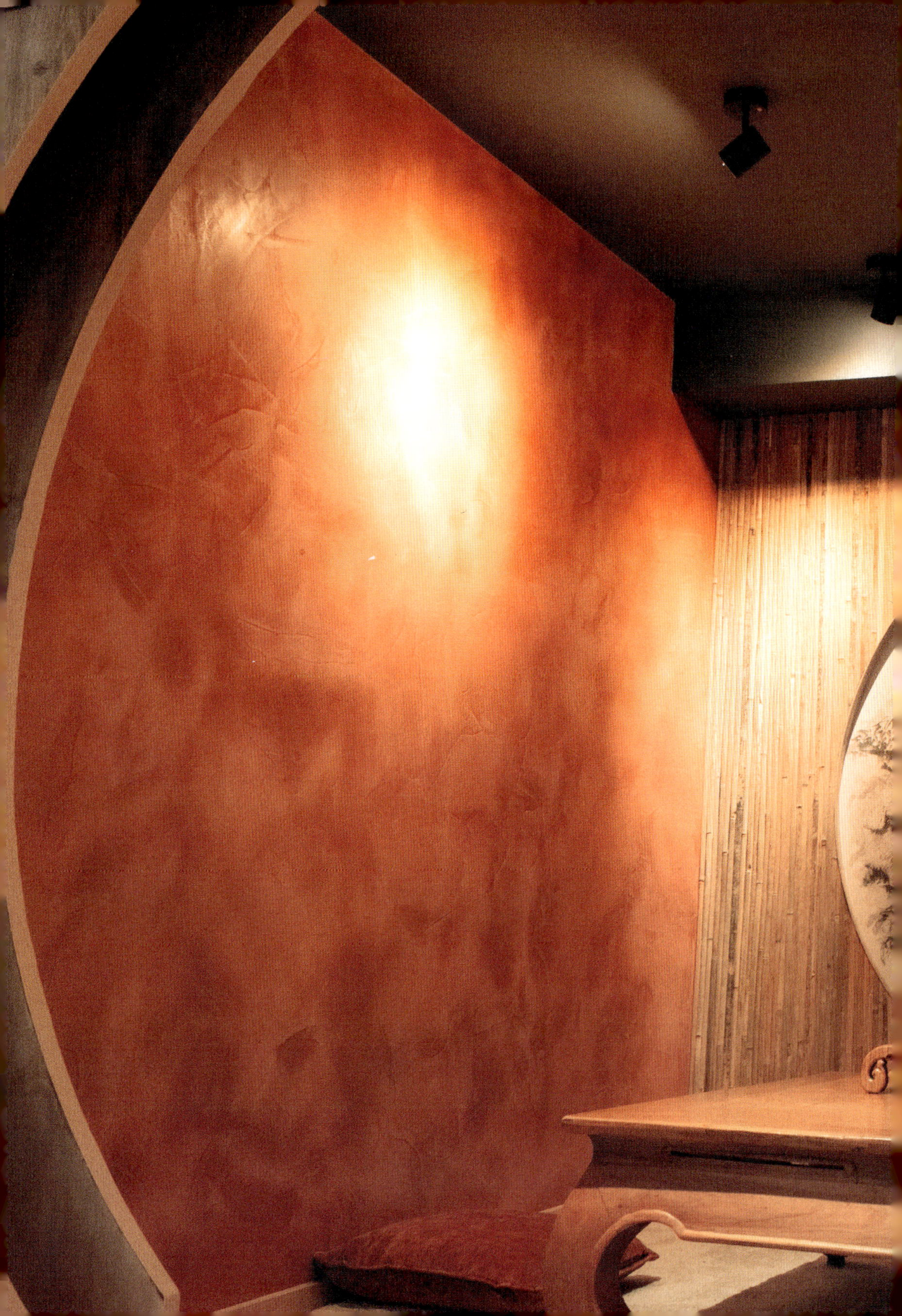

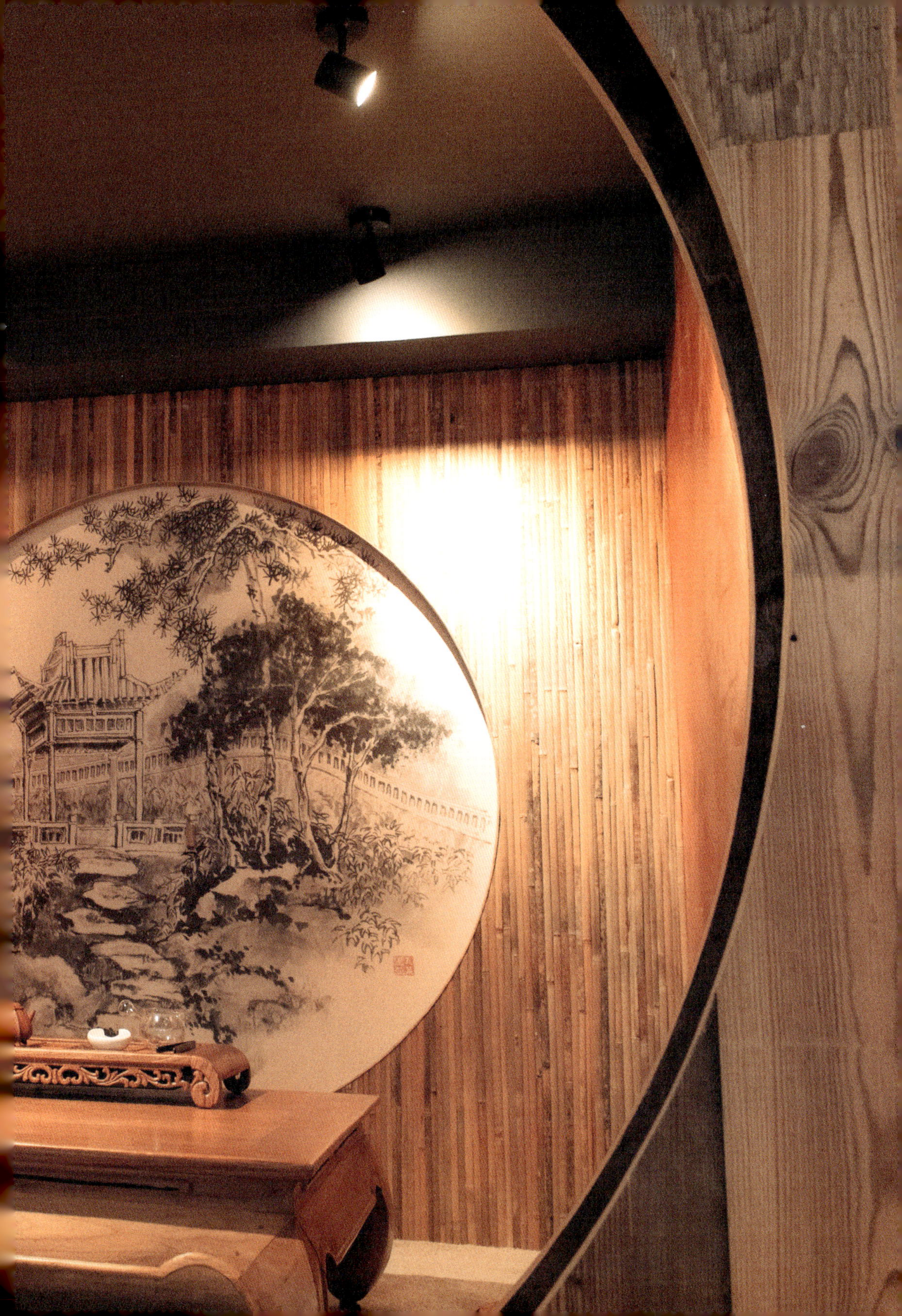

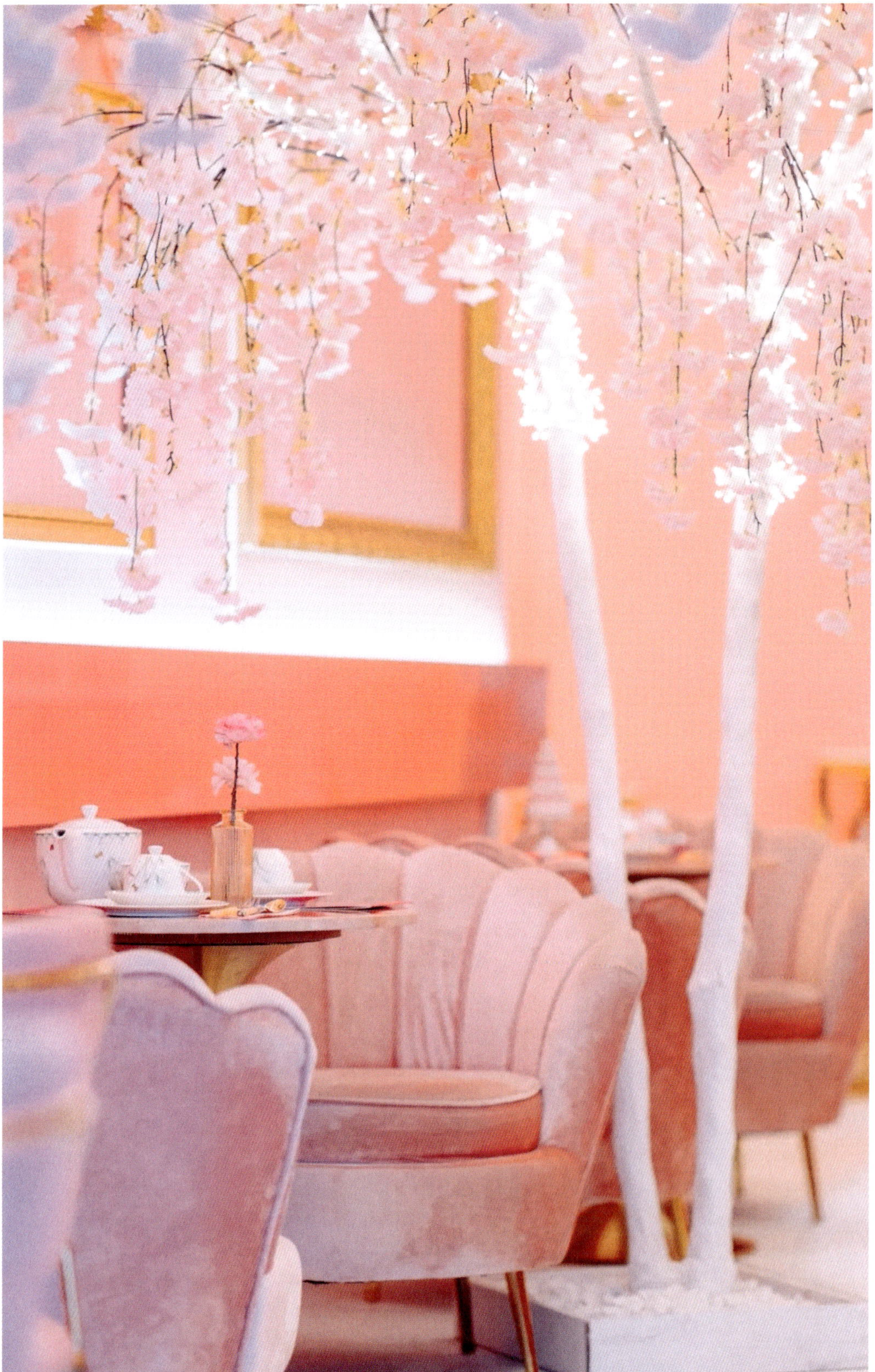

EUROPE · ANTWERP

44 PINK VELVET

Nassaustraat 38, 2000 Antwerp, Belgium

TO VISIT BEFORE YOU DIE BECAUSE

See *la vie en rose* at this over-the-top tea room in Antwerp, which serves a unique mix of fine teas, beautiful cakes and… sushi.

With its blooming cherry trees and flower-lined walls, this Antwerp tea room is unabashedly pink – and so are its teas. Sit on a pink velvet scalloped armchair and choose from flavoured black teas such as Strawberry Popcorn, Cherry Lips and even Unicorn Sprinkles (with apple, candied pineapple, hibiscus flowers, vanilla and pink and white sprinkles). Not such a sweet tooth? Go for the more subdued Jasmine Jade Pearl, Miyazaki Sencha or Earl Grey Special. Uniquely, the three-tiered stands usually seen on afternoon tea tables are used here to serve delicious colourful sushi prepared by skilled sushi chefs. Come the weekend, though, and the delicate Wedgwood porcelain tableware, a classic Royal Albert design with gold rims and burgundy, pink and yellow roses, is used for high tea. It includes savoury snacks such as avocado sandwiches and pretty desserts by Louise Sofia, from cupcakes with pink icing to cake pops decorated with butterflies and pastel macarons. You can also order beautifully decorated cakes and gift boxes.

pinkvelvetantwerp.be +32 487 450 739

TO TSAI

19 Alexandrou Soutsou, Kolonaki, Athens, 10671, Greece

TO VISIT BEFORE YOU DIE BECAUSE

Choose from about 500 varieties of teas and infusions in an award-winning interior by leading architect Georges Batzios.

Owned by specialist Ceylon tea importer Mlesna, To Tsai opened its doors in 1993. Inspired by Japanese architecture, the sleek space by Georges Batzios Architects is divided into a boutique and a tea room, where tea is served in a variety of teapots (porcelain, cast iron or clay), depending on its origin. Classics such as Earl Grey, jasmine and matcha are always popular, but the teahouse is a real treasure trove of hard-to-find teas, such as an organic Orange Pekoe, grown near Etseri in the mountains of Georgia, and mastic tea, a tea flavoured with natural mastic oil (a key Greek ingredient), from Dimbula, Sri Lanka. Another local favourite is mountain tea, or *Sideritis scardica*, grown on an organic farm on Mount Olympus – a delicious infusion with notes of mint, chamomile and citrus. The range of blended teas is, as you can imagine, pretty extensive, with seasonal creations such as Falling Snowflake, a mix of white and green tea with coconut, orange peel and spices.

EUROPE BARCELONA

46 ČAJ CHAI

Carrer de Salomó Ben Adret 12, Barri Gòtic, Ciutat Vella, Barcelona, Spain

TO VISIT BEFORE YOU DIE BECAUSE

The very first teahouse in Barcelona to offer teas from around the world, Čaj Chai specialises in organic and wild teas.

Inspired by Prague's bohemian tea rooms but set in the heart of Barcelona's Gothic Quarter, Čaj Chai was founded by Antonio Moreno to share his passion for tea with the public. 'We place importance on terroir, the art of recollection and harvest, traditional handmade production and proper tea preparation,' he says. The menu includes 140 varieties of tea: a seasonal selection; a chai and yogi section, with special supplements like reishi and lion's mane; and a large selection of herbal teas. Last but not least are the house's signature *matchai*, a blend of freshly ground chai with matcha, and the Ice Tea Float, with homemade iced tea and vegan tea gelato by DeLaCrem. Or simply enjoy a classic Chinese oolong, along with a selection of Japanese, Indian and Arab pastries, in the cosy tea room. There are workshops and special services, including gong fu cha and *chanoyu* matcha. 'We host tea ceremonies as a type of meditation where people connect to themselves, to this wonderful plant and to each other through tea,' explains Antonio.

47 THE PUMP ROOM

Searcys at the Pump Room, Stall Street, Bath, BA1 1LZ, United Kingdom

TO VISIT BEFORE YOU DIE BECAUSE

Follow in the footsteps of Jane Austen and Charles Dickens to have tea in this grand Georgian dining room overlooking the Roman baths.

With a glittering chandelier illuminating its Corinthian columns, this noble room built in the 1790s was once the heart of the Georgian social scene, when high society flocked to the city for the waters they believed would relieve all their illnesses. Jane Austen used it as a setting in her novels *Northanger Abbey* and *Persuasion*; it was the place where 'every creature in Bath was to be seen in the room at different periods of the fashionable hours'. It is now home to The Pump Room restaurant operated by Searcys, where you can sample the spa water as well as Assam, Darjeeling and Earl Grey with breakfast, brunch or afternoon tea – think Victoria sandwiches, and cheddar and chive scones. All this to the soundtrack of spa water trickling out of the marble fountain and live music from the resident pianist. There has been music here since the opening of the original building in 1706, when Richard 'Beau' Nash, the legendary gambler and socialite, put together his own band to perform there.

thepumproombath.co.uk   +44 1 225 444 477

EUROPE   BERLIN

48 GARDENS OF THE WORLD

Blumberger Damm 44, 12685 Berlin, Germany

TO VISIT
BEFORE YOU DIE
BECAUSE

Enjoy both Eastern and Western tea traditions surrounded by lush gardens in Berlin's vast Marzahn Recreational Park.

Opened by the East Berlin city government in 1987 to commemorate the city's 750th anniversary, Marzahn Recreational Park is perhaps best known for its Gardens of the World, a series of themed gardens, from Balinese to Korean. Built to mark the city's reunification, the Chinese Garden is called the Garden of the Waxing Moon – the moon being the Chinese symbol for perfect harmony. It is home to Berghaus zum Osmanthussaft, a classic Chinese teahouse named after the osmanthus flower, where you can sample 30 original Chinese tea rarities or book an appointment for a Chinese tea ceremony. If you prefer your teas sweetened and with a few drops of milk, head next door to the English Garden, where you will find another tea room, this time in a traditional thatched-roof cottage. Sip on an Earl Grey on the terrace surrounded by rose bushes and snack on cucumber sandwiches, shortbread and flapjacks. If you're looking for something more central, there's also a great British tea room in the Tiergarten's English Garden.

EUROPE　　　　　BERLIN

49　PAPER & TEA

Fasanenstraße 22, Kurfürstendamm, 10719 Berlin, Germany

TO VISIT BEFORE YOU DIE BECAUSE

This welcoming tea bar and shop by German tea retailer Paper & Tea has won a prestigious award for its unique design.

With its ash wood shelves and cabinets, houseplants and oak parquet flooring, this brand-new store and tea bar around the corner from Berlin's famous Kurfürstendamm avenue looks more like a chic kitchen than a retail space. The till and samples are hidden away in drawers to let the green tea bar take centre stage, with a series of stools providing seating to enjoy Paper & Tea's hundreds of teas. With a focus on 'people, community, and the feeling of being welcome', this tea company is on a mission to become Europe's leading premium tea brand by providing what it calls 'mindful moments'. A collaboration with Pluspunkt Architektur, the boutique and tea bar has just won a Red Dot Award for its unique design. Sit at the linoleum-clad bar and enjoy hot and cold teas, such as Perfect Day, an organic blend of white and green tea with apple and peach flavours. Also on offer are a selection of tea-infused chocolate, accessories and gift sets, as well as items featuring the brand's innovative paper, made using leftover tea.

paperandtea.com　　　+49 15 123 223 003

PAPER & TEA P & T

EUROPE   BERLIN

50   TADSHIKISCHE TEESTUBE

Oranienburger Street 27, KunstHof, 10117 Berlin, Germany

TO VISIT BEFORE YOU DIE BECAUSE

This candlelit Tajik teahouse in the centre of Berlin is a magical place to enjoy a Russian tea and rum raisins.

The sandalwood columns, Persian rugs and colourful paintings of this teahouse are the real deal: they were first displayed in the Soviet Pavilion at the Leipzig Trade Fair in 1974 and were then given to East Germany by the Tajik Soviet Socialist Republic. As the bold green walls of this cosy space indicate, Tajikistan's national drink is green tea, one of the treasures transported along the Silk Road. Although it is drunk with milk, butter and salt in the Tajik mountains, here in Berlin, you can discover the Russian influence over the Central Asian country. There is borscht and plov stew, as well as pancakes served with cranberries and whipped cream. Take your shoes off and sit on a floor cushion before ordering a Russian tea (served in a samovar, with jam, cakes and cookies); Caravan tea, a mix of *lapsang souchong* and green tea; or Lommonossow, a Black Sea tea served with jam and rum raisins. For summer days, there is also a beautiful shaded courtyard terrace.

tadshikische-teestube.de   +49 302 041 112

EUROPE　　　　　　　　BRIGHTON

51　LEMAN TEA ROOM

15A Madeira Place, Kemptown, Brighton and Hove, Brighton, BN2 1TN, United Kingdom

---

TO VISIT BEFORE YOU DIE BECAUSE

Have a delicious afternoon tea at this small but mighty tea room, a welcoming spot next to Brighton Beach serving delicious scones.

Brits prefer to have tea at home (strong dark tea with milk, Earl Grey or peppermint) and love the reassuring noise of the boiling tea kettle (there is even a 'tea kettle effect', a surge in energy demand when millions make tea during popular TV shows). But they do make an exception when it comes to cream tea (with scones, after a nice walk) or afternoon tea (with sandwiches and pastries, for special events). This is why all around the country you can find cute little tea rooms such as this tiny one in Brighton. With its cosy vintage décor and floral chintz, Leman Tea Room is a happy place for a cuppa made with fine loose-leaf tea and a slice of delicious lemon drizzle cake. Try a pot of one of the house's special teas, such as Mystic, with cardamom, cinnamon and black pepper, or Blue Lady, with apple and hibiscus – and come hungry, as the portions are generous. Make sure to try the freshly baked, still warm scones, served with the traditional clotted cream and jam – simply scrumptious.

EUROPE   COPENHAGEN

52 A.C. PERCH'S THEHANDEL

Kronprinsensgade 5, 1114 Copenhagen, Denmark

TO VISIT BEFORE YOU DIE BECAUSE

This *hygge* tea room is located next to a perfectly preserved historic tea shop in the heart of the Danish capital.

Not much has changed since Niels Brock Perch opened his first tea shop in central Copenhagen in 1835. There are rows of tea canisters on wooden shelves lined with gilded leather wallpaper, and the old apothecary scales still stand proud on the counter. Happily for us, there has been one big transformation, in 2005, when the tea company opened a lovely tea room above the landmark shop. Now located at street level, next to the original store, the tea room is the best place to sample A.C. Perch's 150 different teas, including Morning Tea, its oldest and bestselling blend – a rich and powerful mix of Assam and Ceylon tea. There are also matchas, chais, rare green teas and lovely aromatic black teas with quince and bergamot, plus great afternoon tea options. As well as a classic tea stand, you can try a seasonal shortcake with berries or Ferdinands Fryd, a heavenly combination of tea and scones served with jam, lemon curd and whipped cream. There's also a gift shop selling beautiful tea canisters, and branches of the shop all over Scandinavia.

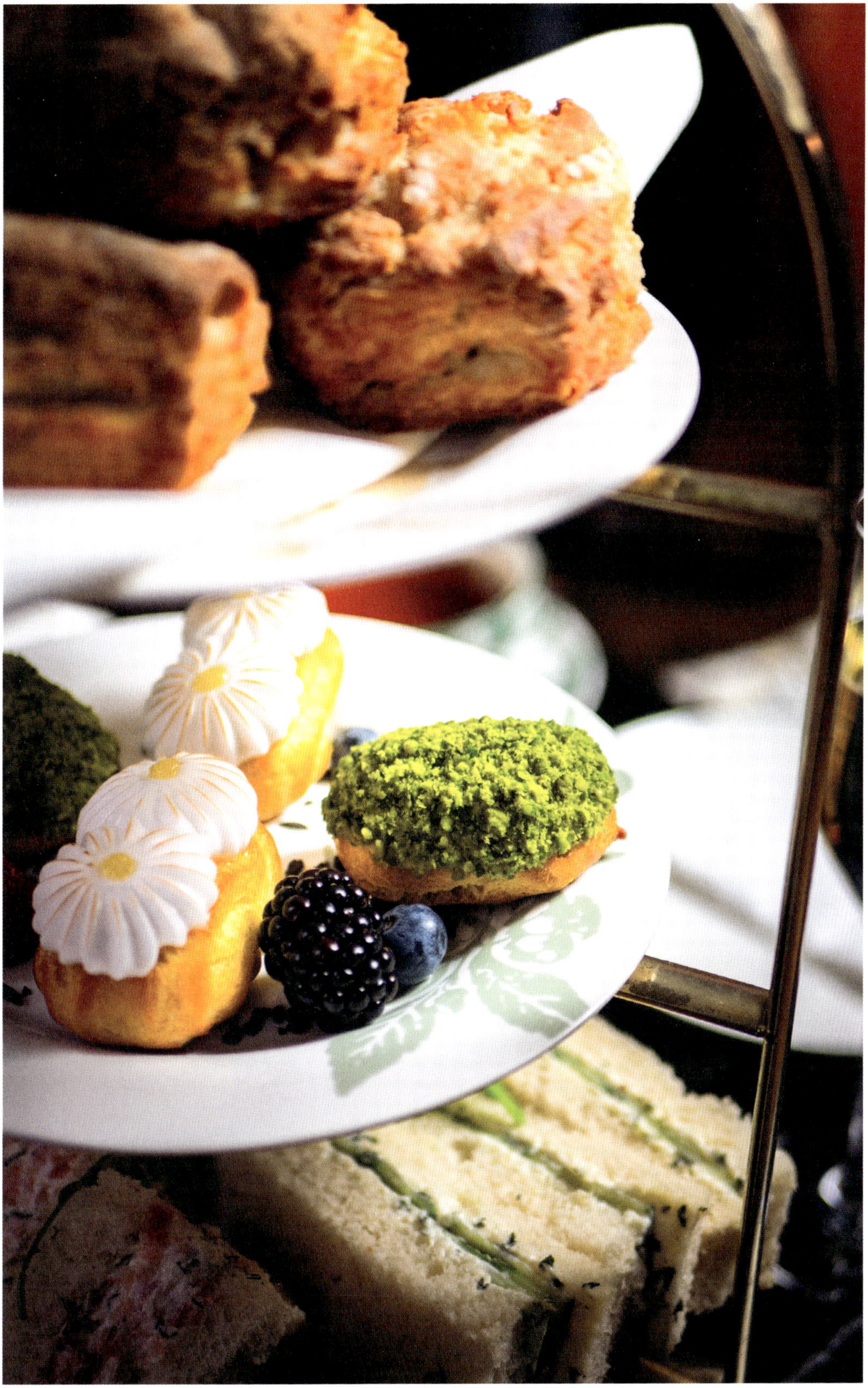

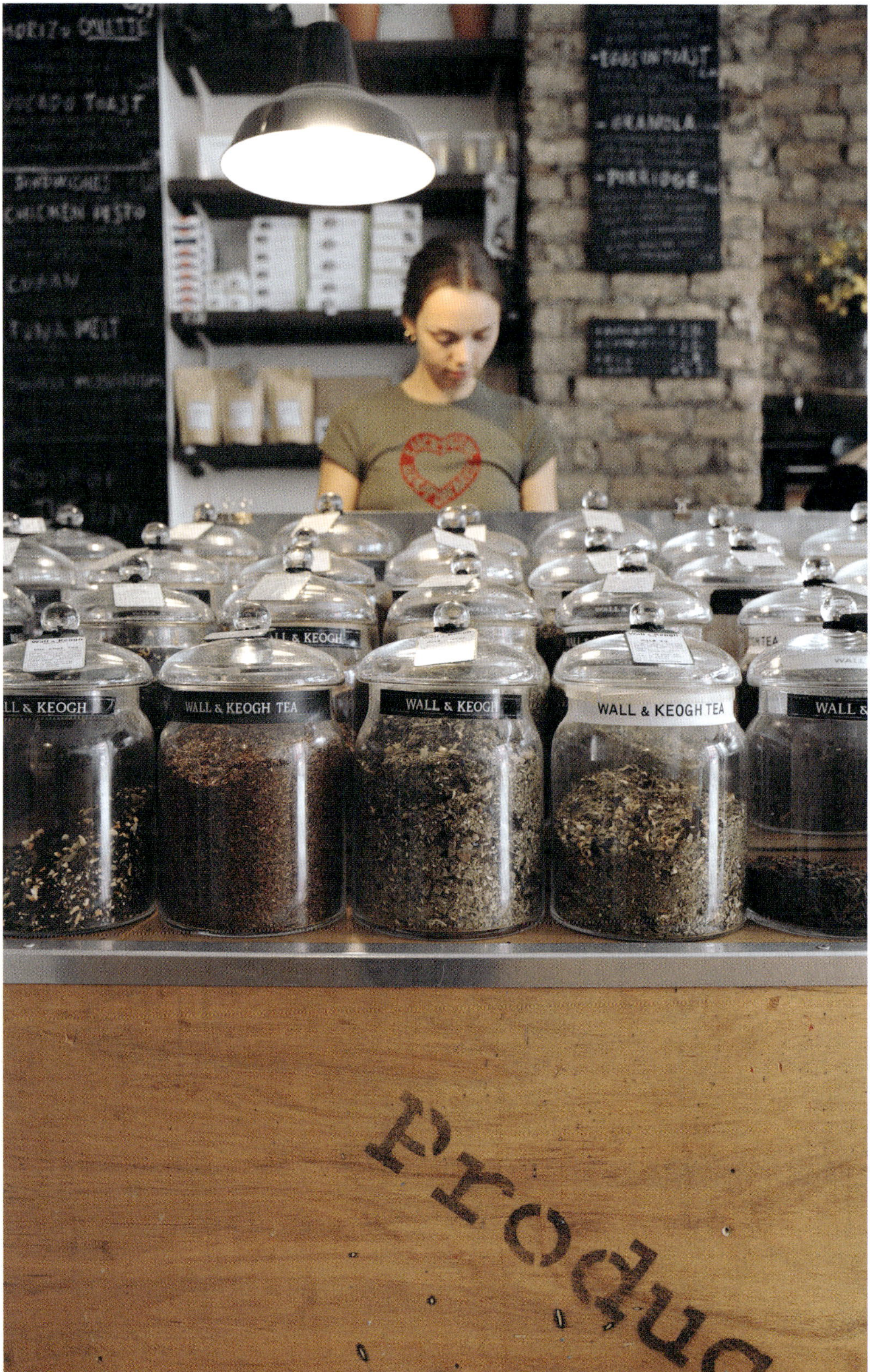
GRANOLA
PORRIDGE
WALL & KEOGH TEA
Produc

EUROPE · DUBLIN

53 WALL & KEOGH

45 Richmond Street S, Portobello, Dublin, D02 XD93, Ireland

TO VISIT BEFORE YOU DIE BECAUSE

This neighbourhood spot sells 150 different loose-leaf teas as well as freshly baked bread and homemade cakes.

Ireland ranks second when it comes to tea consumption per capita, so it's no wonder there's a blend of tea named after the country – the famous Irish Breakfast. A dark mahogany brew perfect with milk and sugar, it's one of the bestselling teas here at Wall & Keogh, a Dublin specialist in superior loose-leaf tea since 2010. Other popular blends include Put the Cat Out (an infusion of chamomile flowers, lime blossom and lavender) and Life of Brian (a green tea with sandalwood and papaya), and you can sample them at Wall & Keogh's great local café in Portobello. As the team says, 'Life is just too short for low-grade tea; enjoy it as it was meant to be!' Start the day with the aforementioned Irish Breakfast and eggs on sourdough toast, or head there on a grey afternoon for a cup of Rooibos Unicorn Tears (with strawberries and raspberries) and a slice of homemade carrot cake or banana bread. There's also a cute little patio at the back – it has a clear roof so can be used even when it's raining.

wallandkeogh.com

EUROPE — EDINBURGH

54 ROYAL DECK TEAROOM

The Royal Yacht *Britannia*, Ocean Drive, Edinburgh, EH6 6JJ, United Kingdom

---

TO VISIT BEFORE YOU DIE BECAUSE

Have a chic cream tea on the deck of Queen Elizabeth II's former floating palace, in Edinburgh's port of Leith.

Launched in Scotland in 1953, Queen Elizabeth's Yacht *Britannia* served the royal family on 968 official voyages, stopping at 600 ports and in over 135 countries. Today, you can have a cup of tea in the very same spot where the royal family would have played deck games and entertained friends and leading figures such as Nelson Mandela and Winston Churchill. The teas are supplied by Brodies of Musselburgh and include Duchess Earl Grey, a take on Earl Grey with lemon verbena and orange blossom; the fragrant Gopaldhara TGBOP Second Flush Darjeeling, harvested high in the foothills of the Himalayas; and the HMY *Britannia*'s homemade sweetened iced tea. Baked by HMY *Britannia*'s on-board pastry chefs, treats include three types of scones and Dundee cake, a rich fruitcake with candied citrus peel, currants and almonds. Note that you'll need to buy a tour ticket to access the tea room (all proceeds go towards preserving the historic ship), and there's more tea on offer next door at the Fingal, a floating luxury hotel.

royalyachtbritannia.co.uk +44 1 315 555 566

EUROPE · GENEVA

55 PAGES & SIPS

37 Grand-Rue, 1204 Geneva, Switzerland

TO VISIT BEFORE YOU DIE BECAUSE

Pair fine loose teas and classic reads at this great bookstore and tea room, open seven days a week (unheard of in Geneva!).

Geneva is better known for its lake and Jet d'Eau fountain than its old town, yet the historic, hilltop heart of the city is a great place to meander, with terraces spilling out onto pretty squares and bubbling stone fountains. A stone's throw from the cathedral and historic Maison Tavel, and opposite Jean-Jacques Rousseau's birthplace, is this charming bookstore and tea shop, which caters to both English readers and scone lovers. Scones are freshly baked every morning and served with Gruyère double cream – a Swiss speciality that some would say trumps the original Cornish clotted cream. As well as plain, chocolate and fruit scones, there are also quiches and salads, which you can enjoy with a selection of 30 loose-leaf teas from Betjeman & Barton (see page 127) or homemade iced tea. Speaking of which, we suggest that after finishing your teapot at Pages & Sips, you grab a classic iced tea – Switzerland's unofficial national drink – from the local Migros supermarket and head to the city's Bains des Pâquis for a dip.

EUROPE · GLASGOW

56 MACKINTOSH AT THE WILLOW

215–217 Sauchiehall Street, Glasgow, G2 3EX, United Kingdom

TO VISIT BEFORE YOU DIE BECAUSE

Enjoy afternoon tea in Modern Style splendour at this unique tea room by the great Scottish designer Charles Rennie Mackintosh.

Located on Glasgow's main shopping street, Mackintosh at the Willow is the only surviving tea room designed by Charles Rennie Mackintosh and his wife Margaret Macdonald for Miss Catherine Cranston. The daughter of a baker and hotelier and sister of a tea dealer, she commissioned Mackintosh to create stunning tea rooms as part of the popular temperance movement, which sought an alternative to male-centred pubs. The last surviving example, opened in 1903 on Sauchiehall Street, is still in use today, so you can admire its breathtaking Art Nouveau interiors while sitting on a ladder-back chair and nibbling on spiced shortbread. Teas include Scottish chai, orange blossom oolong and the bespoke 1903 blend. Created by PekoeTea Edinburgh, it contains teas from Sri Lanka and China and rose petals referencing Mackintosh's rose motif. For special occasions, afternoon tea is served in the Salon de Luxe, a jewel-like purple private dining room. Make sure to book a tour and visit the permanent exhibition to learn more about this architectural masterpiece and the four-year restoration project.

EUROPE　　　　　　　　　　　HARROGATE

57　**BETTYS**

1 Parliament Street, Harrogate, HG1 2QU, United Kingdom

TO VISIT BEFORE YOU DIE BECAUSE

Try a strong, bespoke tea blend and Fat Rascals scones at this Yorkshire institution in the spa town of Harrogate.

Swiss orphan Frederick Belmont learned the art of baking as he travelled across Europe in search of work, before settling in Yorkshire and opening Bettys in 1919. Today, the fourth-generation family business celebrates both its Swiss heritage and its Yorkshire roots, which is why you can have bircher muesli or rösti for breakfast and alpine macaroni and Fendant wine for lunch, before sampling a cream tea or afternoon tea (of which there's also a high-end version, served upstairs in the Imperial Room, with accompanying pianist). Make sure to try the signature Fat Rascals – big, fruity scones decorated with a cheeky glacé cherry and almond face and served with butter. Teas are bespoke blends supplied by sister company Taylors of Harrogate, the maker of Yorkshire Tea, widely considered the only purveyor of a 'proper brew' by some British milk tea drinkers – including myself! (Although those in camp PG Tips would disagree.) Bettys also has a branch on York's St. Helen's Square.

bettys.co.uk　　　　　　　　+44 8 004 561 919

EUROPE · HELSINKI

58 THÉHUONE

Eerikinkatu 10, 00100 Helsinki, Finland

TO VISIT BEFORE YOU DIE BECAUSE

Sample teas from all corners of the globe at this Scandi-chic tea shop and tea room, the oldest in Finland.

As you'd expect for a boutique located in the Design District, the décor at Théhuone is pure Scandinavian minimalism – no floral teacups here, I'm afraid. Instead, tea is served in sleek white porcelain cups and gorgeous transparent teapots, which are perfect to watch flowering teas (available in flavours such as peach and pineapple) unfurl. There's only a handful of tables and a seating area with floor cushions by the window from which to enjoy a selection of over 400 teas, carefully selected by sisters Nina and Nea, who founded the tea room in 2005. Flavoured teas are particularly popular here, such as classic Earl Grey and cherry-flavoured Sencha Sakura, as well as rare pu-erh varieties from Yunnan (which you can buy in cakes) and the finest oolong teas from Taiwan. The knowledgeable team also organises tea tastings and private sessions. In keeping with the pared-back décor (by local studio Pure Design), which lets the teas do the talking, there is no food menu – but drinks do come with little biscuits, mochis or a piece of green tea chocolate on the side.

thehuone.com +35 8 505 510 711

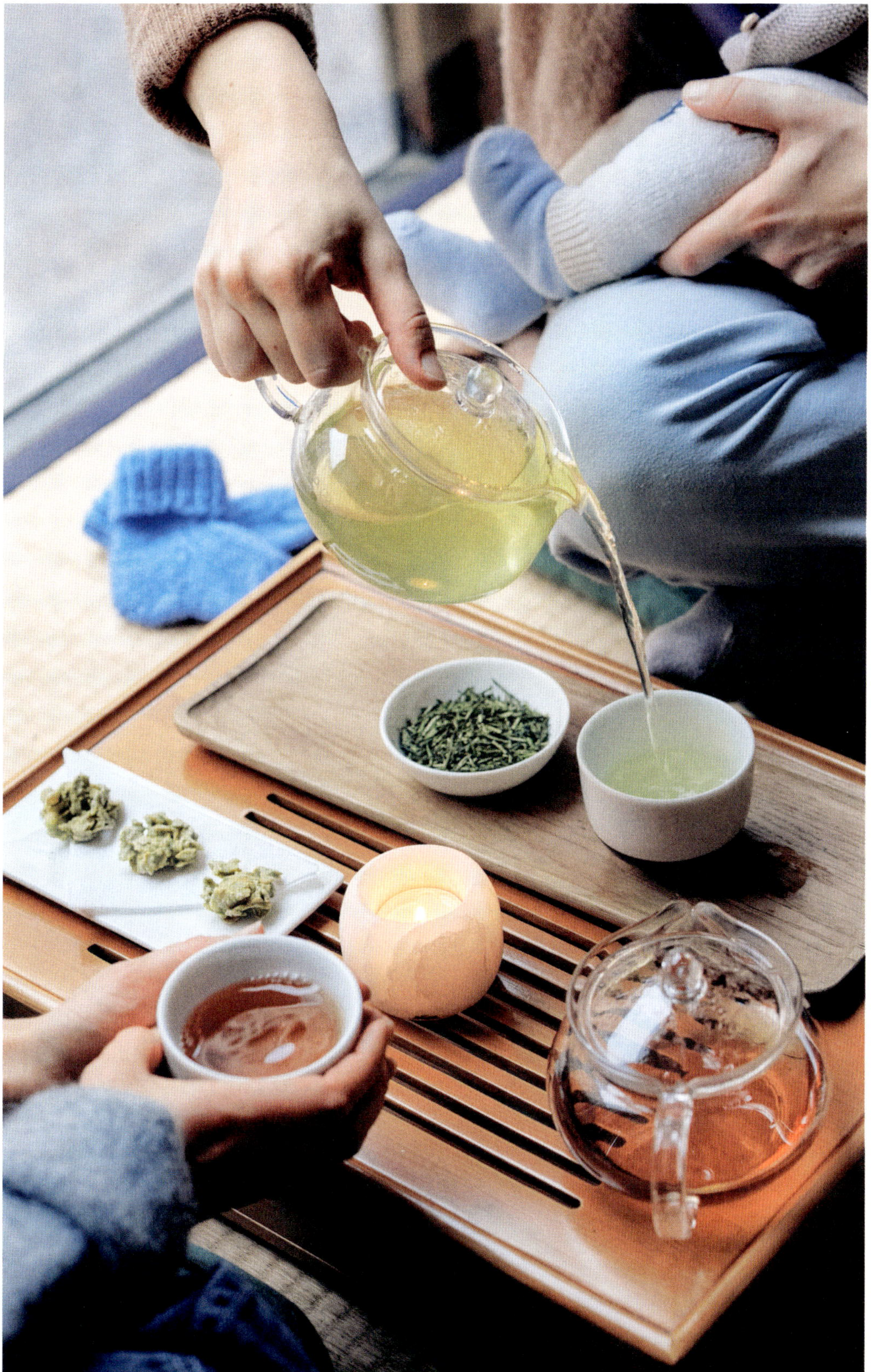

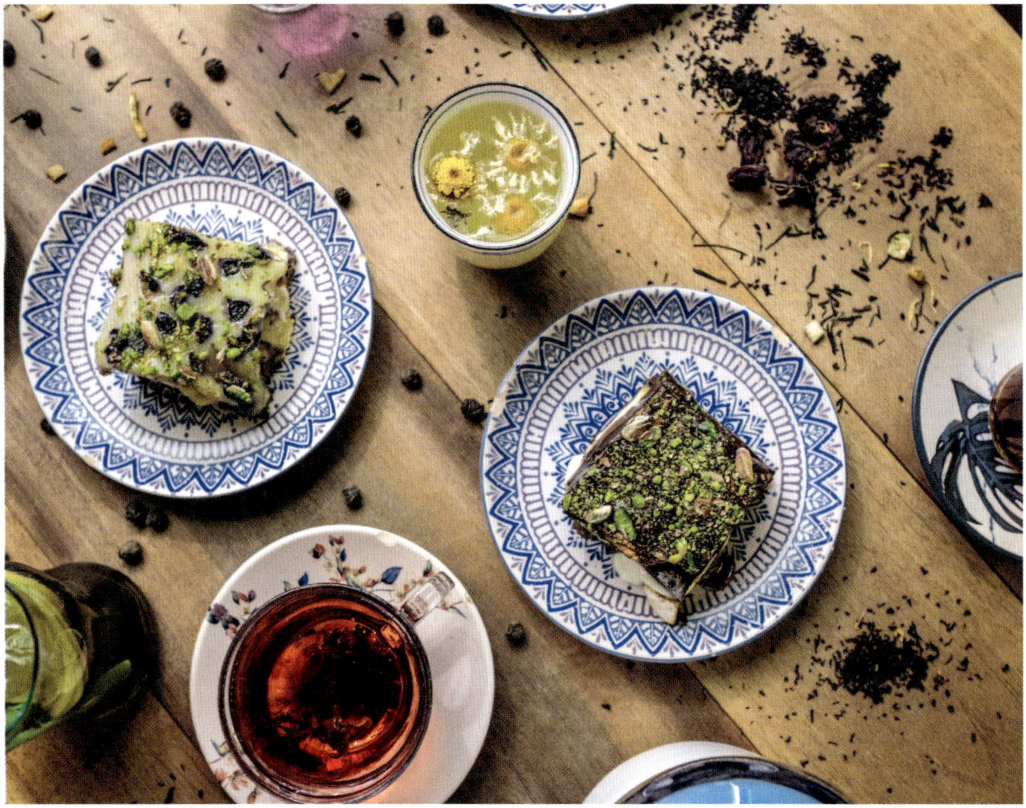

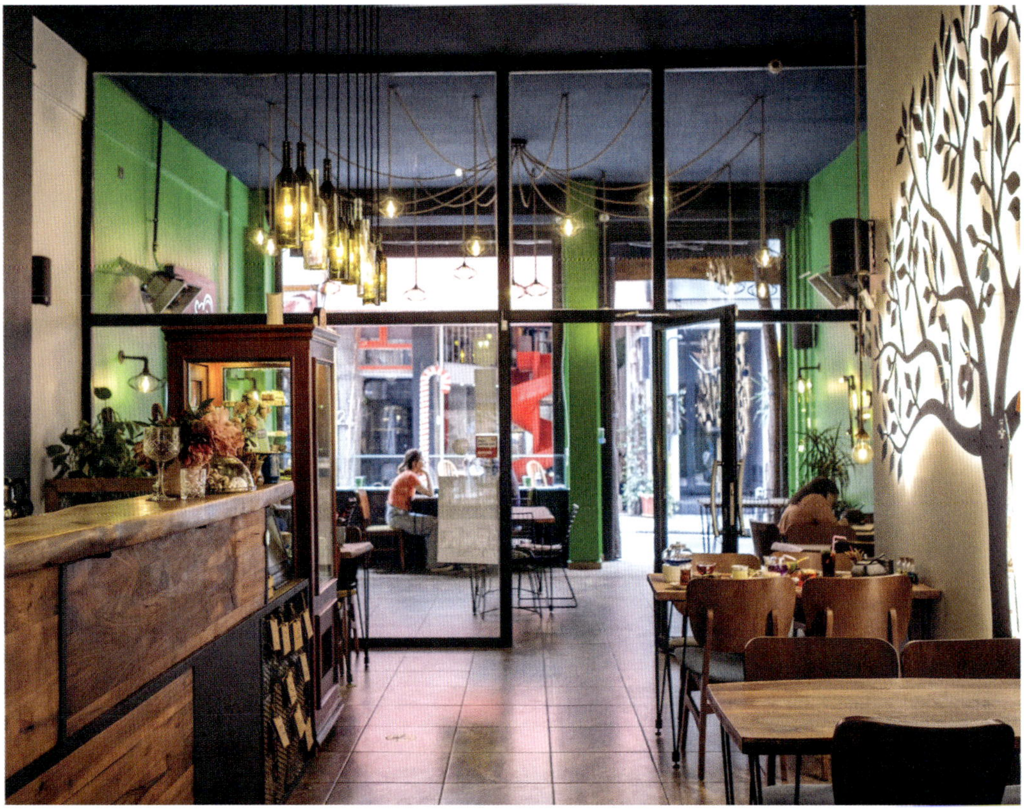

EUROPE   ISTANBUL

59 CHA'YA MODA

Caferağa Mahallesi Bademaltı Sokak 17/B,
34710 Kadıköy/Istanbul, Turkey

TO VISIT BEFORE YOU DIE BECAUSE

This great local tea room serves fine teas from Turkey and abroad, as well as amazing signature cakes and sweet treats.

Located on the Asian side of Istanbul, the Moda neighbourhood of Kadıköy has seen a boom in new cafés, boutiques and restaurants opening in the past few years. Away from the tourist crowds of Galata, it's a great place to soak up the city's atmosphere in a more relaxed setting. So, hop on the ferry to reach this charming local tea room, named after the Japanese word for teahouse. It offers authentic teapots, mugs and teacups as well as nearly 60 teas, including the bestselling Pink Wishes (silver needle white tea with raspberry, strawberry and hibiscus), lapsang souchong, strawberry white chocolate matcha latte and blue butterfly pea tea with elderflower. If you prefer a traditional Turkish black tea, you will be treated to a rare first-harvest organic tea from Hemşin, in the country's main tea-producing district, Rize, near the Black Sea. Last but not least is the dessert menu, including original recipes such as baklava cheesecake and *İncir uyutması*, a fig pudding served on walnut *kadayıf*. Enjoy it in the little back garden, where the resident cats like to nap.

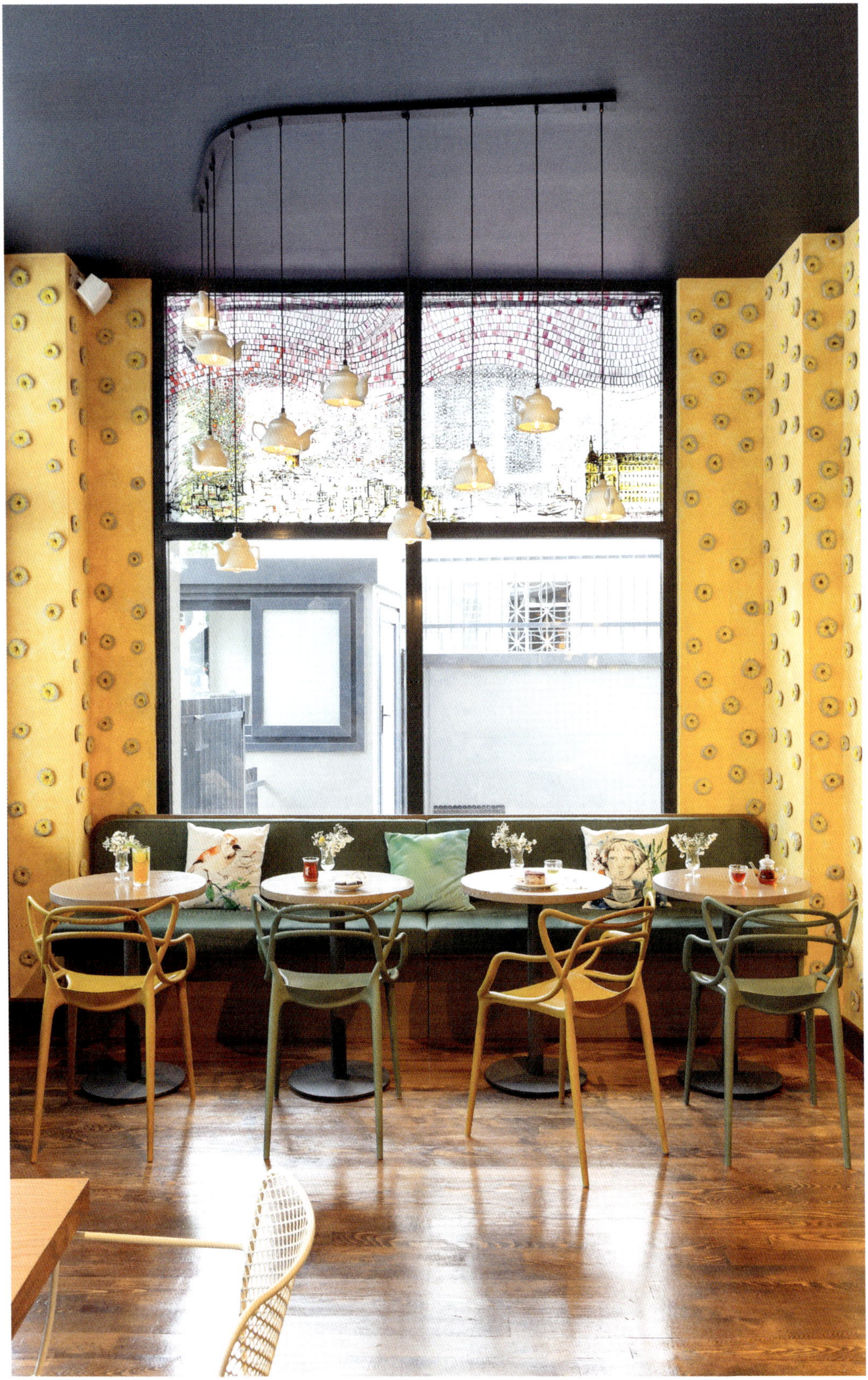

EUROPE ISTANBUL

60 DEM MODA

Caferağa, Şair Nefi Sokak 9/1, 34710 Kadıköy/Istanbul, Turkey

TO VISIT BEFORE YOU DIE BECAUSE

This warm and welcoming tea room in the new cultural centre of Istanbul serves premium teas from around the world.

'Our tea room is named after the Turkish word *dem*, which refers to the heart, fragrance and smell of tea and unfortunately has no exact translation in English,' explains owner Ömer Çağatay. Opened in 2013 in Karaköy, Dem was the first café dedicated to the world of tea in the city. It moved to Moda in 2019, where it continues to offer premium Turkish teas; homemade iced teas, such as Velvet and White Lemonade; and its own Teastar Collection of handpicked high-quality rare teas. On the menu are over 60 teas from around the world, served differently to honour the culture they come from. Can't decide? Ask the staff to help you with a 'tea smelling' session and information on the various sources and qualities of the tea. Treats include afternoon tea, while house specials range from a dulce de leche cheesecake to a bruschetta made with *simit* (a Turkish sesame ring). For spectacular views of the Sea of Marmara, continue your tea tour of Moda and head to the seaside park, where you can have more tea at the ever-popular Moda Aile Çay Bahçesi.

@demistanbul

61 MELEZ TEA LAB

Reşitpaşa, Kongre Caddesi 81/A, 34400 Sarıyer/Istanbul, Turkey

TO VISIT BEFORE YOU DIE BECAUSE

This unique multisensory tea experience in northern Istanbul pairs artisanal blends with bespoke music playlists.

After a walk in Istanbul's enchanting Belgrad Forest, head to this peaceful haven located in the city's northeastern suburbs. It was founded in 2015 by tea sommelier Liliana L. Aslanoba and Emre Aslanoba with the mission of sharing the benefits of tea for mind, body and soul. Designed by Aslı Baysan, the zen-like space reimagines the Japanese tea room to convey the essence of Melez Tea, 'harmony between east and west, old and new,' says Liliana. Melez offers tea-tasting flights, as well as signature creations including matcha affogato and chai-spiced hot chocolate. There are also artisanal blends, each story and recipe created by a tea sommelier and blended locally in Istanbul. Each has its own playlist, assembled as attentively as the tea itself, so you can listen to jazz while sipping Sleep Tea, or indulge in classical tunes over a cup of Beauty Tea. 'We're committed to creating a multisensory experience; a place where you find yourself fully immersed in the moment as the tea notes hit your taste buds,' says Emre.

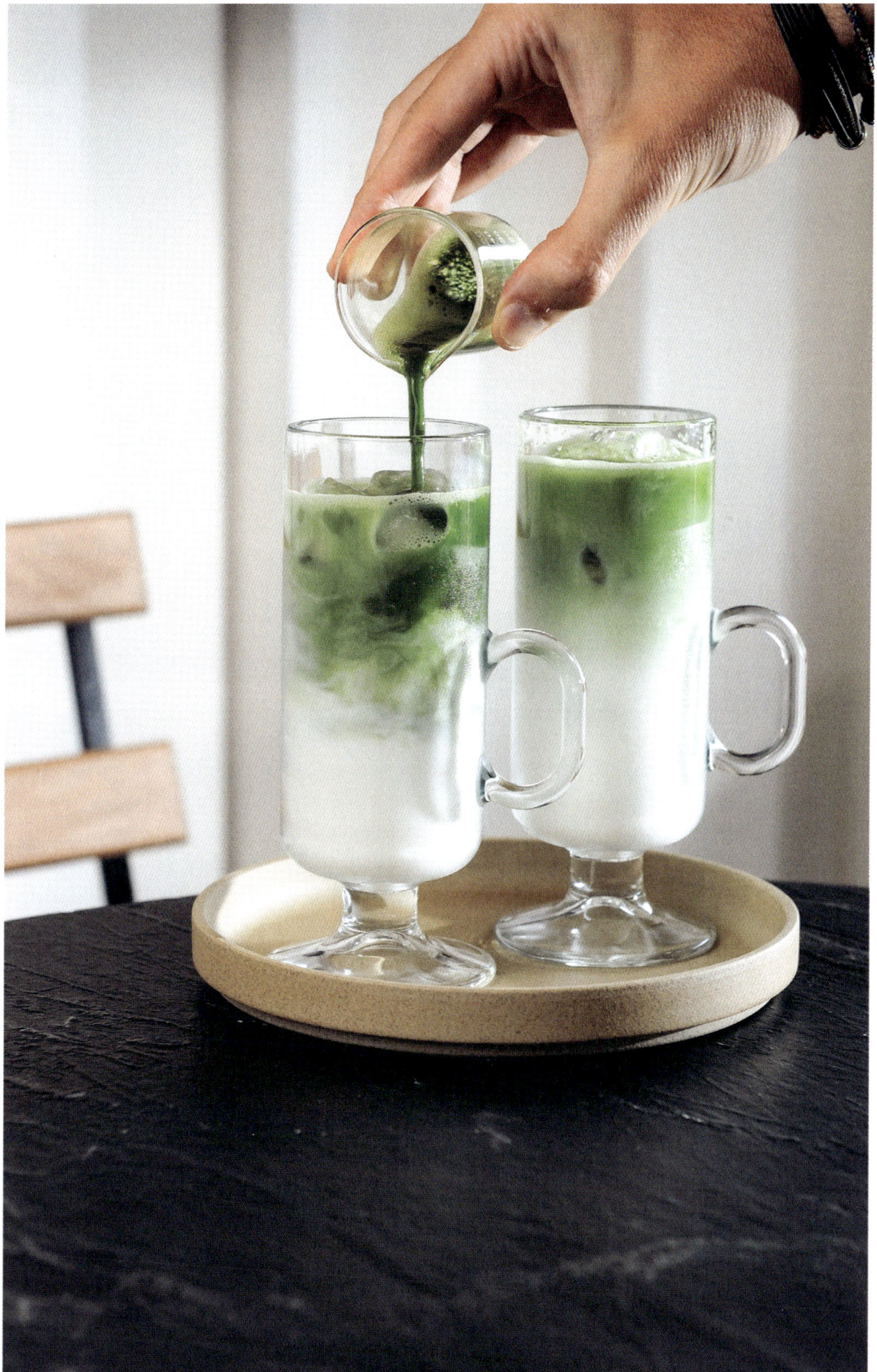

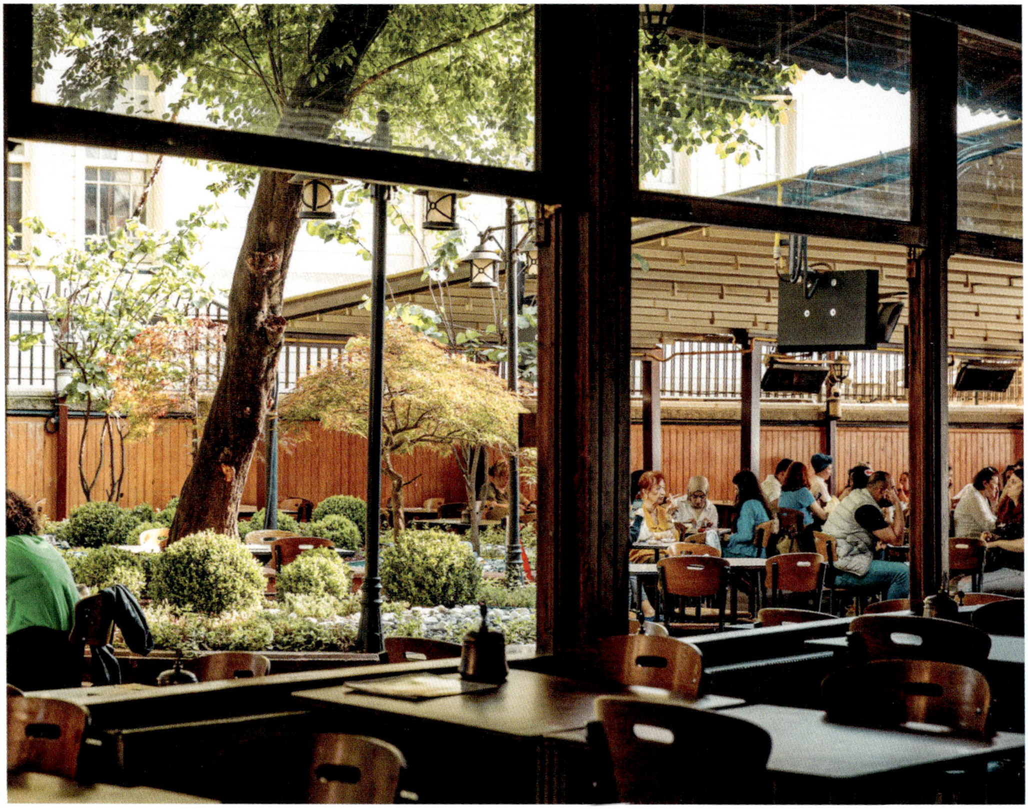

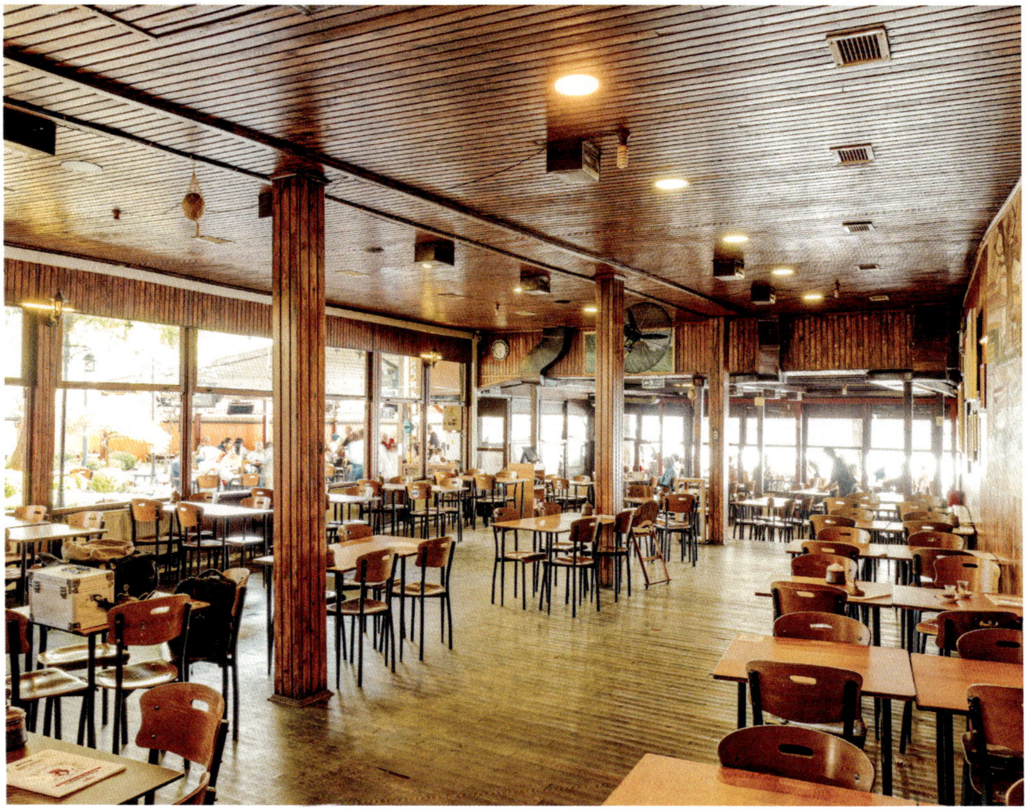

EUROPE　　　　　　　ISTANBUL

62　TARIHI ÇINARALTI

Çengelköy Mahalle, Çengelköy Caddesi, Çınarlı Cami Sokak No. 4, 34680 Üsküdar/Istanbul, Turkey

TO VISIT BEFORE YOU DIE BECAUSE

Cross the Bosphorus for a fabulous view of the skyline of the Old City and cups of strong traditional black tea.

Lined with old Ottoman mansions, the Asian shore of the Bosphorus Strait is popular with locals, who head to the waterfront promenade of towns such as Çengelköy to enjoy the riverside views… and drink countless cups of tea, of course. Turkey is the world's leading tea-drinking country, with each Turk consuming an average of 1,300 cups of tea per year. Join them under a thousand-year-old sycamore tree on the terrace of Tarihi Çinaraltı, which offers panoramic views of the Bosphorus Strait and the European side of Istanbul. It's great for breakfast, but you can also just turn up for a cup of black tea or apple tea. Turkish tea is served boiling hot in tulip-shaped glasses, so make sure to hold them by the rim unless you want to burn your fingers. You can bring your own pastries, too, such as a sesame bagel from the Çengelköy bakery next door. But be warned, you'll have to share the space with stray cats and seagulls, and it gets really busy at the weekend.

@tarihicinaralti

EUROPE — LEICESTER

63 CHAIIWALA FOSSE PARK

Fosse Park Avenue, Leicester, LE19 1HQ, United Kingdom

TO VISIT BEFORE YOU DIE BECAUSE

The flagship tea room of this halal chain is the place to enjoy an authentic masala chai and sample some Indian street snacks.

The UK is not short on chains, but still something was missing: a nice place to go for a cup of tea and a chat, in the daytime or the evening – somewhere that wasn't a pub or an American coffee chain. Enter chaiiwala, which has been on quite a journey, opening new locations around the country – including drive-throughs in Bolton and Blackburn – at breakneck speed. Established in 2015 by Muhummed Ibrahim, the great-grandson of a New Delhi tea seller, it now operates over 100 sites, and it's even a hit in London's trendy Dalston. Its flagship location, at Fosse Park in the brand's hometown of Leicester, tells the story of a tea room empire that attracts a young, friendly and diverse crowd of tea lovers. The signature *karak* chai is pre-steeped for at least 40 minutes for maximum flavour and is included in the popular Desi breakfast, a spiced omelette with masala beans or daal, with rotis, parathas or toast. Also on offer are a pink chai cake and *ghulab jamun* cheesecake.

fossepark.chaiiwala.co.uk

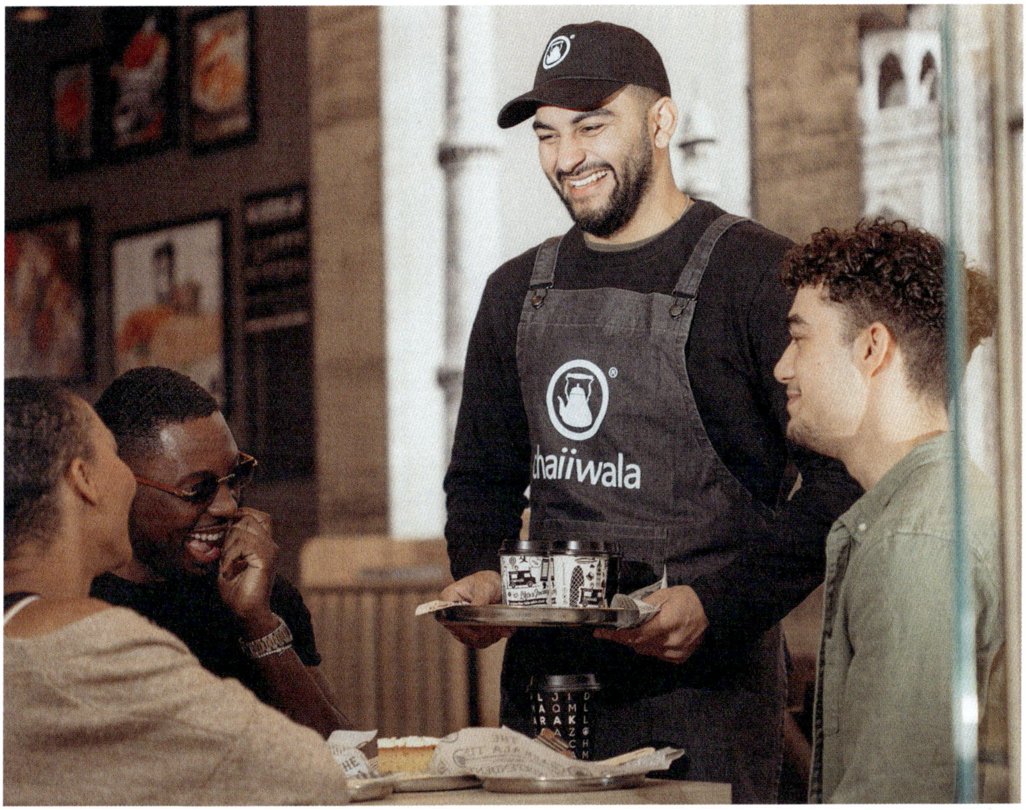
chaiiwala

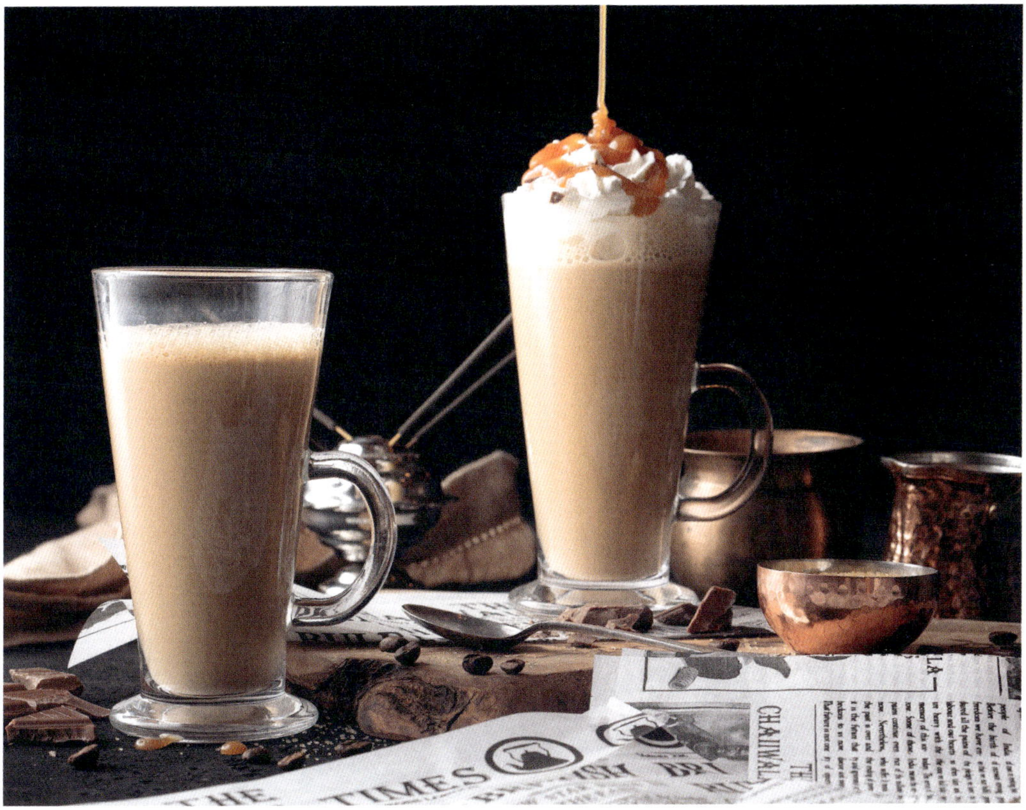
TIMES

EUROPE — LIZARD

64 HOUSEL BAY HOTEL

Housel Bay Road, Lizard, Helston TR12 7PG, United Kingdom

TO VISIT BEFORE YOU DIE BECAUSE

Sample an authentic Cornish cream tea with bracing sea views of the Lizard Peninsula, at the UK's most southerly tip.

Although Devon and Cornwall cannot agree on who invented the cream tea and, worse, cannot agree on how to eat it (clotted cream first, or jam first?), the UK's West Country is certainly the best place to enjoy this afternoon treat. Usually served with a pot of English Breakfast tea (a robust blend of Kenyan, Assam and Ceylon black teas), it comprises freshly baked scones, strawberry jam and clotted cream – the rich, thick and delicious cream that is a local speciality. One of the best places to enjoy it is at Housel Bay, an award-winning small hotel located on the dramatic Lizard Peninsula. Here, depending on the 'predictably unpredictable weather', you can enjoy a cream tea in the Terrace restaurant overlooking the Lizard Lighthouse, in the sea-front garden, or even take it with you to the nearby beach or for a walk along the South West Coast Path. The scenery is truly breathtaking, while head chef Joseph Fallowfield ensures the ingredients – from local producers including the Trewithen Dairy and Cornish Tea Company – are first-rate. An afternoon tea version comes with sandwiches and seasonal miniature cakes.

EUROPE — LONDON

65 CLARIDGE'S

Brook Street, London, W1K 4HR, United Kingdom

TO VISIT BEFORE YOU DIE BECAUSE

This Art Deco landmark in London's Mayfair district has been serving luxurious afternoon teas for over 150 years.

Housed in a building designed by Charles William Stephens, the architect of Harrods, and decked out in full Art Deco glory in the 1920s by Basil Ionides, Claridge's is a pretty unique place – and they know it full well: 'There are many five-star hotels in London but nowhere quite like Claridge's.' The attention to detail here is simply jaw-dropping: sit in the foyer under a Dale Chihuly glass sculpture and admire the original Art Deco screens and mirrors, the bespoke cutlery and porcelain tableware (sporting the hotel's unique jade-and-white chevron pattern) and the beautifully illustrated menu. To the sound of piano music, you can enjoy a carefully thought-through afternoon tea featuring the classic combination of fine finger sandwiches, scones and pastries. There are tea pairing tips (hō-jicha is suggested for the sandwiches, for example) and fine loose-leaf teas selected by Henrietta Lovell of the Rare Tea Company. The hotel's signature blend has a deep, malty finish, while the Cornish Earl Grey is sourced from Tregothnan, the very first tea estate in England.

EUROPE　　　　　　　　　LONDON

66 FORTNUM & MASON

181 Piccadilly, St. James's, London, W1A 1ER, United Kingdom

TO VISIT BEFORE YOU DIE BECAUSE

The great department store on London's Piccadilly is a world-leading purveyor of rare teas and fine preserves.

Named in honour of Queen Elizabeth II, who inaugurated the room in 2012, Fortnum & Mason's Diamond Jubilee Tea Salon is a real crowd-pleaser, with five types of afternoon tea (including one made without gluten), featuring Fortnum & Mason's own strawberry and Champagne preserve or lemon curd. Marmalades and jams are one of the department store's specialities; the other is, of course, tea, which has been sold here since 1707. Fortnum & Mason's team of experts sources the finest, rarest small-batch teas from around the world, resulting in an incredible tea menu (tea-tasting experiences are also available). House blends include the original Smoky Earl Grey, dating from 1835, while fine teas range from Chinese bi luo chun and *rose pouchong* to the latest innovation, a non-alcoholic sparkling tea. There are just too many to mention, and all are available to purchase, beautifully packaged, in the adjoining ground-floor boutique. There is also another Fortnum & Mason tea room in the spectacular courtyard of The Royal Exchange at Bank, which tends to be less crowded.

EUROPE   LONDON

67   PETERSHAM NURSERIES TEAHOUSE

Petersham Road, off Church Lane, Richmond, London, TW10 7AB, United Kingdom

TO VISIT BEFORE YOU DIE BECAUSE

Enjoy a dreamy afternoon tea in an enchanting plant-filled glasshouse in leafy Richmond – the perfect English country garden setting.

Located just between the Thames and Richmond Park, this garden centre and slow food hotspot was opened in 2004 by Gael and Francesco Boglione. Inspired by Francesco's travels to India and Gael's love for nature and ability to draw beauty out of the simplest things, Petersham Nurseries is a mix of plants, furniture, antiques and gifts. One of the large glasshouses is a restaurant, the other a magical tea room filled with fresh flowers and a table full of delicious homemade cakes. Under climbing bougainvillea, vines and fragrant jasmine, you can enjoy teas such as English Breakfast ('big, beautiful, exuberant'), Jade Tips green tea ('cut grass, succulent, verdant') and freshly made herbal infusions. From Thursday to Sunday, you can also book a garden afternoon tea featuring a series of seasonal bites, such as a roast beef, rocket and horseradish cream sandwich with pumpkin sunflower choux or a slice of pistachio loaf with cream cheese and a spiced pear éclair. Many ingredients are sourced from the company's own farm in Devon.

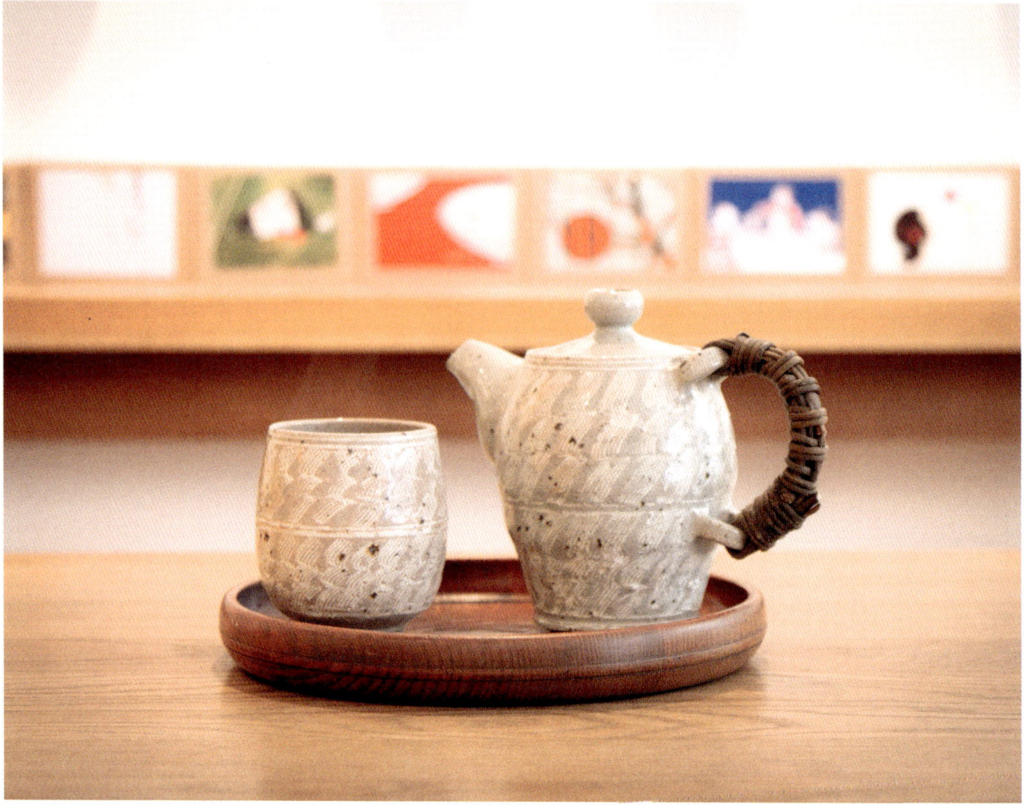

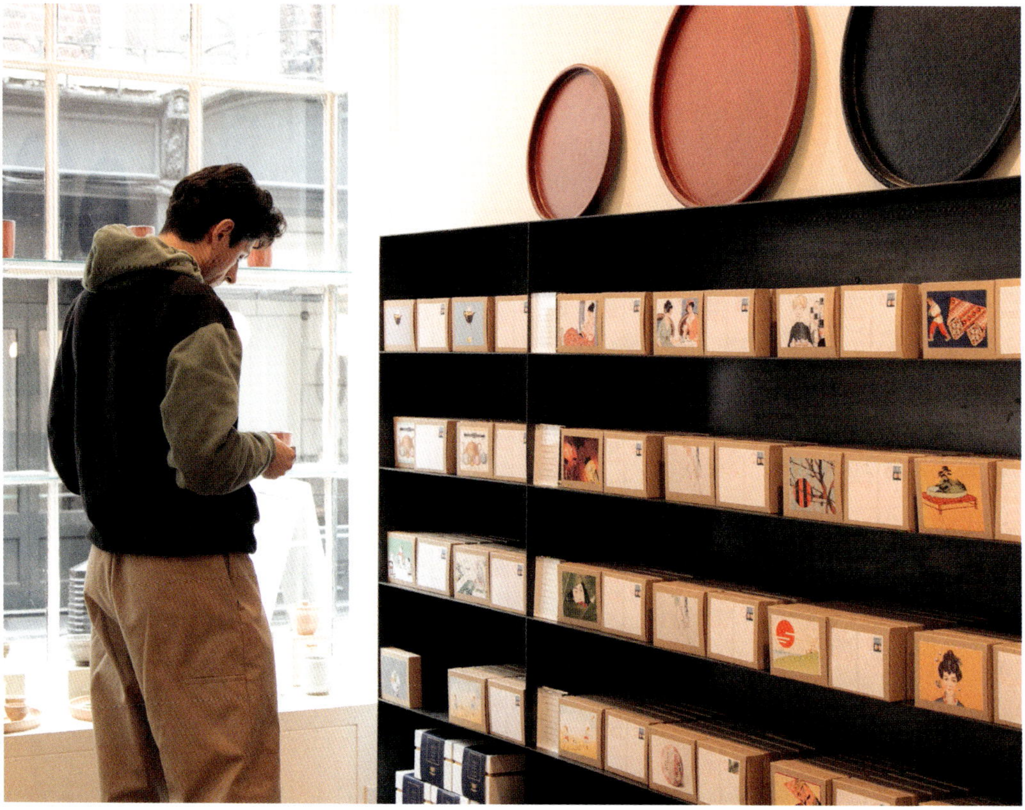

EUROPE — LONDON

68 POSTCARD TEAS

9 Dering Street, London, W1S 1AG, United Kingdom

TO VISIT BEFORE YOU DIE BECAUSE

Learn all about 'small tea' at this London specialist shop and tasting room opened by a pioneering team nearly 20 years ago.

There are very few tea shops in London, or at least none of the tea chains that are common in European cities. What we do have, though, are a handful of specialist tea boutiques, and the most famous of them all is Postcard Teas, near New Bond Street. Led by a team of experts who scour the world's tea-growing regions, it was the first company to put the maker's name and location on all of its 70 teas in 2008. Then, in 2012, it decided to sell only 'small tea' sourced from micro-farms (with an average size of two football fields), as it is 'better for the people, the local economy, and the planet'. On Saturdays, the beautiful teaware display table turns into a tasting table for the Tea School, a fascinating one-hour session with a focus on a different type of tea every week. A green tea tasting, for example, will take in Longjing teas by Master Luo, a Korean sparrow's tongue and a Fuji sencha by Master Akiyama in Shizuoka.

postcardteas.com +44 2 076 293 654

EUROPE — LONDON

69 THE GALLERY AT SKETCH

9 Conduit Street, Mayfair, London, W1S 2XG, United Kingdom

TO VISIT BEFORE YOU DIE BECAUSE

This destination tea room in Mayfair has the motto 'Eat, Music, Drink, Art' and an exquisite menu featuring fine teas by Lalani & Co London.

The concept of afternoon tea appeared only in the 1840s, when Anna Maria Russell, Duchess of Bedford, started the trend by inviting her friends to join her for tea, bread and butter in the afternoon. Combined with the Earl of Sandwich's own invention, afternoon tea became a fashionable social event, with ladies dressing up for the occasion. Continue the tradition at The Gallery at Sketch, a chic tea room known for sunshine-yellow walls and well-dressed customers (the novelty egg-shaped toilet pods are also a hit). Redesigned by India Mahdavi, with art by Yinka Shonibare, the space is complemented by eye-catching patisseries such as Battenberg cake and opera cake. But it's not all about the looks: the menu also features fine teas by specialists Lalani & Co London, including a traditional iron Buddha from Dazhai Garden in Fujian and an organic Darjeeling second flush from Okayti and Pussimbing gardens. Founded in 2003 by Mourad Mazouz, Sketch is located in an 18th-century townhouse once home to Christian Dior's London studio and comprises many bars and restaurants, including the three-Michelin-starred Lecture Room and Library by Pierre Gagnaire.

sketch.london +44 2 076 594 500

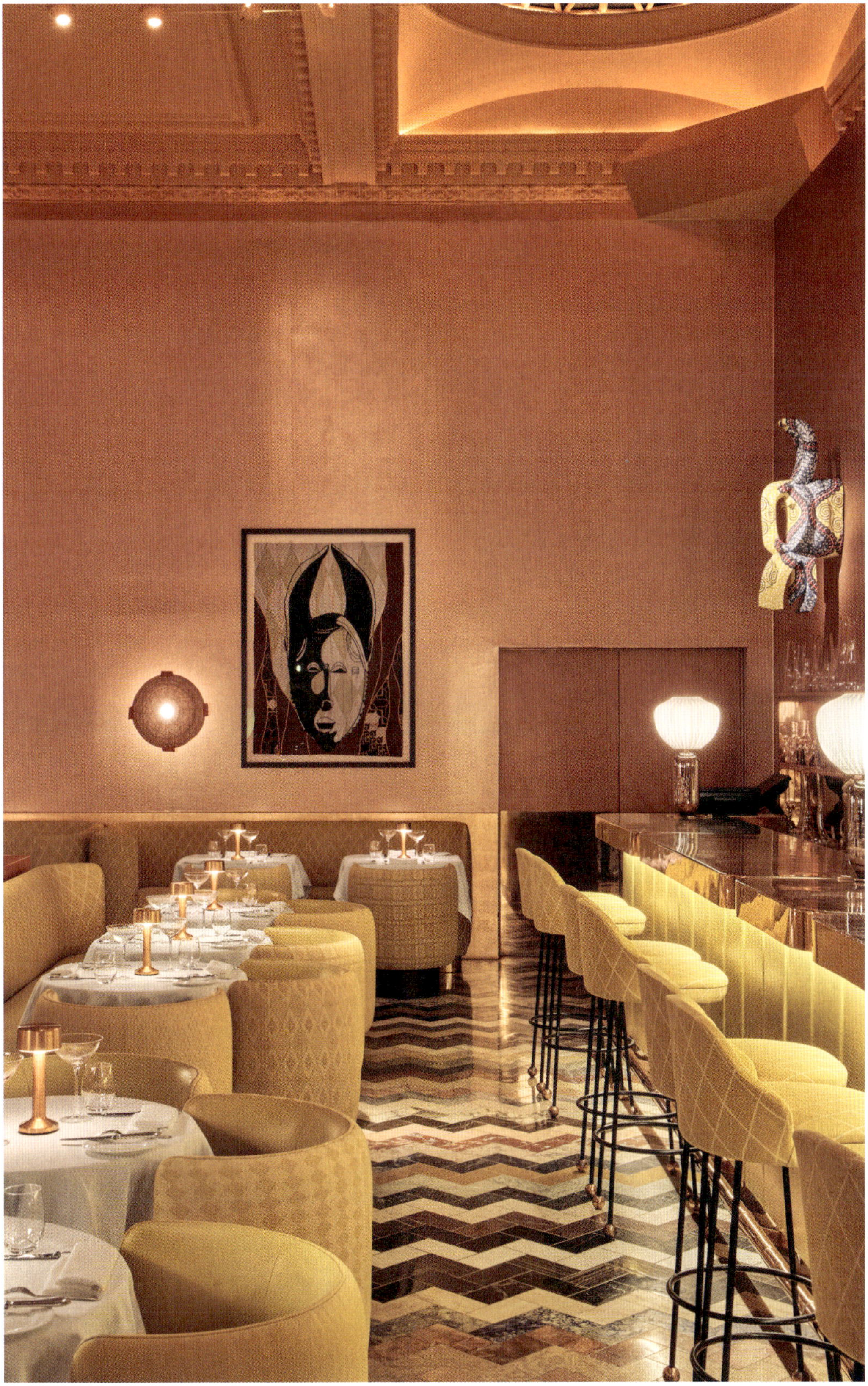

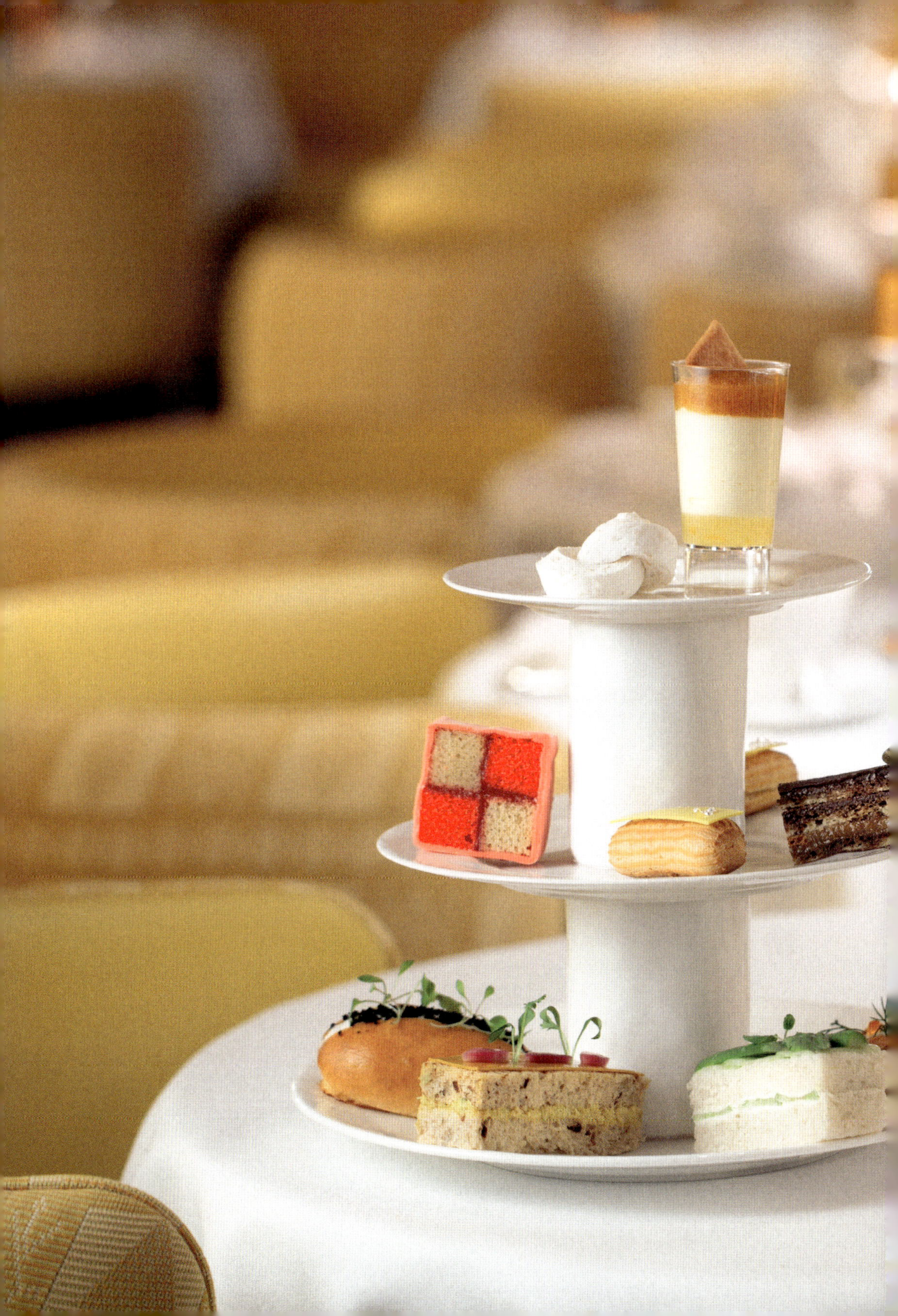

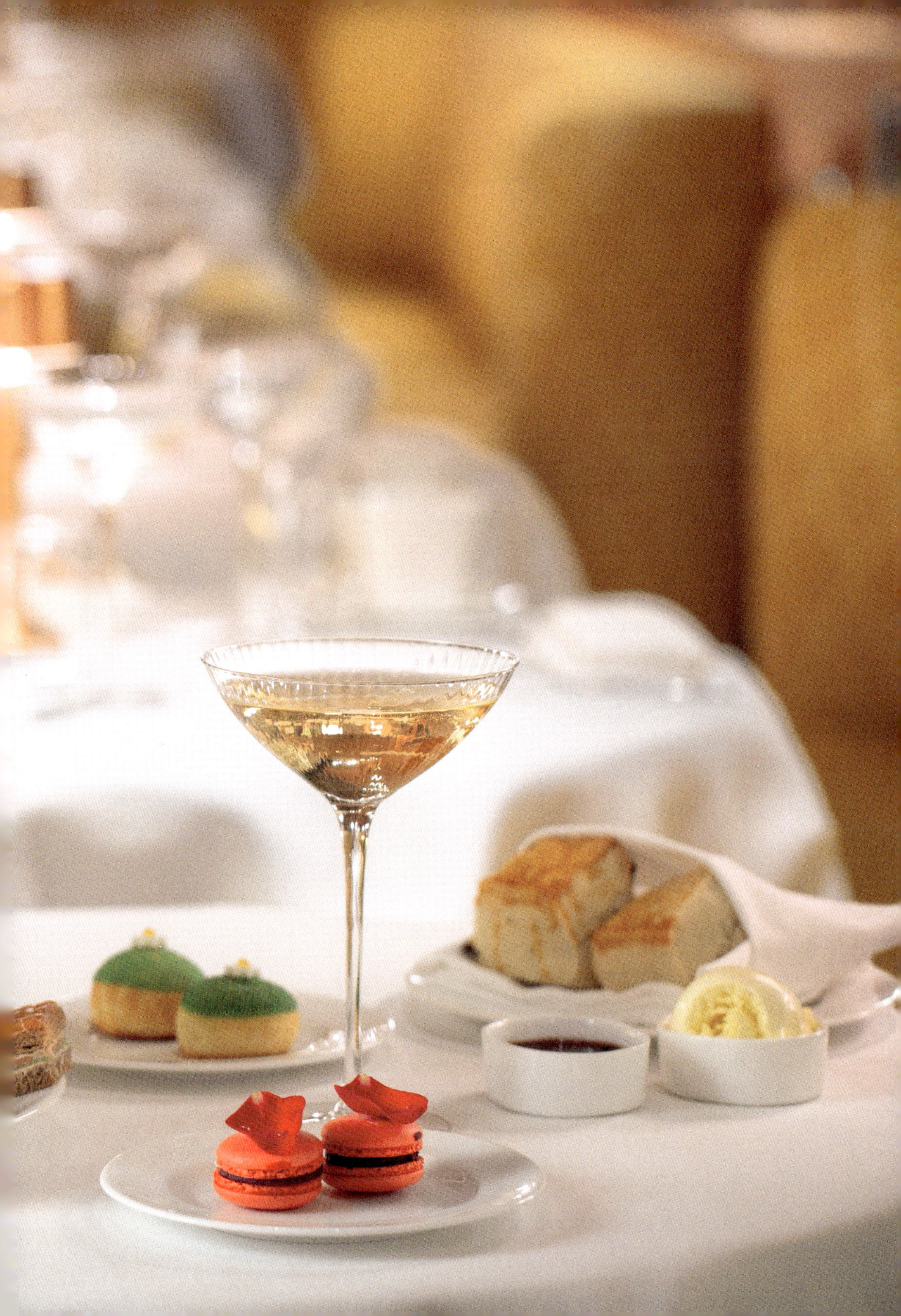

EUROPE — LONDON

PALM COURT AT THE LANGHAM

1C Portland Place, Regent Street, London, W1B 1JA, United Kingdom

TO VISIT BEFORE YOU DIE BECAUSE

This London grande dame spearheaded the fashion for hotel afternoon teas and has served fine teas, sandwiches and scones for 160 years.

When The Langham opened in 1865 at the top of Regent Street, it became the first hotel in the world to serve afternoon tea – a ritual until then reserved for the private salons of high society. And with its first tea (a meal costing one shilling and sixpence), the hotel started a trend still popular today in luxury hotels around the world. At The Langham, tea is served on bespoke floral chinaware in the Palm Court, a classic salon with a resident pianist. While the food menu reflects chef Michel Roux's British-French heritage (think classic cucumber sandwiches and almond madeleines), the tea was selected with the help of Jing Tea and comprises a bespoke breakfast blend of Phoenix Honey Orchid and Jasmine Silver Needle. There's also a cute children's menu served on miniature stands, and you can sample executive pastry chef Andrew Gravett's Victorian-inspired treats along with tea-based cocktails. Next door is the world's best bar, Artesian, for more tea-infused drinks, and Chuan Spa, which serves teas inspired by traditional Chinese medicine.

palm-court.co.uk +44 2 076 361 000

EUROPE   LONDON

71   TĪNG AT THE SHARD

Level 35, Shangri-La The Shard, 31 St. Thomas Street, London, SE1 9QU, United Kingdom

TO VISIT BEFORE YOU DIE BECAUSE

This sky-high Asian-inspired afternoon tea with a choice of signature blends offers panoramic views over London.

The Shard is London's tallest building, and the Shangri-La's TĪNG restaurant is the building's highest dining experience – so it's safe to say that it offers unparalleled views across the capital, which looks like a toy town from the 35th floor, with model trains whizzing in and out of London Bridge station below. Served here every day, afternoon tea comprises classic finger sandwiches, cakes and scones, and a Shard-shaped centrepiece served on a bed of dry ice. There are signature teas, such as the hotel's Ceylon black tea from Waltrim and a Gong Mei white tea, and London-specific blends by the family-run Camellia's Tea House. These include Welcome Tea, with apricot and jasmine, and a breakfast blend of Assam, Sumatran and Yunnan teas. Interesting infusions range from orange and cactus fig rooibos to Iranian rosebud tea, while seasonal menus include Bees in Bloom, a pink *sakura* extravaganza, and a festive tea with a Santa's hat made with chai tea mousse.

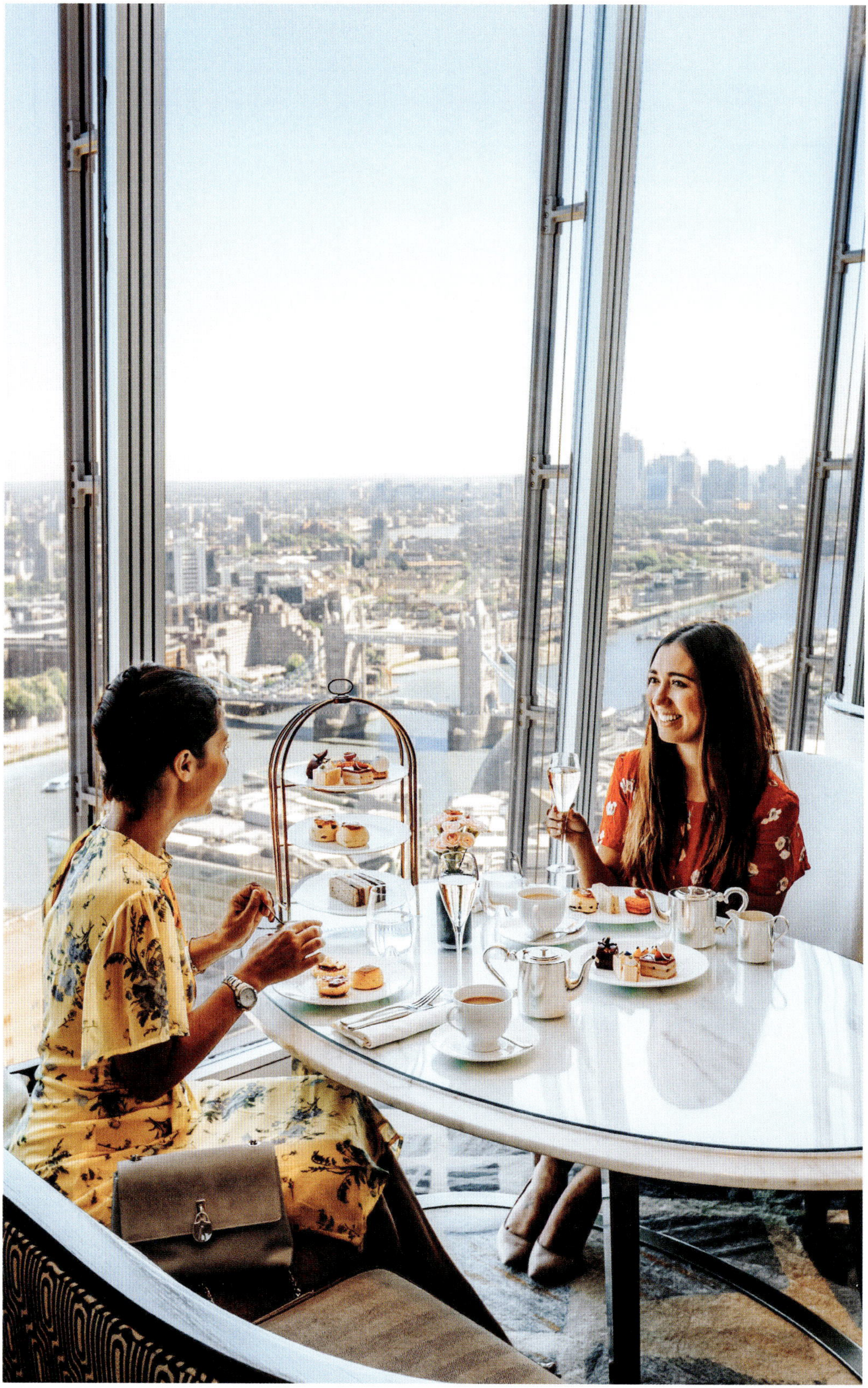

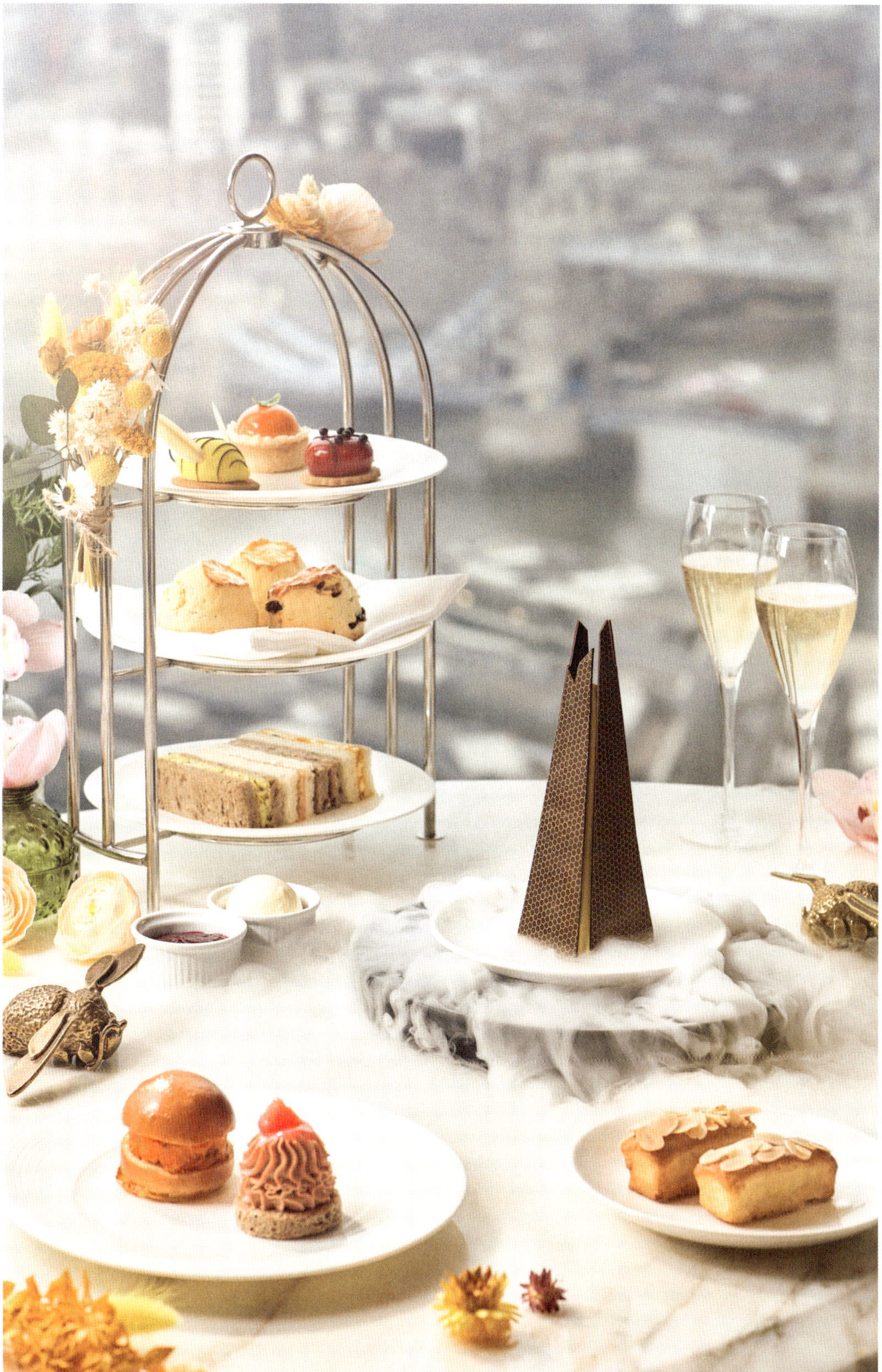

EUROPE — LONDON

72 TWININGS – THE STRAND

216 Strand, Temple, London, WC2R 1AP, United Kingdom

TO VISIT BEFORE YOU DIE BECAUSE

Build your own pick-and-mix box of fine tea or sample some fine blends at the oldest tea shop in London, 'under the golden lion on the Strand'.

Blink and you'll miss it: Twinings' flagship shop is only a few metres wide, but it's a wonderful slice of history, with a beautiful frontage depicting two Chinese figures framing a golden lion. It opened over 300 years ago, not long after tea drinking became popular in England – a trend started in the 1660s by King Charles II and his Portuguese wife, Catherine of Braganza. Thomas Twining was quick to seize the opportunity, turning a coffeehouse in a prime location into a place for ladies, including Jane Austen, to shop for tea without damaging their reputation in one of the city's seedy coffeehouses. Today, the shop houses a pick-and-mix wall and a tea bar where you can sample all Twinings' teas, from the classic English Breakfast to a London Strand Earl Grey. There are also masterclasses focusing on the six types of tea, the brand's history and herbal infusions, as well as bespoke blending sessions. And if you're after an afternoon tea, Twinings has devised a menu of 27 loose-leaf tea blends, including a bespoke blend for the Sheraton Grand London Park Lane.

twinings.co.uk/pages/twinings-flagship-store-216-strand

+44 2 073 533 511

EUROPE   LYON

73   LE LUMINARIUM

9 Rue des Trois-Maries, Vieux Lyon, 69005 Lyon, France

TO VISIT BEFORE YOU DIE BECAUSE

This cute tea room in Lyon's old town offers a slice of local history, flavoursome teas and tisanes, and delicious desserts.

French people like their tea flavoured with fruit or flowers, and most of all, they like their tisanes – herbal teas that are often part of a calm ritual or sipped to wind down in the evenings. This is why infusions are such a big part of the menu here at Le Luminarium, a *salon de thé* in Lyon's old town also serving great desserts such as baked cheesecake and Earl Grey cake. Located in a beautiful stone building, it is surrounded by the city's famous *traboules*, not-so-secret shortcuts that take you through Renaissance courtyards and dark passageways. You'll find one at 6 Rue des Trois-Maries, but there are many more in the vicinity. Once you've finished exploring, take a break at Le Luminarium, where you will find many variations on the classic verbena, as well as flavoured rooibos, milky oolong and golden Yunnan. The house's own tea range, Luminosity, has 40 blends, such as Tarte Tatin (a black tea with apple and caramel) and Souvenir d'Enfance (a green tea with orange and vanilla).

EUROPE   MADRID

74   TEAPOTS

Calle de Postas 26, Centro, 28012 Madrid, Spain

TO VISIT BEFORE YOU DIE BECAUSE

Enjoy unique teas and homemade cakes in this welcoming tea room on a pedestrian street in the heart of the Spanish capital.

Madrid's imposing Plaza Mayor is lined with bars and cafés, but for a good cup of tea and a bit of peace and quiet, you'll have to go just around the corner to Teapots. Opened in 2021 by partners Iñaki, an ace baker, and Edwin, a specialist tea blender, the boutique boasts a contemporary interior and a lovely terrace. It offers over 100 different teas, which you can either enjoy in the tea room or buy by weight. 'You can drink pure white teas such as the exclusive organic *bai hao yin zhen*, or a great first-flush Darjeeling *puttabong*, or an aged royal pu-ehr,' explains Iñaki, who also serves light lunches and homemade bakes, such as Basque cheesecake, carrot cake with cinnamon tea, and apple and pear tarte tatin. You could also pair amazing Japanese pure teas, such as gyokuro saemidori, ceremonial Uji or Kagoshima matcha, with Japanese treats like matcha rolls and mochis. Particular favourites include dong ding and Ikebana, a floral tea blend created by Edwin.

teapots.es   @teapotsmadrid

EUROPE NORDEN

75 OSTFRIESISCHES TEEMUSEUM

Am Markt 36, 26506, Norden, Germany

TO VISIT BEFORE YOU DIE BECAUSE

Drink tea in layers and learn all about the region's fascinating tea ritual at this local museum full of surprising facts.

The region of East Frisia, on Germany's North Sea coast, stands out from the rest of the country for its passion for tea. Here, tea is served up to six times a day and is the star of a ritual that is almost as elaborate as Asian tea ceremonies. After rinsing the teapot and brewing the tea, the host places rock sugar in a teacup, then pours freshly brewed tea over it. Last but not least, they use a special spoon to top the drink with cream, along the rim. The cream sinks and rises again to form a little cloud called a *wulkje*. The drink should never be stirred, but rather enjoyed layer by layer – first the cream, then the strong tea, then the sugar. The teaspoon next to the cup is not used to stir, but is placed in the empty cup at the end, to signal that you do not want any more tea. You can also enjoy East Frisian tea at the nearby Café ten Cate or at Is Teetied, in the pretty town of Greetsiel.

EUROPE OSLO

76 TO SØSTRE

Sommerro Hotel, Sommerrogata 1, Oslo 0255, Norway

TO VISIT BEFORE YOU DIE BECAUSE

Admire the hotel's glorious Art Deco features before sipping on a teapot cocktail in the elegant light-filled lounge.

Originally the headquarters of the city's electrical company, the Sommerro was designed in 1931 by renowned architects Andreas Bjercke and Georg Eliassen. Lit by a skylight and filled with greenery, its lobby lounge is an Art Deco paradise designed by GrecoDeco to celebrate the country's unique folklore and aesthetics. Inspired by Asbjørnsen & Moe's fairy tale *East of the Sun and West of the Moon*, a beautiful vintage-style yellow motif featuring a polar bear extends from the teapots by William Edwards to the rattan chairs. It's a stunning place to enjoy a classic, seasonal afternoon tea prepared by highly skilled pastry chefs while listening to the self-playing Steinway grand piano. The drink menu ranges from a Scandinavian herbal detox tea with birch, sea buckthorn, cranberry and blueberry, to blends by leading French tea seller Palais des Thés, including Thé des Gourmets (with sour notes of cherry, cranberry and almond) and a lavender-flavoured pu-erh. There's also a non-alcoholic sparkling blue tea, as well as teapot cocktails, such as spritz (sparkling wine, botanicals and citrus).

EUROPE PARIS

77 BETJEMAN & BARTON'S TEA BAR

24 boulevard des Filles-du-Calvaire, 75011 Paris, France

TO VISIT
BEFORE YOU DIE
BECAUSE

This chic white tea bar serves over 200 different teas, also available to buy in covetable colourful canisters.

Next to the historic Cirque d'Hiver, on one of Paris' grand boulevards, you will find France's first tea bar, opened in 2012 by Parisian tea company Betjeman & Barton. Its story started in 1919, when English tea merchants Arthur Betjeman and Percy Barton opened the first tea-only shop in the French capital. With its white walls, silver lighting and pops of red, the tea bar makes for a welcoming spot and reflects the brand's commitment to elegance and refinement, but with a touch of whimsy. It offers 200 different teas, including rare Asian teas and a wide range of the flavoured teas so popular in France. Bestsellers include Pouchkine (bergamot and citrus) and Malesherbes (passion fruit, peach, rose and strawberry), while blends often have evocative names such as the Un Gentleman à Deauville black tea; the Escale au Port de la Lune (Stopover at Moon Harbour) green tea; and Comme une Étoile (Like a Star), a green tea flavoured with violet, kiwi and peach.

betjemanandbarton.com +33 967 496 686

EUROPE   PARIS

78   BONTEMPS 'LE JARDIN SECRET'

57 Rue de Bretagne, 75003 Paris, France

TO VISIT BEFORE YOU DIE BECAUSE

Enjoy great sablés and floral teas in the courtyard garden of this chic patisserie and tea room in Paris' Marais district.

Located a few steps away from the foodie heaven that is the Marché des Enfants Rouges, Bontemps is a beautifully designed take on the classic French neighbourhood patisserie. It was opened in 2015 by Fiona Leluc, who ditched her career in banking to become a pastry chef. Her speciality? A super crumbly shortcrust pastry used to make amazing sablé biscuits and tarts. Once you've gawked at the stunning cakes and floral décor, head to the equally pretty tea room and secret garden at the back to try them. Other teatime treats include lemon cake and pear tart, as well as house blends such as Premier Amour ('First Love'), a mix of Chinese green tea, orange blossom, strawberry and blackberry, and a black tea blend called Un Matin au Jardin Secret ('A Morning in the Secret Garden'). Herbal teas range from flavoured rooibos to a classic tisane with linden flower, chamomile and orange blossom. Bontemps' Sunday brunch is very popular and includes more tea, freshly baked pastries and savoury bites such as an avocado bun with smoked salmon from Maison Barthouil.

bontemps.paris/jardin-secret   +33 142 741 155

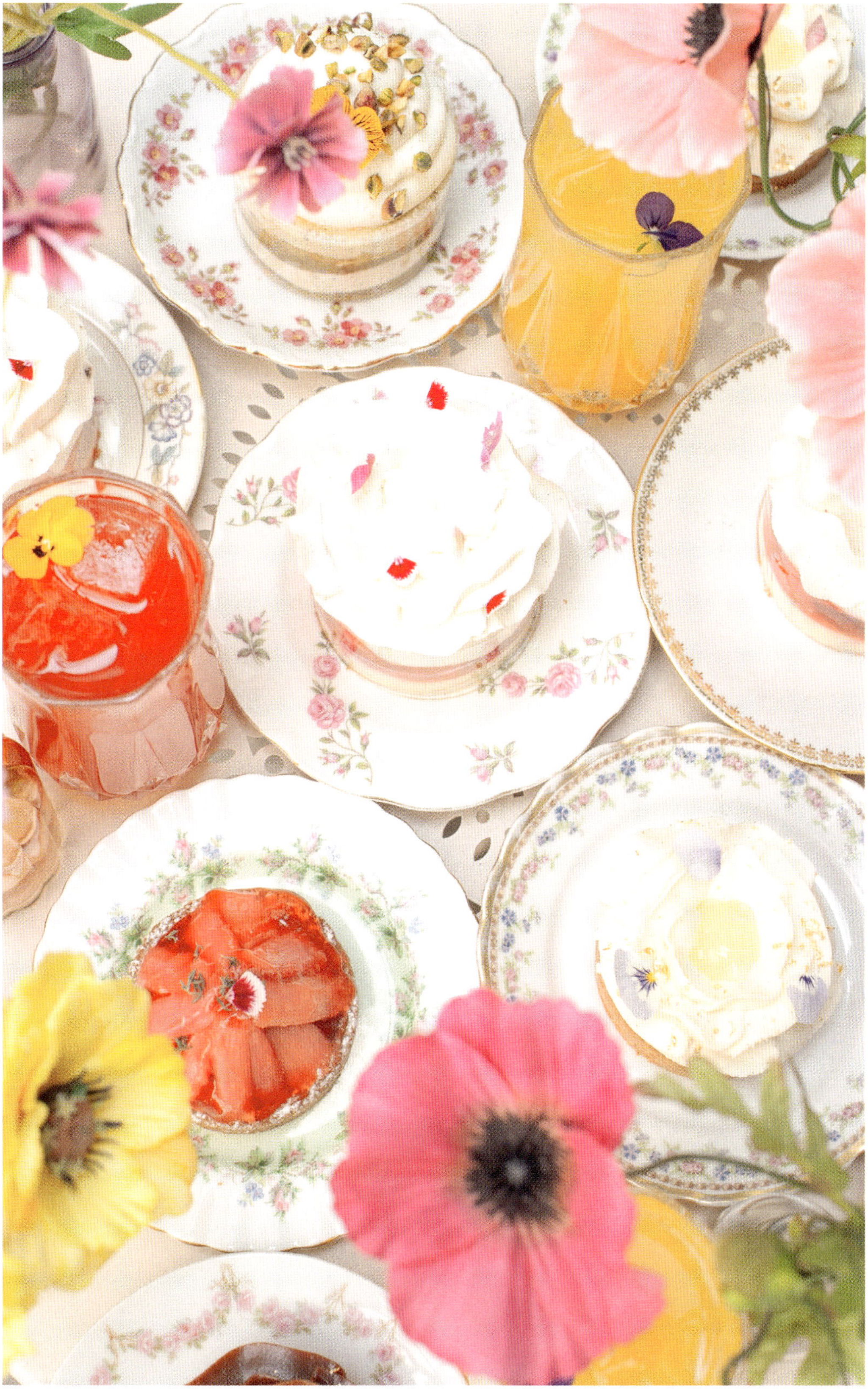

EUROPE　　　　　　　　PARIS

79　LE NÉLIE

158 Boulevard Haussmann, 75008 Paris, France

TO VISIT
BEFORE YOU DIE
BECAUSE

Savour a unique teatime experience under a Tiepolo-painted ceiling in a sumptuous 19th-century Parisian mansion.

Built for Edouard André and his wife Nélie Jacquemart at a time when Paris was being completely remodelled by Baron Haussmann for Napoléon III, this *hôtel particulier* is now a public museum, its grands salons filled with the couple's extensive art collection. The former dining room has been turned into a restaurant, Le Nélie, where you can dine under a ceiling originally painted by Giovanni Battista Tiepolo for a villa in Italy – one of the many treasures the couple brought back from their travels. Every weekend from 3 to 5.30pm (the perfect time for a *goûter*, or an afternoon snack) is Le Nélie's teatime, where you can pair a cup of tea with one of the freshly baked treats from the patisserie counter. These are sourced from the city's best pâtissiers and include French classics such as apple tarte tatin and tarte au citron meringuée. As well as tisanes, such as verbena, chamomile and peppermint, the tea menu includes jasmine green tea, vanilla black tea and Japanese sencha.

musee-jacquemart-andre.com/en/nelie

EUROPE · PARIS

80 MARIAGE FRÈRES

30 Rue du Bourg-Tibourg, 75004 Paris, France

TO VISIT BEFORE YOU DIE BECAUSE

This historic Parisian tea shop has over 1,000 teas to choose from, as well as a lovely tea room and a small tea museum.

Their forefathers having explored Persia, India and Madagascar as private envoys to King Louis XIV, Henri et Édouard Mariage were steeped in the family tradition of selling exotic teas and spices. The brothers opened their first teahouse in Paris in 1854, importing tea for hotels and delicatessens, but Mariage Frères started selling to the public in only 1984. Today, the wood-panelled shop and tea room in the heart of the Marais district is still filled with vintage tea crates and antique scales. It sells over 1,000 different teas, from *grands crus* like Taiwanese blue oolong to house blends such as Full Moon, a black tea with vanilla and almonds. The salon de thé serves tea-infused brunches and patisseries such as dark chocolate marble cake with Marco Polo Sublime black tea, and even the scones are served with tea jelly. Tucked neatly between the tea room and the shop is a staircase leading to the small tea museum, which is filled with painted tea chests, precious tea caddies and unique teapots.

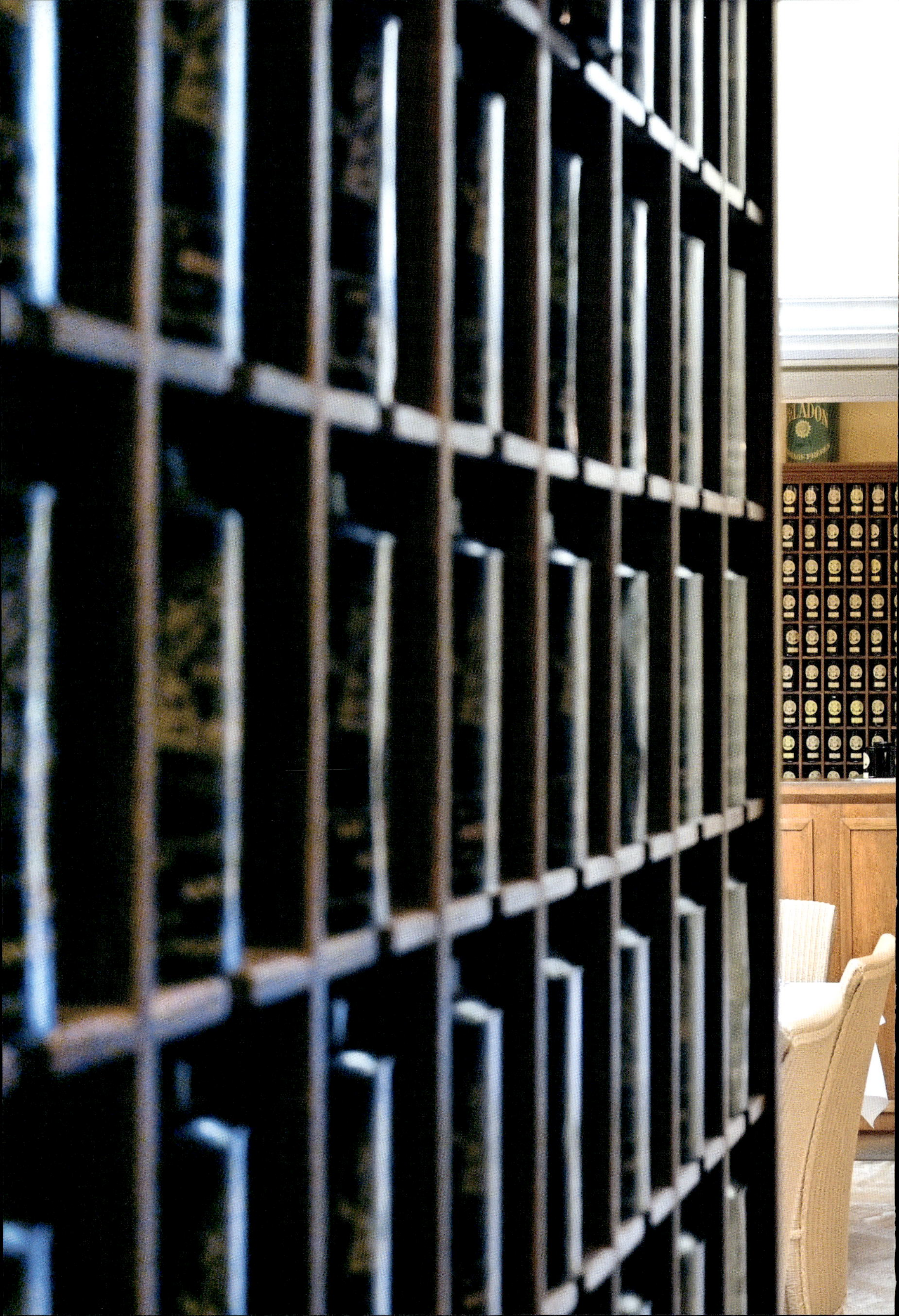

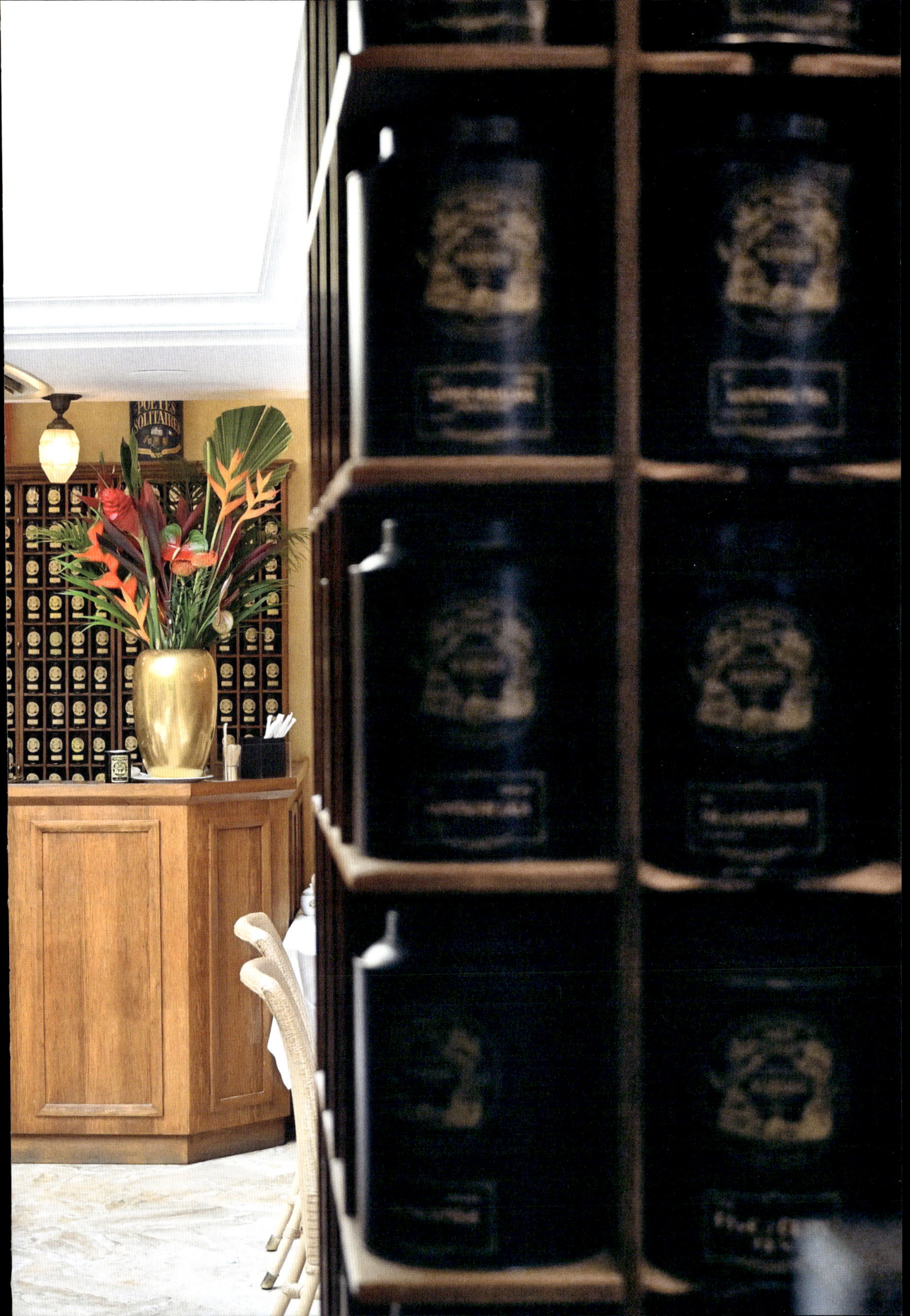

EUROPE   PARIS

81   YAM'TCHA

121 Rue Saint-Honoré, 75001 Paris, France

TO VISIT BEFORE YOU DIE BECAUSE

This Michelin-starred fusion restaurant located near the Louvre is known for its exquisite food and tea pairings.

The clue is in the name: *yam'tcha*, in Chinese, means 'to drink tea', and the magic of this restaurant lies in the combination of great dishes with fine teas. A passion project by chef Adeline Grattard and her husband, Hong Kong-born tea sommelier Chi Wah Chan, yam'Tcha is a tiny place serving a daily menu based on the freshest ingredients. Although they also offer wine pairings – we're in France, after all – the focus is clearly on the teas. 'We offer mostly teas from China and Taiwan,' explains Chi Wah. 'These are pure, unflavoured teas with a great variety of tastes, which can be compared to fine wines, with floral, mineral, fruity notes.' A tuna and foie gras dish, for example, is served with a pu-erh tea. Like the ingredients, the tea menu is also seasonal: 'In autumn, for example, we feature tea with intense fruity notes, such as Tieguanyin,' says Chi Wah. There is also a yam'Tcha boutique on nearby Rue Sauval, which offers Hong Kong-style milk tea, tea tastings and baos.

EUROPE · PRAGUE

82 DOBRÁ ČAJOVNA

Václavské náměstí 778/14, 110 00 Nové Město, Prague, Czech Republic

TO VISIT BEFORE YOU DIE BECAUSE

This long-established tea room just off Wenceslas Square attracts tea lovers with its atmospheric décor and immense choice of teas.

During the last days of communism in Czechoslovakia, a group of young tea lovers met to sample rare Indian, Chinese and Japanese teas smuggled into the country and otherwise available only to political party members, government officials and the military elite. After the Velvet Revolution, in 1992, they started the Society of Tea Devotees, and the year after, in 1993, their first bohemian-style tea room was born: Dobrá čajovna, or 'the good tea room'. A narrow passage leads to an ochre courtyard with a little terrace, while inside, the eclectic interiors have a cosy, welcoming feel. Here, you can sample delicious treats such as carrot cake, as well as high-quality artisan tea sourced from farmers who practise healthy, sustainable methods. You'll be spoilt for choice – the brick-like menu is 50 pages long, with highlights including silver needle tea from Rwanda and maté rancho from Brazil. The knowledgeable staff also run workshops and even host a podcast to share their passion. Dobrá čajovna has 30 tea rooms in the Czech Republic, Poland, Hungary, Slovakia and the United States.

dobratea.eu · +420 224 231 480

EUROPE RIGA

83 TĒJO TEA HOUSE

Krišjāņa Barona iela 2A, Centra rajons, Rīga, LV-1050, Latvia

TO VISIT BEFORE YOU DIE BECAUSE

Enjoy teas from around the world in this tranquil teahouse located in one of Riga's beautiful parks.

The lucky inhabitants of Riga have not one lovely teahouse with park views, but two: the first is called Tabu, in the Vērmane Garden, and the other is this octagonal beauty, Tējo Tea House, in Bastejkalna Park, just next to the city's old town and opera house. The Japanese-style wooden pavilion is set right by the city's canal, and you can sit either outside on the terrace, surrounded by the park's greenery, or inside, in a cosy, two-level space filled with plants. As well as pastries and cakes, including cinnamon buns, carrot cakes and tiramisu, you can sample teas from all over the world, sourced by local tea sommelier Gundega Silniece, a board member of the European Speciality Tea Association. Teas are priced by category (everyday, special and premium), and the globetrotting selection ranges from seasonal iced matcha to Chimarrão yerba maté. You can also book a gong fu cha tea ceremony, featuring premium teas from China, Taiwan and Japan, served in authentic teaware.

tejoteahouse.lv +371 27 330 055

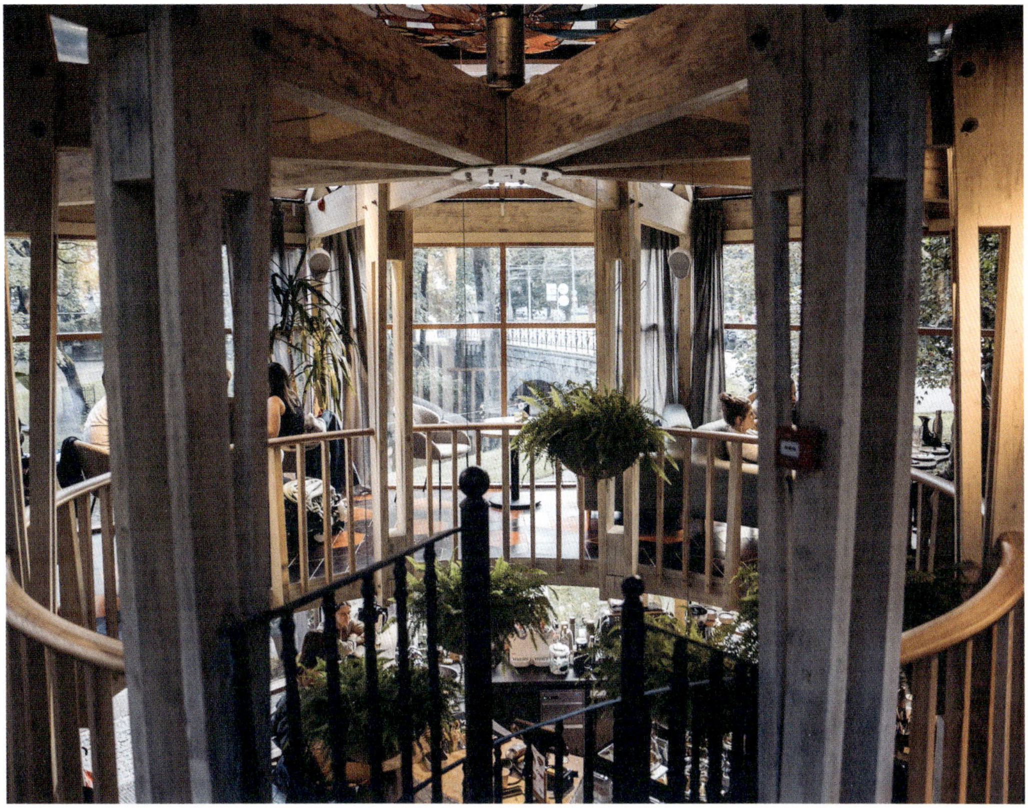

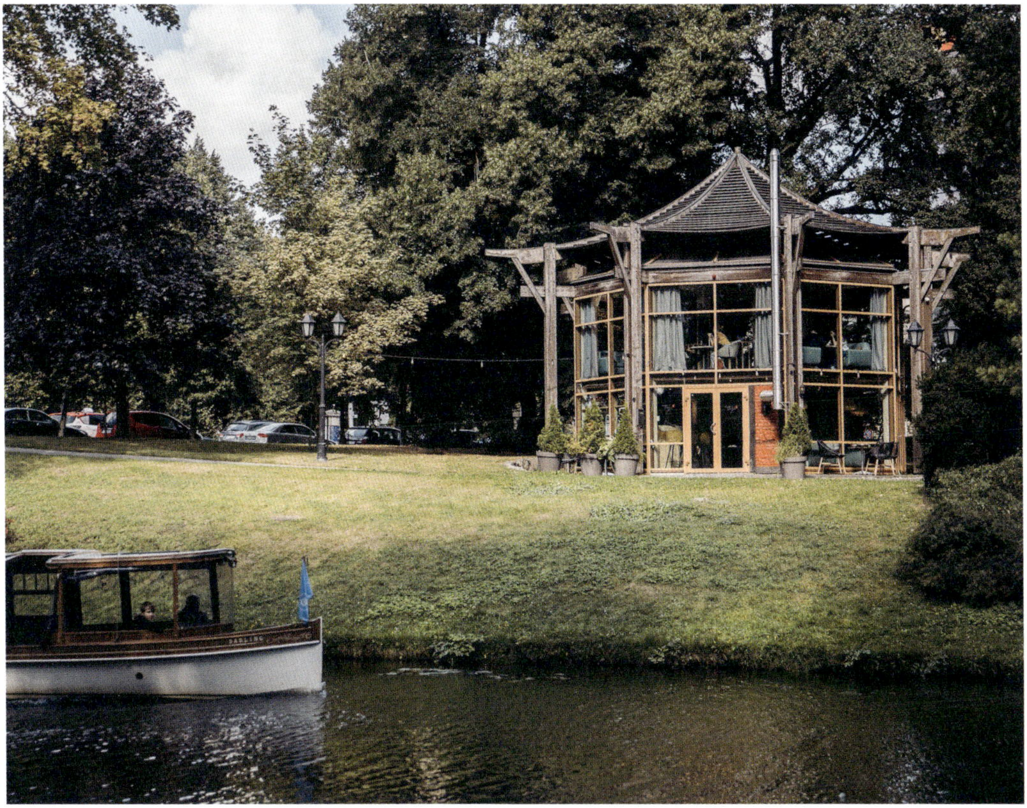

EUROPE SÃO MIGUEL

84 CHALET DA TIA MERCÊS

Rua das Caldeiras s/n, 9675-045 Furnas, São Miguel, Azores, Portugal

TO VISIT BEFORE YOU DIE BECAUSE

Watch the steam rise from the *caldeiras*, geothermal vents, and enjoy a cup of local violet tea at this unique tea room in the Azores.

A former bathhouse set on the banks of Ribeira Amarela in Furnas, on the island of São Miguel, Chalet da Tia Mercês offers a series of unique tea experiences, showcasing local teas or explaining the chemistry of the volcanic mineral waters. These include a tea-tasting session focused on a rare Azorean tea flight (the island is home to the oldest tea plantation in Europe) and a thermal tea tasting highlighting teas and infusions made with different waters from Furnas (as they say in Japan, 'it is the water that makes the tea'). The house speciality is the violet volcanic tea, made with geothermally heated iron- and acid-rich volcanic water that turns a unique shade of purple as it reacts with the antioxidant-rich green tea. Accompany this with homemade desserts such as banana cake, cooked in the hot springs or underground using the heat of the earth in Furnas Volcano, like many of the dishes on the seasonal menu, which features ingredients from all nine islands of the Azores.

EUROPE — STOCKHOLM

85 CAFÉ SVENSKT TENN

Strandvägen 5, 114 51 Stockholm, Sweden

TO VISIT BEFORE YOU DIE BECAUSE

Sample rare teas and seasonal dishes selected by chef Petter Nilsson at the stylish café of Swedish homeware brand Svenskt Tenn.

Leading Swedish interiors brand Svenskt Tenn was founded in 1924 by Estrid Ericson, an entrepreneur and a great tea lover who is said to have drunk five cups of tea every day: two and a half in the morning and two and a half at lunch. Fittingly, the brand's beautiful shop in central Stockholm is also home to a café serving a wide range of teas, with everything from delicate, grassy Japanese green teas and Indian Darjeeling, to its own flavoured blend of Chinese Keemun/Yunnan. The teas were selected by the team at Petri, a fine-dining restaurant that is known for its focus on tea pairings, so expect some pretty special drinks here, such as rare Jungle Teas from the Monsoon Tea Wat Ket in Thailand (see page 27) and Dongfang meiren ('Oriental beauty') from Nantou County in Taiwan. These can be accompanied by dishes such as smoked salmon on French toast, beef brisket with fennel, and parsley and ramson capers, or sweet treats such as rhubarb cheesecake, canelés or chestnut tartlets.

svenskttenn.com/fr/en/the-store/cafe-svenskt-tenn

EUROPE STRASBOURG

86 LE THÉ DES MUSES

19 Rue Sainte-Barbe, 67000 Strasbourg, France

TO VISIT BEFORE YOU DIE BECAUSE

Located in the old town of Strasbourg, this tea room offers 300 different types of teas from around the world, plus homemade desserts.

In most salons de thé in France, tea is just a little extra to go with the main act, pastries and petits gâteaux (in fact, traditional tea rooms here are often simply extensions of existing patisseries). Not so at Le Thé des Muses, where visitors are greeted by shelves lined with burgundy tea canisters, filled with precious leaves from around the world. There are 300 types of loose-leaf teas, sourced from everywhere from Shree Antu in Nepal to Zomba in Malawi, which you can enjoy in one of the comfy armchairs. Signature blends include Un Parfum d'Alsace, a mix of flavoured green and black tea inspired by the local vineyards, and A Peaceful Nap, a green tea with melon, fig, peach, apricot and almonds. Strasbourg is known for its Christmas market and gingerbread (*pain d'épice*), so try the Plein d'Épices, a Chinese green tea with orange, cinnamon, cardamom and cloves. And yes, this being France, there are also excellent homemade cakes, as well as cherry pies, caramel hazelnut tarts and even mochi.

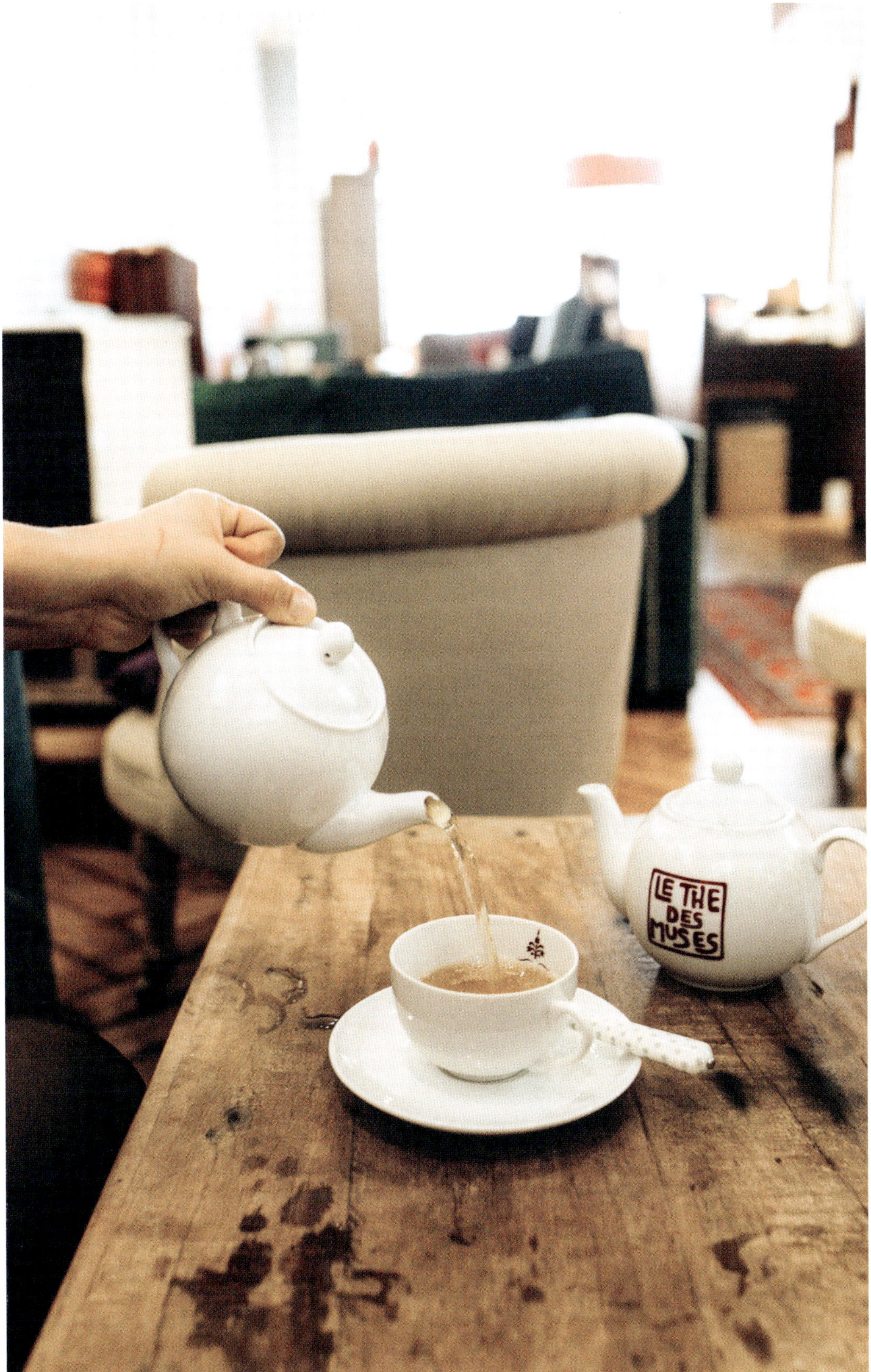
LE THE
DES
MUSES

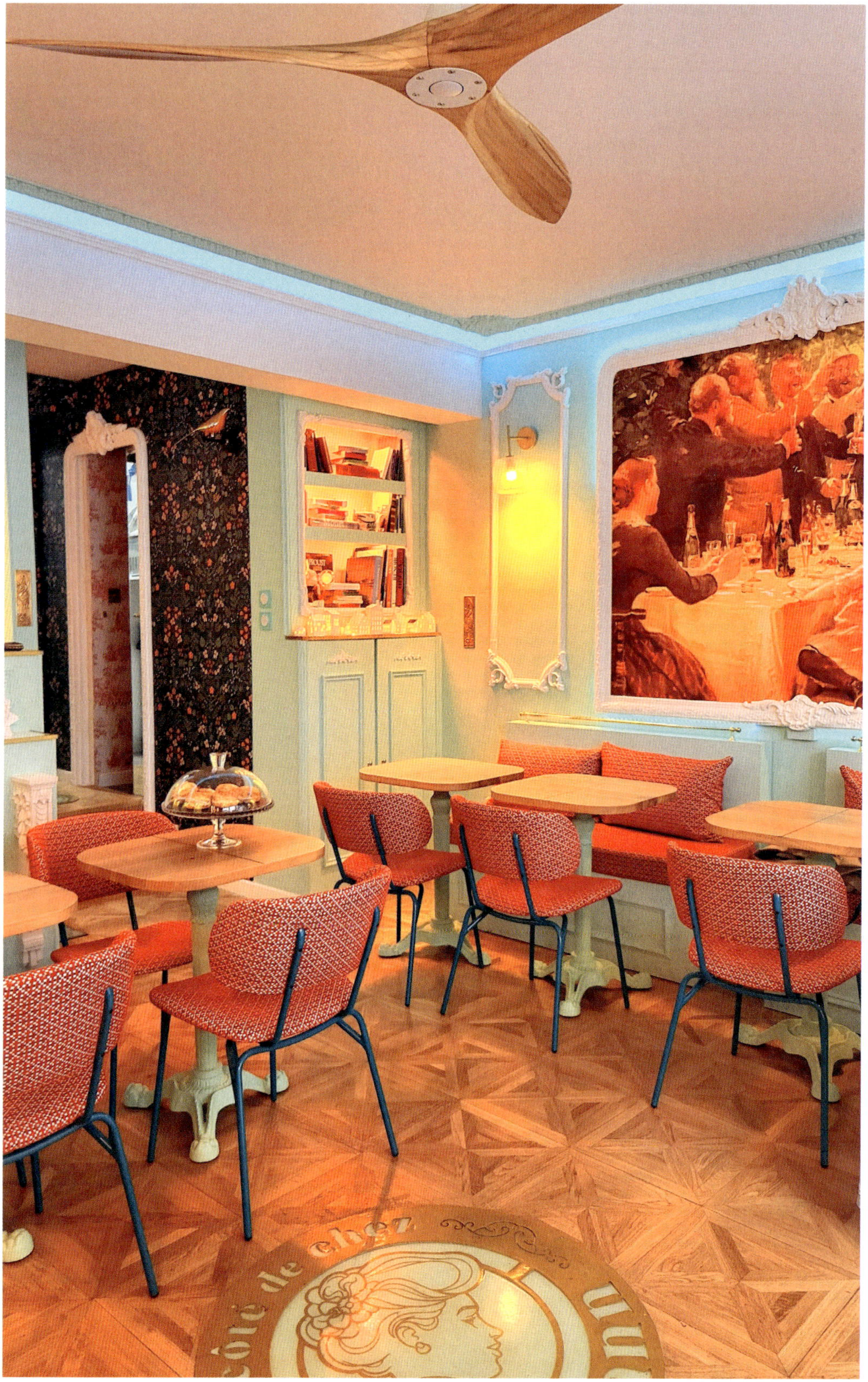
côté de chez

EUROPE — TOULOUSE

87 DU CÔTÉ DE CHEZ SWANN

20 Rue Tolosane, 31000 Toulouse, France

TO VISIT BEFORE YOU DIE BECAUSE

This French tea room in the centre of Toulouse is a dreamy and colourful space to enjoy Dammann Frères teas and homemade patisserie.

Named after the first volume of French novelist Marcel Proust's *In Search of Lost Time*, this newly opened tea room is the passion project of Raphaël Drommelschlager, a comic book author and interior designer. Like his grandmother Lucie, he'd always dreamed of opening his own salon de thé, and he has poured his creativity into every single detail of the space, from the blue electric stove to the wood panelling. There is also an heirloom buffet that once belonged to his grandmother and Raphaël's own watercolours on the walls. As well as Proust's famous madeleines, there are plenty of sweet treats in store, including a popular lemon and basil meringue pie and a chocolate cake made by the in-house pastry chef, Marie, following a recipe by Raphaël's grandmother. Dishes are named after Proust's characters, and the flavoured teas come from Dammann Frères, a French luxury tea specialist since 1825. They include Paul & Virginie (a red fruit and black tea blend named after another famous French novel) or A Night in Versailles (a green tea with bergamot, kiwi and peach).

@swann_toulouse +33 663 465 568

EUROPE   VIENNA

88 HAAS&HAAS

Stephansplatz 4, 1010 Vienna, Austria

TO VISIT
BEFORE YOU DIE
BECAUSE

This specialist tea room in the heart of Vienna holds forth in coffee country, with a tea menu spanning Japanese gyokuro to Austrian fruit teas.

There are many, many great cafés in the old town of Vienna – but only one great tea room. Just behind the gothic cathedral, you will find Haas&Haas, a family business whose team has been travelling the world for 30 years sourcing fragrant teas, 90 of which you can sample in their cosy tea room and courtyard terrace. Located in a historic building a stone's throw away from Mozarthaus Vienna, the tea room has vaulted ceilings and serves homemade cakes and scones made using flour from the UK. There are eight types of afternoon tea, ranging from Moroccan tea with marzipan pastries to East Frisian tea (see page 125) with a crab on rye open-faced sandwich. The breakfasts are equally international, taking in Chinese dim sum, röstis and local Kornspitz bread rolls. The adjoining shop sells tea gifts, jams and gelées. And although Austrians drink far less tea than their other European neighbours, there is, in fact, another lovely little tea shop not too far away in Mariahilf, called Sir Harly's Tea.

haas-haas.at   +43 15 122 666

EUROPE WARSAW

89 SAME FUSY

Nowomiejska 10, 00-271 Warsaw, Poland

TO VISIT
BEFORE YOU DIE
BECAUSE

There is something to please every type of tea lover at the oldest teahouse in Warsaw, hidden in a medieval cellar in the Old Town.

This welcoming teahouse in Warsaw's Old Town is a bit of a hidden gem, as you have to head down a stone staircase to find Same Fusy's atmospheric 16th-century cellar, lit by the warm glow of candles. Opened in 1998 by tea enthusiast Mariusz Kowalewski, it's a unique place to enjoy some unusual teas and infusions. 'The menu is brimming with surprises,' says manager Ula Janczuk. 'You'll find classic teas from far-flung corners of the globe alongside original blends crafted from local herbs and fruits. For traditionalists, there's Tieguanyin, brewed in the gong fu cha style, or matcha, whisked with a traditional *chasen*. Another treat is Dragon Eyes, a hand-rolled green tea infused with a subtle hint of jasmine, or baozhong, a light and intensely floral tea, handpicked with exceptional craftsmanship.' Or you could simply enjoy an infusion like Little Red Riding Hood, with strawberry leaves and rose petals, and a slice of traditional cheesecake, apple pie or Slovenian *gibanica* poppy seed layer cake.

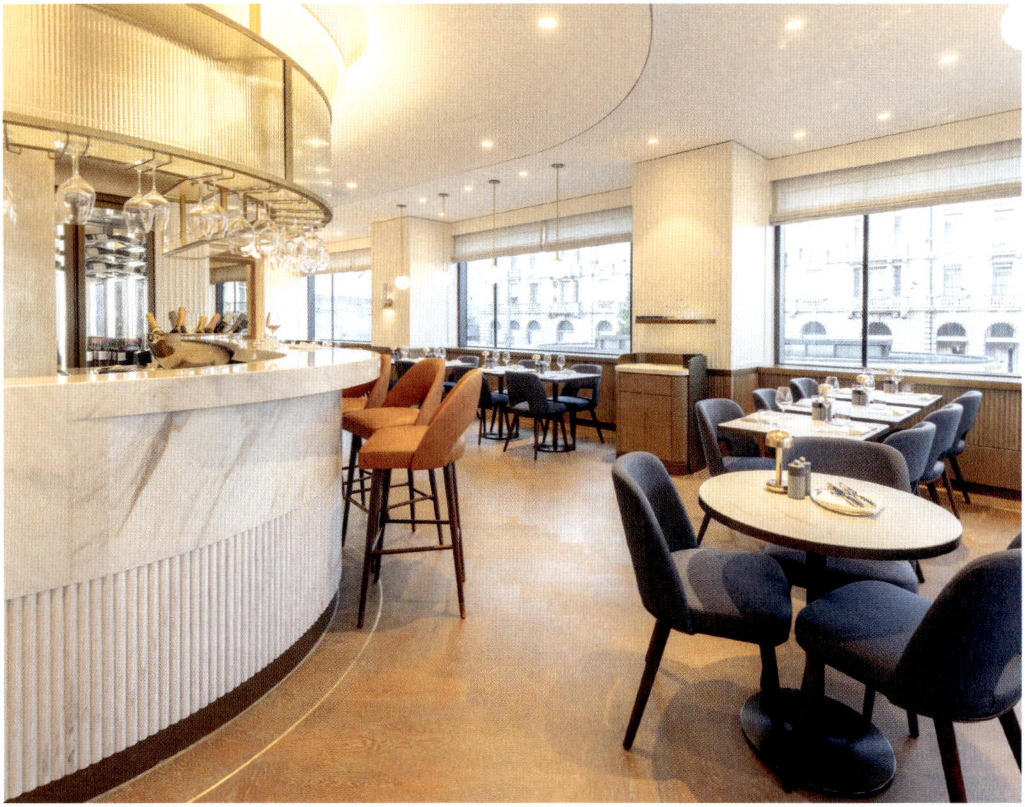

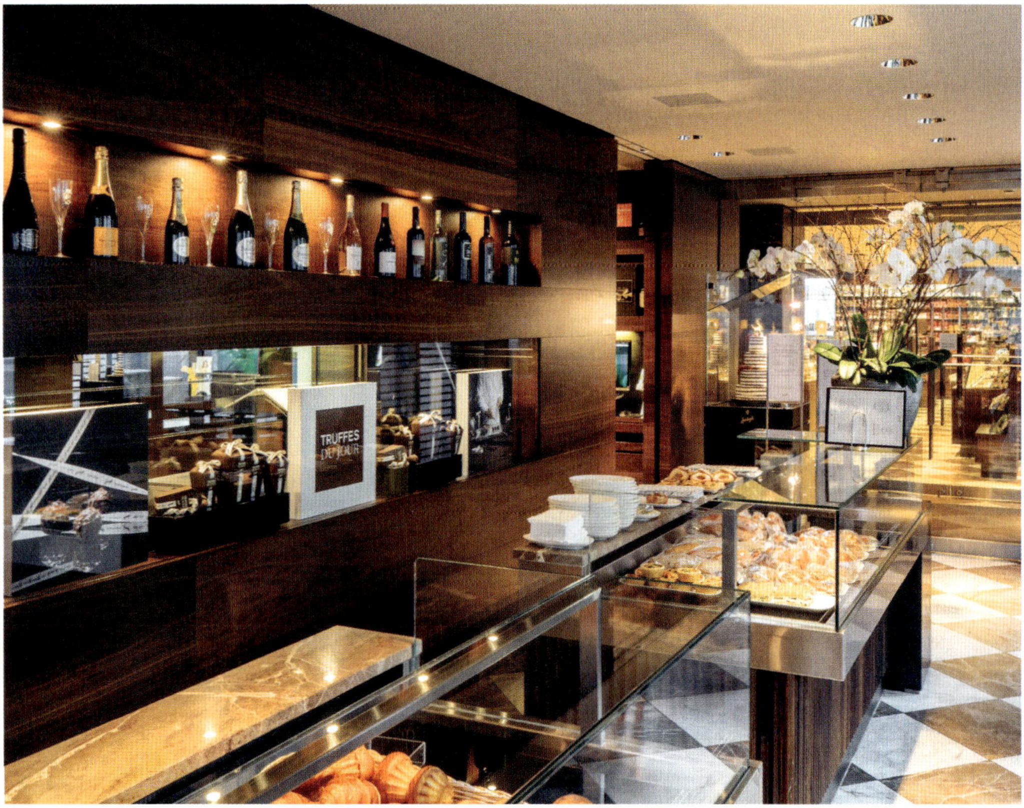
TRUFFES
DU JOUR

EUROPE   ZÜRICH

90   CONFISERIE SPRÜNGLI

Bahnhofstrasse 21, 8001 Zürich, Switzerland

TO VISIT BEFORE YOU DIE BECAUSE

This landmark chocolate shop and tea room in Zürich's Central Square is the place to indulge in a spot of tea and chocolate pairing.

Forget wine and cheese pairings; instead, try tea and chocolate at Confiserie Sprüngli, one of Switzerland's leading chocolatiers. Opened in 1859, its great tea room overlooking the trams whizzing by on the city's Paradeplatz has welcomed guests such as *Heidi* writer Johanna Spyri, and is today known for its Luxemburgerli macarons and chocolate truffles. Go for healthy bircher muesli or indulgent truffle cake, and choose from teas including sencha, *genmaicha* and even Zealong oolong (see page 239). Recommended pairings include a Grand Marnier or lime Maracaibo chocolate truffle with Earl Grey, as both fit perfectly with the fruity yet tart aroma of the tea; a Praline Grand Cru Arriba-Nut to go with the Zealong; and a creamy Bourbon vanilla truffle with the vanilla black tea. Make sure to also try two Swiss favourites: the homemade iced tea and the Piz Palü, an infusion of alpine herbs. Named after a mountain in Graubünden, it should be paired with a Praliné Spéciale, with a walnut on top, as walnut tart is one of the canton's specialities.

spruengli.ch   +41 442 244 740

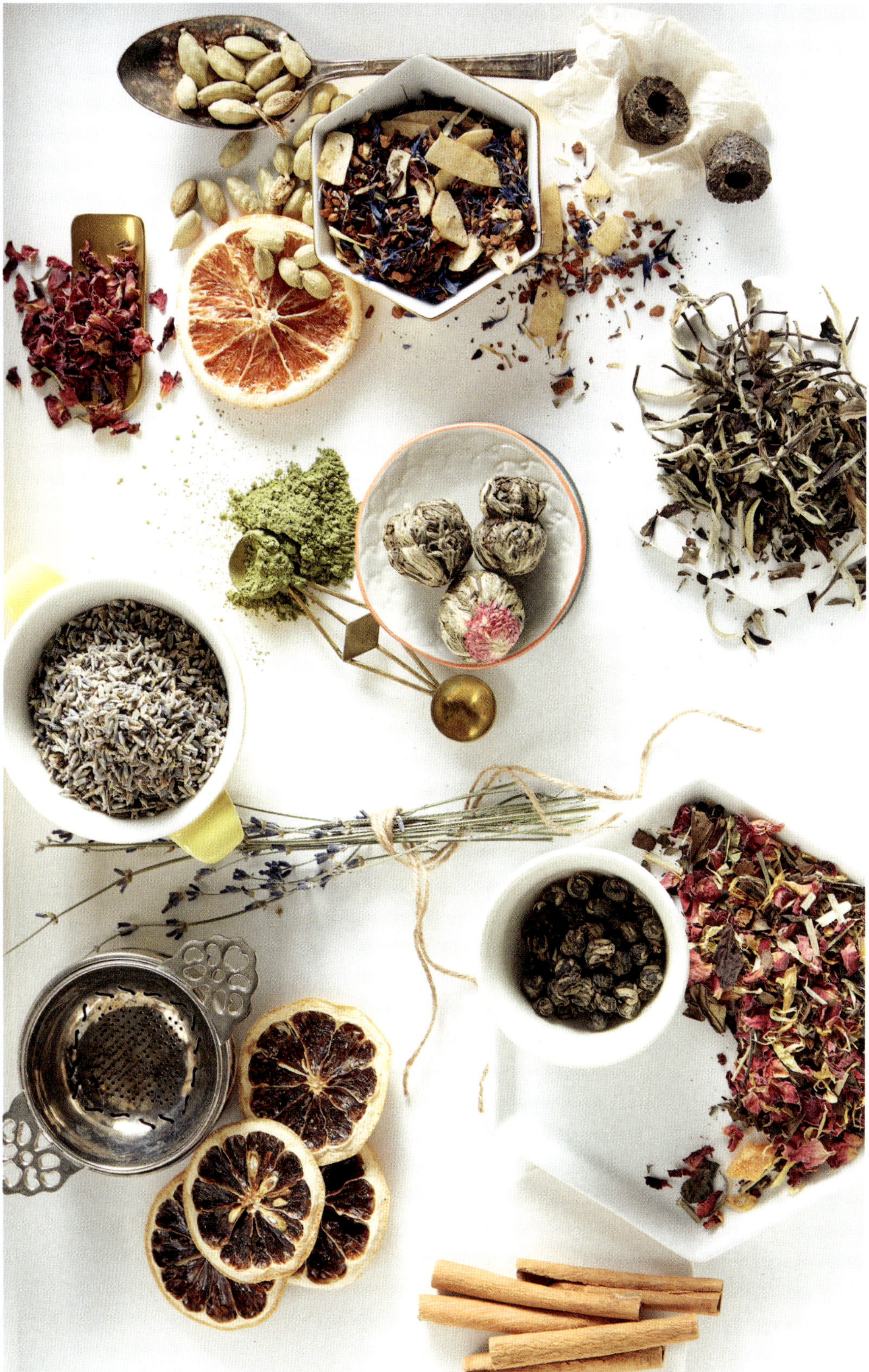

THE AMERICAS   ATLANTA

91 JUST ADD HONEY

684 John Wesley Dobbs Avenue NE, Unit E, Atlanta, Georgia, 30312, United States

TO VISIT BEFORE YOU DIE BECAUSE

Enjoy a refreshing iced tea and unique flavoured blends at this lovely Black-owned tea room in Atlanta's leafy Inman Park.

Southerners are known for their sweet tooth, especially when it comes to tea – or iced tea, more accurately. Served at every meal and made with black tea and sugar, sweet tea is the 'table wine of the South'. You'll find this regional staple served on tap and with extra sweetness at Just Add Honey, a friendly tea room established in 2006 by Brandi Shelton. Located in Atlanta's Inman Park, a leafy neighbourhood known for its cafés and bars, it is just steps away from the Atlanta Beltline, a 22-mile-long green loop – so you can stay for a drink on the charming patio or grab a tea to go and head for a walk in the Historic Fourth Ward Park. Brandi, who runs the tea room with her husband Jermail, specialises in thoughtfully blended loose-leaf tea, with creations ranging from Georgia Peaches, which makes a great iced tea, to the hibiscus-based Berries on the Beltline – but there are also oolongs, pu-erhs and matchas to choose from, as well as an afternoon tea with all the trimmings, including a delicious chicken salad sandwich.

THE AMERICAS   BOGOTÁ

92   TEMPLO TÉ

Avenida Carrera 24, #37–60, Parkway, Bogotá, Colombia

TO VISIT BEFORE YOU DIE BECAUSE

Discover Colombia's unique teas and local infusions such as guayusa and coca leaf at this bright and colourful tea room in central Bogotá.

It's a little-known fact that Colombia has been producing tea since the 1950s, growing a mix of *sinensis*, *assamica* and Cambodian tea bushes at high altitudes. Here at Templo Té, you can try a black tea with malty notes from the Bitaco plantation in the country's Valle del Cauca. The flagship store in Parkway is a great place to come for a slice of cake and a cup of pu-erh tea, or silver needles, as well as more unique local specialities. Colombians love their *aromática*, a drink made by steeping fresh fruit, herbs and other ingredients in hot water, but at Templo Té they offer tea and freeze-dried fruit blends ranging from Wild Orange, combining red berries and citrus, to Piña Melange, a hot take on a piña colada. There are herbal options, too, mostly chamomile or lemongrass based. Make sure to try the infusions of *guayusa*, a traditional medicinal plant native to the Amazonian rainforest, and coca leaf, once a staple of Inca feasts and religious rituals. Templo Té also has two other outposts in central Bogotá.

93 ABIGAIL'S TEA ROOM & TERRACE

Boston Tea Party Ships & Museum, 306 Congress Street, Boston, Massachusetts, 02210, United States

TO VISIT BEFORE YOU DIE BECAUSE

Taste the historic blends at the centre of the Boston Tea Party rebellion in this cosy waterside tea room in the heart of Boston Harbor.

Located on the site of Boston's historic Griffin's Wharf, the Boston Tea Party Ships & Museum is a tourist attraction complete with costumed actors, Hollywood set-worthy replicas… and a great little tea room. Here, you can taste the same varieties of tea that were thrown from the ships on the night of the Boston Tea Party in protest of the British Tea Act of 1773, which allowed the East India Company to sell tea from China without paying taxes. This tea-based rebellion helped accelerate the American Revolution, eventually leading to the country's independence. Thankfully, no one today is throwing tea overboard, but rather enjoying tasty chocolate chip cookies and Boston cream pie along with the five historic tea blends. Selected with the help of the museum's renowned tea master Bruce Richardson, these include the likes of Young Hyson, a green tea from Anhui, and Bohea, a black tea grown in the Wuyi Mountains of northern Fujian. It's crazy to think they once travelled all around the world only to get thrown into Boston Harbor.

bostonteapartyship.com/tea-room +1 8 669 550 667

THE AMERICAS　　　　　BOULDER

94　BOULDER DUSHANBE TEA HOUSE

1770 13th Street, Boulder, Colorado, 80302, United States

TO VISIT BEFORE YOU DIE BECAUSE

Wonder at the exquisite decorative details and exhaustive menu of this authentic Tajik teahouse in the middle of Colorado.

To celebrate their friendships, most sister cities come up with only a little road sign or two. But here in Boulder, they've actually got a whole teahouse – all thanks to an organisation founded by Dwight Eisenhower in 1956 to bring peace through people-to-people diplomacy. Boulder, Colorado, and Tajikistan's capital, Dushanbe, are now forever linked by a beautiful building, created by 40 artisans in the Central Asian country before being shipped to the US in the 1990s. Featuring 12 decorative cedar columns, intricately carved plaster panels and a colourful hand-painted ceiling, it's a stunning place to enjoy the house's signature chai or one of the hundreds of other teas on offer. Sourced from around the world, they include the bestselling Boulder Breakfast, a blend of Keemun, Assam and Yunnan, and Full Moon Spice, a black tea flavoured with almonds, as well as Chinese classics, Japanese senchas and a great selection of rooibos and infusions. The food menu is just as extensive and international and includes afternoon tea as well as dishes such as lapsang souchong bulgogi.

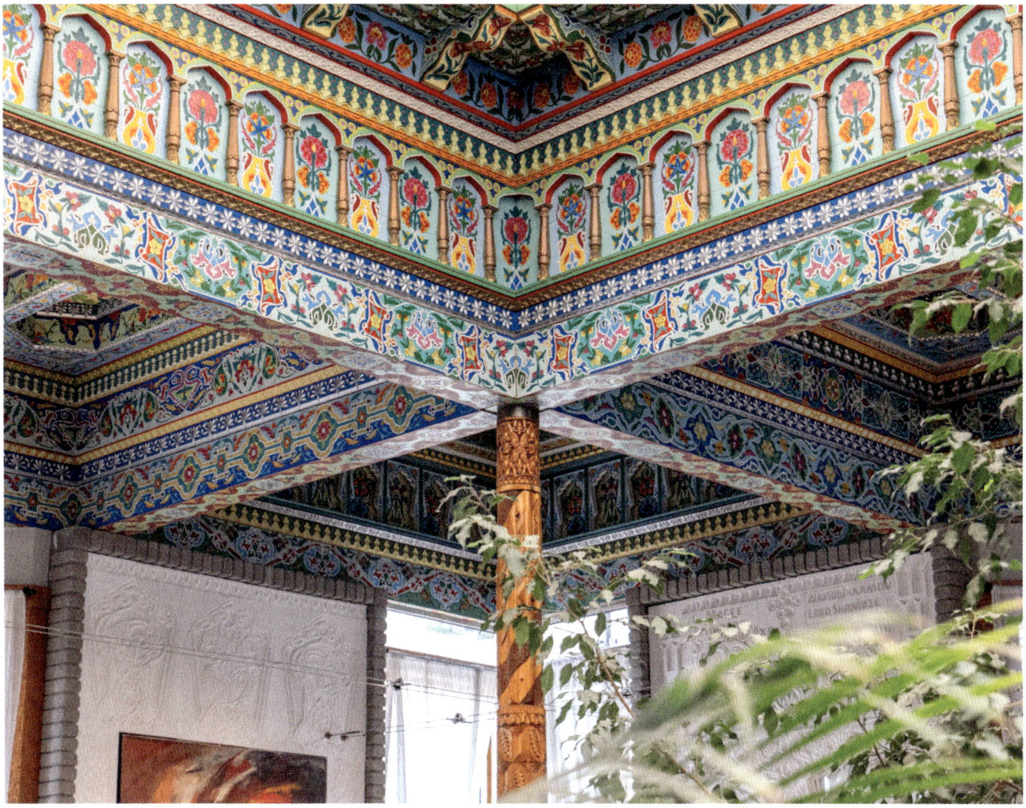

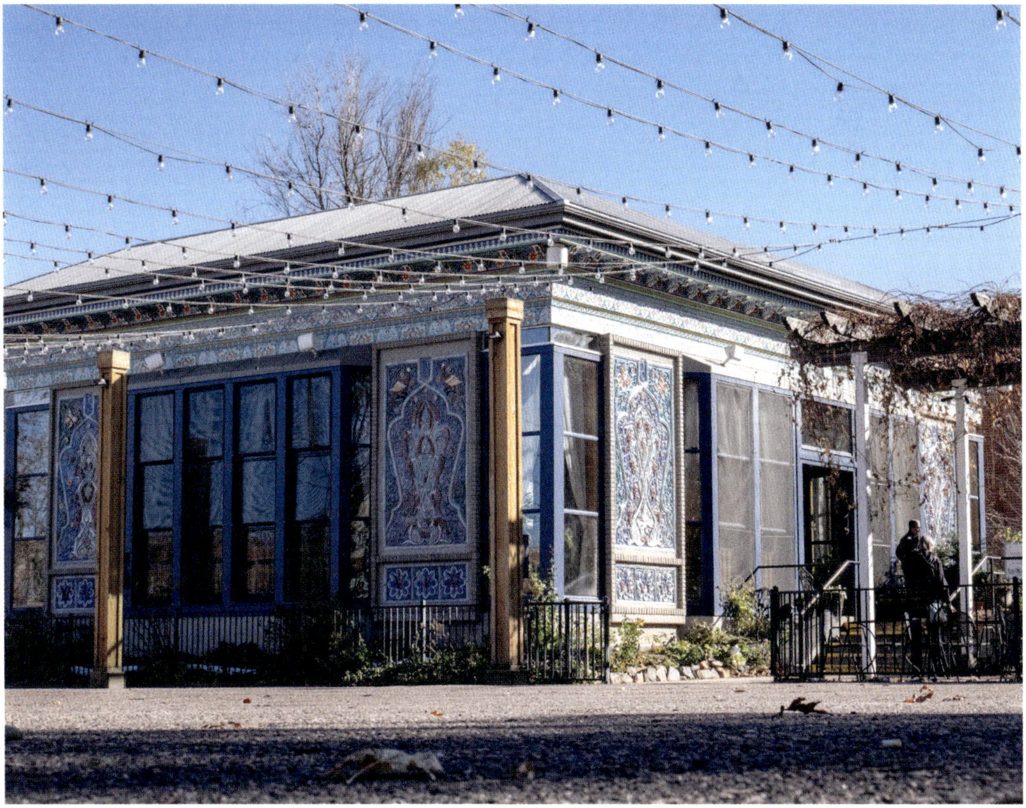

THE AMERICAS · BRASÍLIA

CASA DE CHÁ
95

Praça dos Três Poderes Três, Brasília, Distrito Federal, 70802-140, Brazil

TO VISIT BEFORE YOU DIE BECAUSE

Savour a cuppa in style at this recently refurbished sleek teahouse designed by legendary modernist architect Oscar Niemeyer.

Designed between 1965 and 1966 by renowned architect Oscar Niemeyer, the Casa de Chá was conceived as a meeting point on the monumental Three Powers Plaza, the site of the three branches of the Brazilian government. Half hidden in the square, close to the giant national flag, the recently refurbished Casa de Chá is a unique spot with floor-to-ceiling windows hiding under a long flat white roof, in the great modernist tradition. Inside, you will find classic pieces such as Jean Gillon armchairs and a menu by local chef Gil Guimarães. The café is actually part of the local university and a training ground for its hospitality students. The tea menu includes a good variety of hot and cold drinks, from Itamaraty Chai (black tea with star anise, cloves and pepper) and a house maté to the Congresso infusion, with hibiscus, apple, clove and cinnamon. We'd recommend sampling these with a slice of corn cake or, if really hungry, a Niemeyer tartine with Parma ham and umbu jelly, or a full-blown Dona Sarah afternoon tea.

casadecha.df.senac.br

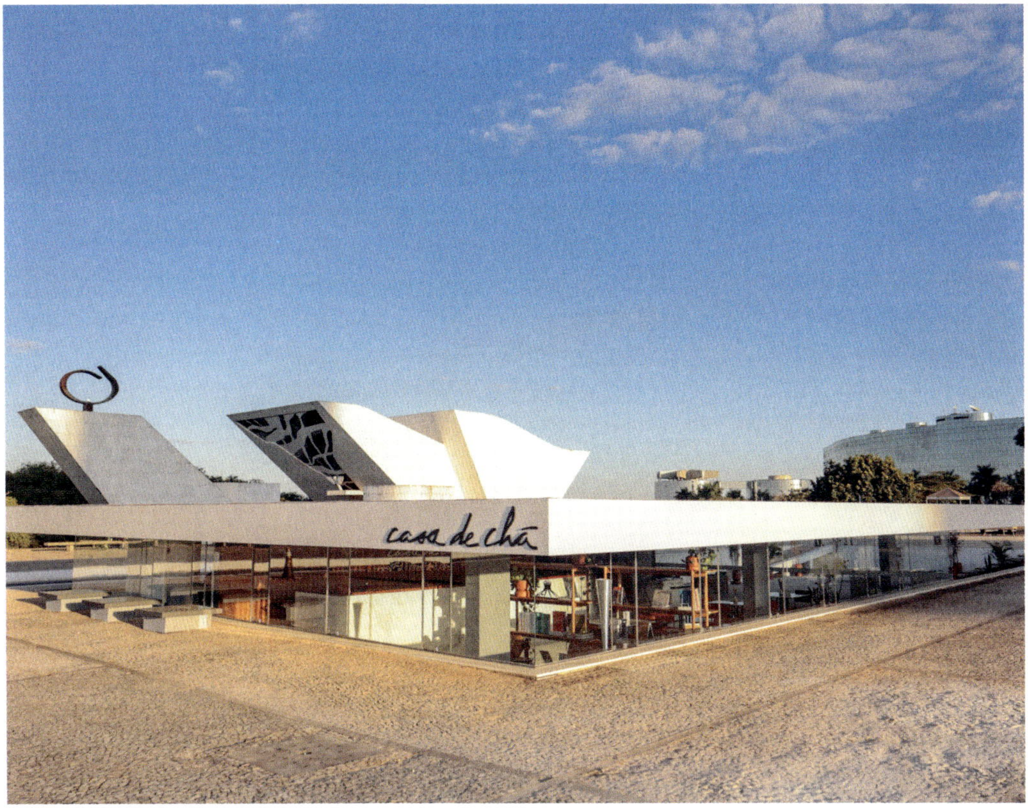
casa de chá

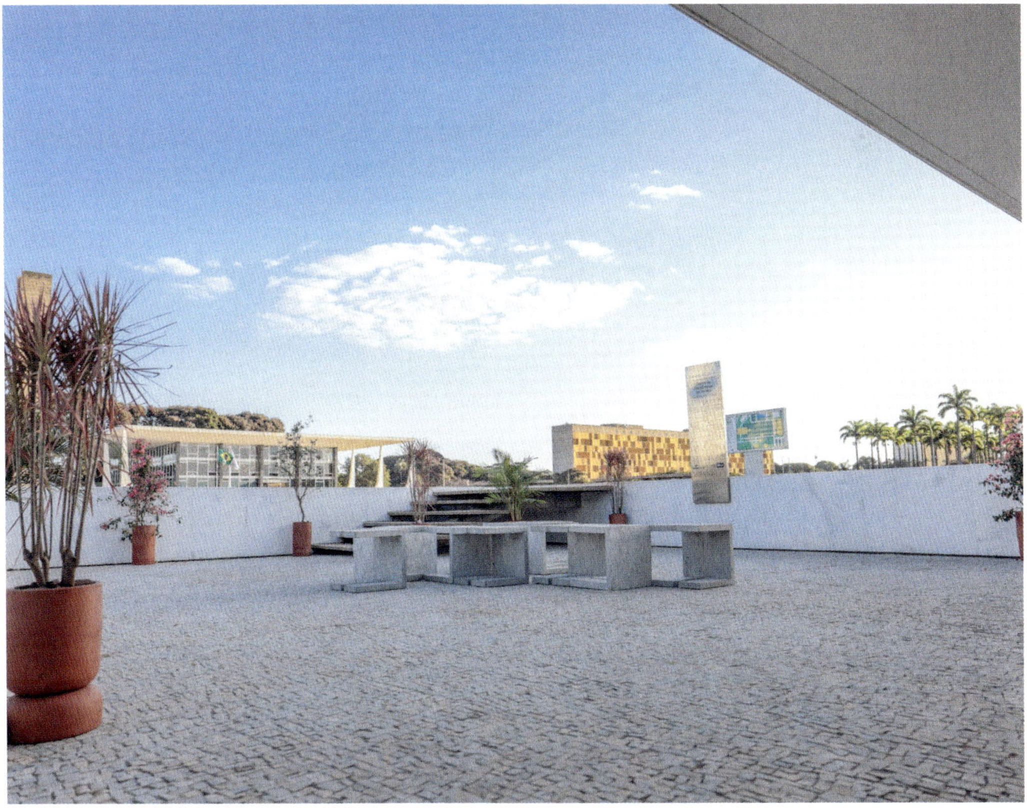

BENEFICIOS DE LA YERBA MATE
ANTIOXIDANTE
Es fuente de
VITAMINAS
MINERALES
REDUCE COLESTEROL
Y PRESIÓN ARTERIAL
PREVIENE DIABETES
POTASIO
MAGNESIO
proteínas
HEPATOPROTECTOR

THE AMERICAS BUENOS AIRES

96 MATEA AROMAS Y SABORES

Ayacucho 1538, Recoleta, Buenos Aires, Argentina

TO VISIT BEFORE YOU DIE BECAUSE

Opened in 2018, this welcoming maté bar in Buenos Aires is the place to discover and sample South America's favourite hot drink.

Made by brewing the leaves and small twigs of the *Ilex paraguariensis* tree, yerba maté is originally from Paraguay but is now enjoyed throughout South America. There are large plantations in the northeast of Argentina, where you can follow the Ruta de la Yerba Mate, but here in Buenos Aires' Recoleta neighbourhood, you will find the only tasting room in Latin America dedicated solely to celebrating the infusion. 'Maté is not just a tea; it is a ritual, an excuse to meet with our friends and talk for hours,' says co-founder Ilan Zaltzman. 'This ritual comes from the Guaraní, from 1,500 years ago, and we still do things the same way today.' Matea's experiences include learning about the beverage's origins and cultural relevance, as well as sampling exclusive blends of yerba maté, paired with Argentinian pastries. You will also learn about traditional drinking vessels and *bombillas*, the straw/filter used to sip on the infusion, which is appreciated for its slightly bitter edge and earthy taste.

somosmatea.com.ar

THE AMERICAS CHICAGO

97 RUSSIAN TEA TIME

77 E Adams Street, Chicago, Illinois, 60603, United States

TO VISIT BEFORE YOU DIE BECAUSE

Drink Russian-style black teas from samovars, or enjoy some fine teas from China and beyond at this welcoming Chicago landmark.

Perfectly located next to The Art Institute of Chicago, this traditional Russian tea room was actually founded by Klara Muchnik, a Ukrainian nurse with a passion for cooking and baking. In the 1990s, she left Uzbekistan for a new life in the US, and soon after opened Russian Tea Time with her son Vadim. Over 30 years later, and the space is still beloved by locals and tourists alike for its cosy dining room lined with red velvet curtains and its wide choice of teas. As well as the house speciality, Czar's Samovar, a dark black tea with a hint of currant served in a glass (traditionally sipped through a sugar cube held between the teeth), you can order teapots of smoky Russian breakfast, top-grade *bai hao yin zhen* silver needle, Keemun *hao ya a* or Earl Grey lavender. (Larger groups can also enjoy tea from a brass samovar.) Rather than going for the afternoon tea, we recommend you sample the Russian teas, along with specialities such as honey cake, latkes, blinis and pelmeni dumplings, or the full house platter, complete with carrot salad, tabouli, stuffed cabbage and kebabs.

Russian tea time
Darjeeling-Black Currant
Tea Blend
LOOSE TEA

THE AMERICAS — DALLAS

98 THE FRENCH ROOM AT THE ADOLPHUS

1321 Commerce Street, Dallas, Texas, 75202, United States

TO VISIT BEFORE YOU DIE BECAUSE

Enjoy a chic afternoon tea with carefully thought-through tea pairings in a landmark 1912 building in downtown Dallas.

Although it is located in the heart of Dallas, Texas, The Adolphus Hotel was modelled after a German Beaux-Arts castle in a nod to its founder's roots. It is also known for its French Room, a grand salon where you can enjoy afternoon tea in style. With gold trim on the walls and gilded Louis XVI chairs, it's a place for special occasions, beautifully lit up by candy-coloured Italian Murano glass chandeliers. As well as exquisite pastries, seasonally flavoured scones and homemade preserves, the menu includes a selection of loose-leaf teas from Zakti, a local purveyor who creates special blends just for the hotel, carefully paired with each course. Savoury dishes such as roast beef brioche come with a light-roasted High Mountain Chinese oolong, while pastries such as lemon tart and raspberry choux are served with cups of Risheehat Tea Garden, a black tea from India. The seasonal Holiday Tea, when the room is decked with twinkling lights, gold ribbons and fir trees and speciality teas are on offer, is particularly popular, as is the children's tea.

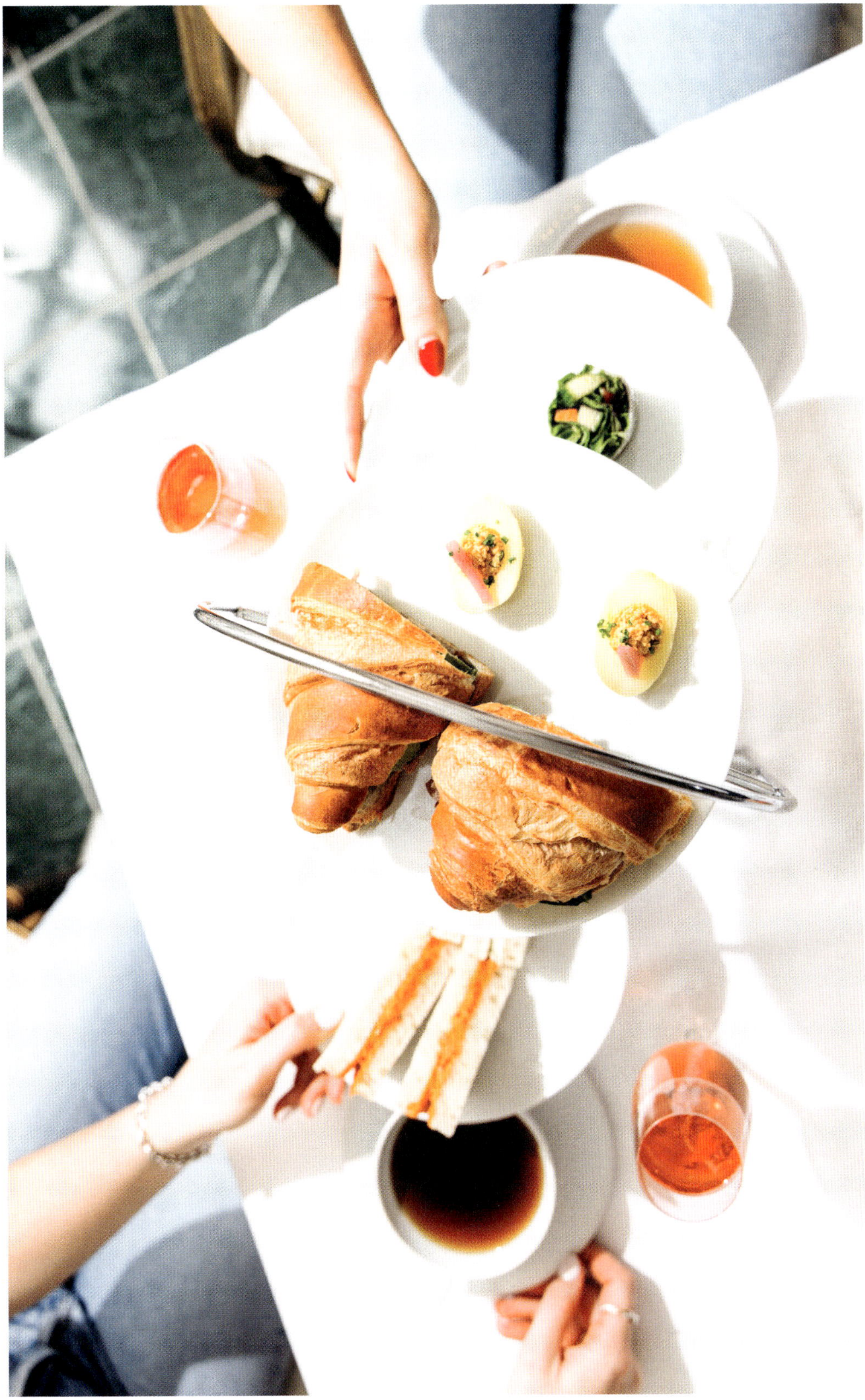

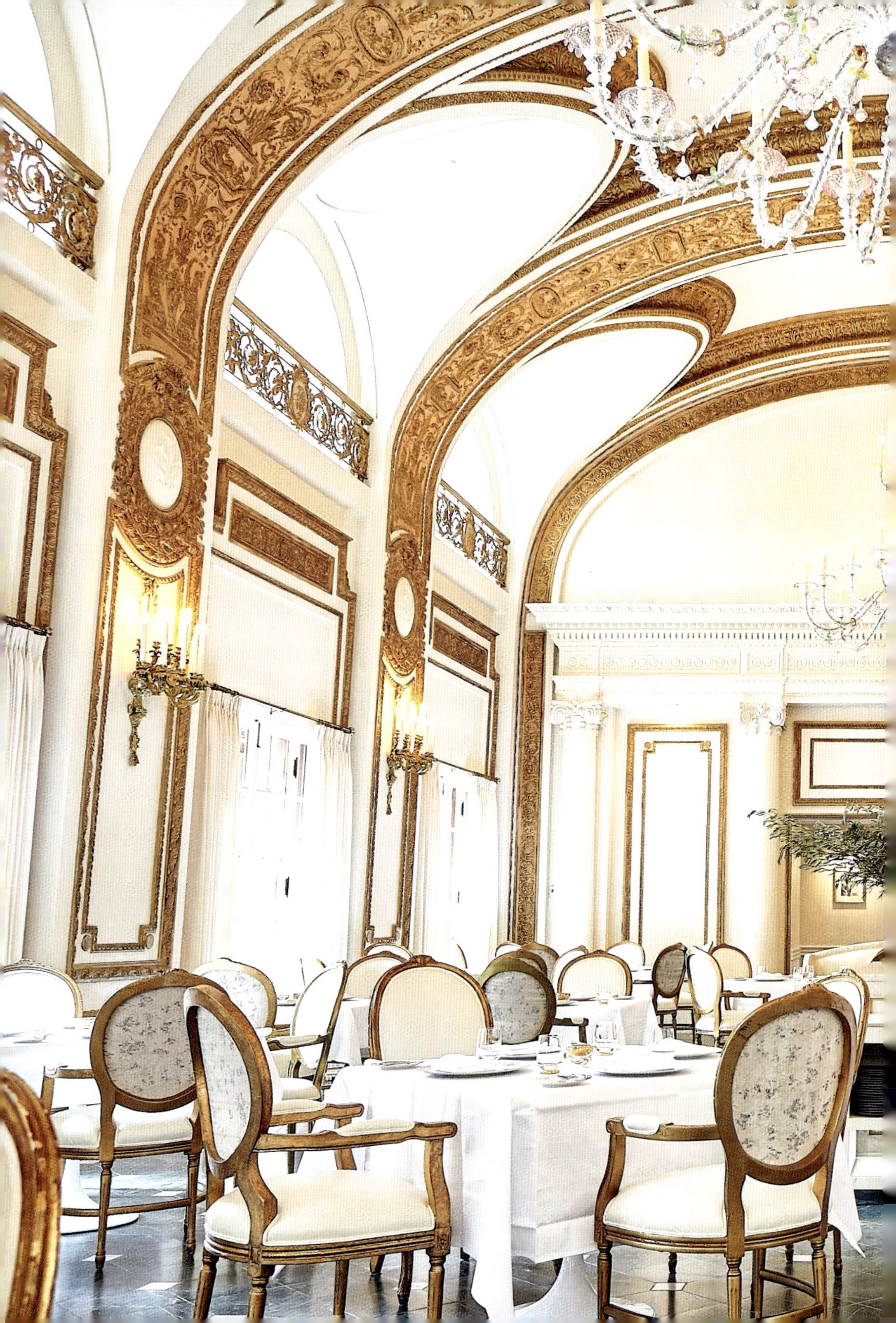

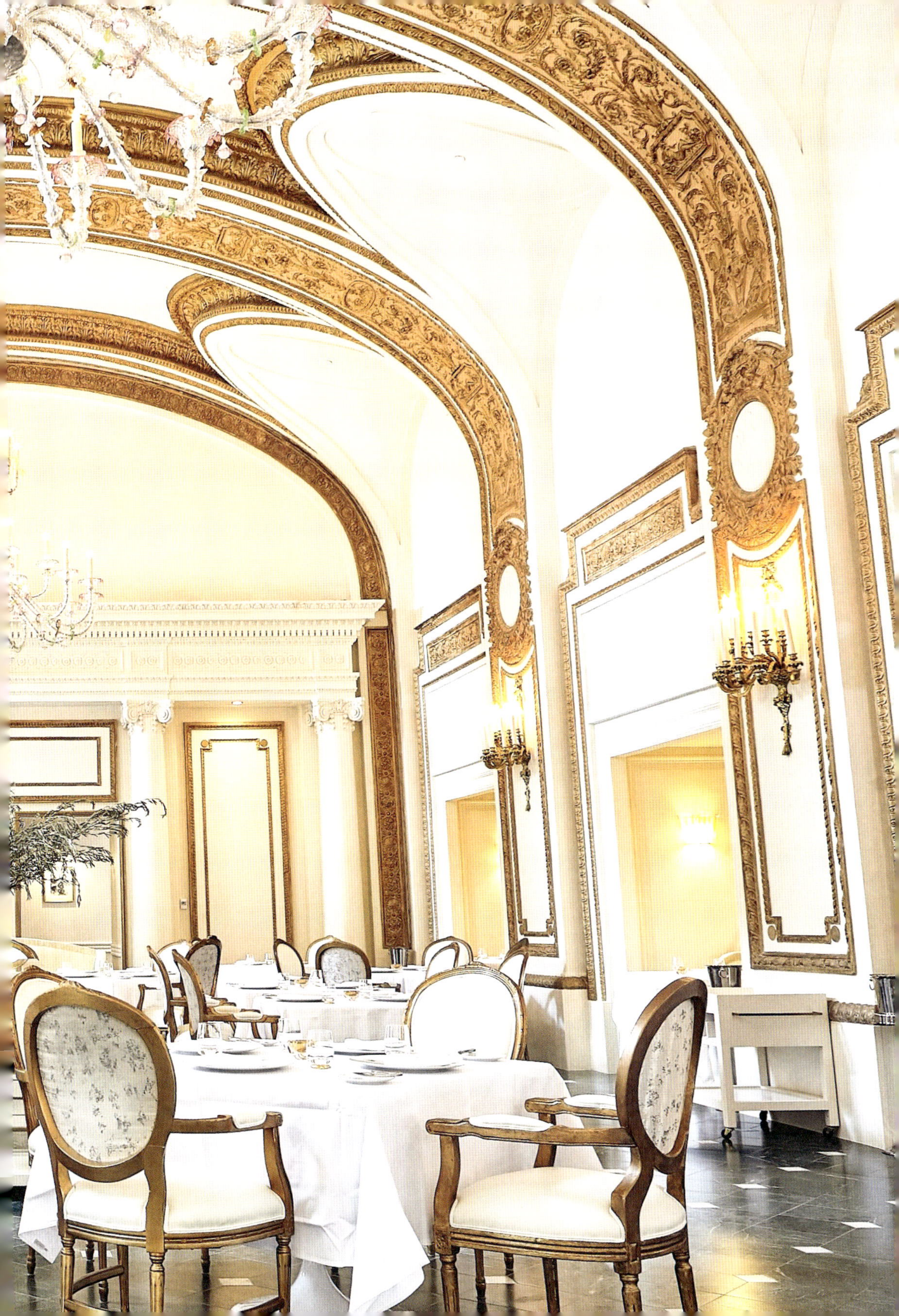

THE AMERICAS · GAIMÁN

99 TY GWYN

9 de Julio 111, U9105 Gaimán, Chubut, Argentina

TO VISIT BEFORE YOU DIE BECAUSE

Have a Welsh afternoon tea with homemade cakes and scones, right in South America's wild Patagonia province.

Patagonia's glaciers and natural beauty put it at the top of many travellers' bucket lists, but there is another – very unexpected – reason that you should consider paying it a visit. In this remote region, you will find not one but a series of Welsh teahouses, set up in and around the town of Gaimán. This is due to around 150 Welsh settling here in the second half of the 19th century, their language and culture having been kept alive by their many descendants until today. Ty Gwyn, located on the north side of the Chubut River and decorated with some of the settlers' items, was founded in the 1970s by María Elena Naso and Carlos Alberto 'Boby' Sánchez, a direct descendant of Abraham Mathews, preacher of the first ship that arrived in Patagonia. More than 150 years later, the family still serves homemade cakes made with seasonal fruit from their farm, including the classic *torta negra galesa* (Welsh black cake), cream cake and apple pie. Black tea is served in porcelain teapots dressed with knitted tea cosies, and enjoyed with milk and sugar, of course.

THE AMERICAS   LAKE LOUISE

100   LAKE AGNES TEA HOUSE

Lake Agnes, Lake Louise, Alberta, T0L 1E0, Canada

TO VISIT BEFORE YOU DIE BECAUSE

This off-the-grid teahouse has been serving up spectacular views of the Canadian Rocky Mountains and fine cups of tea since 1905.

Welcoming hikers from early June to October, this family-run teahouse is perched at an altitude of 2,135 metres near Lake Louise, in Canada's Banff National Park. Built in 1901 by the Canadian Pacific Railway as a refuge for hikers, it still features the original log cabin's windows, tables and chairs. Here, you can take in the stunning scenery of Lake Agnes while listening to a rushing waterfall. As well as homemade bread and soup, cooked on the teahouse's propane stove, the menu includes 100 fine loose-leaf teas from various corners of the world. There are classic flavoured black teas, green teas such as Blueberry Green and an immense selection of speciality teas, from white teas such as Ontario Ice-Wine, to black teas such as Sikkim Temi from the Himalayas. Unusually, there are also 10 different flavoured rooibos to choose from. Due to the remote location, this is a cash-only establishment, with no internet or electricity. The hike there takes about an hour and a half, and you're advised to bring plenty of water with you.

lakeagnesteahouse.com

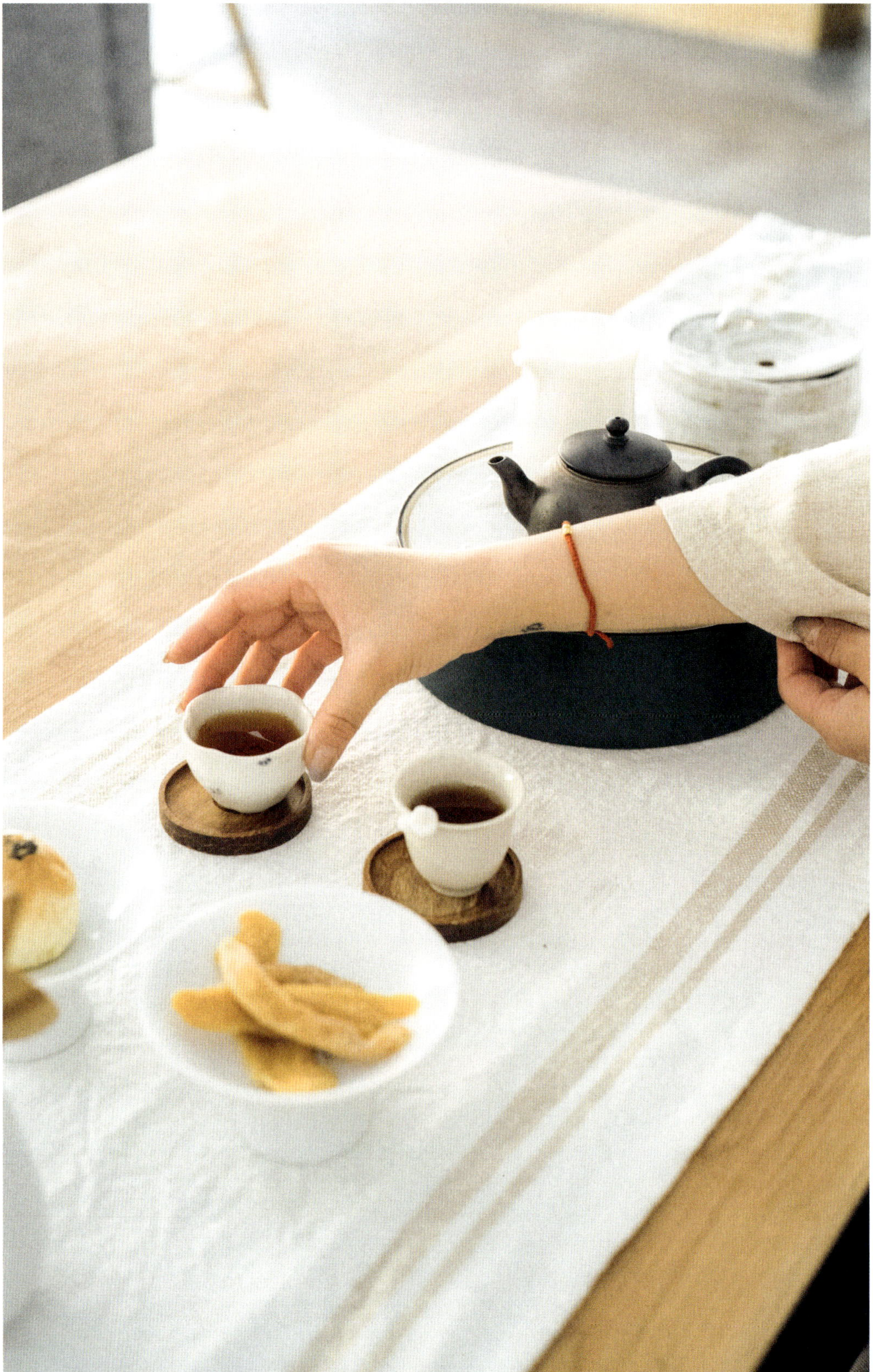

101 STEEP LA

970 N Broadway, Suite 112, Los Angeles, California, 90012, United States

TO VISIT BEFORE YOU DIE BECAUSE

Located in Los Angeles' Chinatown, this tea room and bar puts a contemporary twist on traditional Chinese tea and the art of slow living.

This teahouse, bar and eatery was co-founded by Samuel Wang and Lydia Lin, for whom tea is a family tradition. While Samuel grew up drinking oolong with his dad, Lydia's favourite is pu-erh tea, which her family enjoys while eating dim sum. Their menu focuses on premium teas hand-picked from China and Taiwan, which cover five out of six major Chinese tea categories: black, green, white, oolong and pu-erh – the latter including a refreshing Green Tangerine tea with notes of citrus and freshly cut grass. 'You can choose to pick up a freshly steeped hot tea or a bottle of our cold brew tea to go,' explains Samuel, 'but what sets us apart are the tea ceremonies you can enjoy with friends and family in our clean, sleek tea room.' Come 5pm, Steep LA introduces its After Dark programme, offering tea-infused cocktails such as Winter's Whisper, with Jiaziyuan oolong tea. There is also a food menu with noodle bowls and snacks and a boutique selling pieces by local designers and craft makers.

THE AMERICAS   LOS ANGELES

102   TEA AT SHILOH

2035 Bay Street, Arts District, Los Angeles, California, 90021, United States

TO VISIT BEFORE YOU DIE BECAUSE

This late-night teahouse offers delicate teas, music and conversation in a serene space in a very unlikely corner of the city.

'The teahouse is a portal into possibilities,' says founder Shiloh iii of her slightly mysterious, late-night, reservation-only teahouse, hidden behind a discreet black gate somewhere in the Arts District. 'We are a space for those looking for intimacy, jazz and a moment to be around others seeking softness.' During the day, you can come here to work or study with unlimited hot tea and sample a variety of seasonally crafted Chinese and Japanese traditional teas, such as hōjicha and Taiwanese oolongs. Come evening, the beautifully designed space, with exposed brick walls and soft lanterns, aims to reimagine nightlife by offering a calm and inspiring atmosphere that fosters connection and creation. From 7 to 11pm, Shiloh's hosts blend a variety of herbs to create custom teas. Other surprises include a high-perched stage accessed by a ladder, tarot reading sessions and quiet hours for introverts, as well as books and even watercolours for those inspired by their tea or the unique setting.

teaatshiloh.com

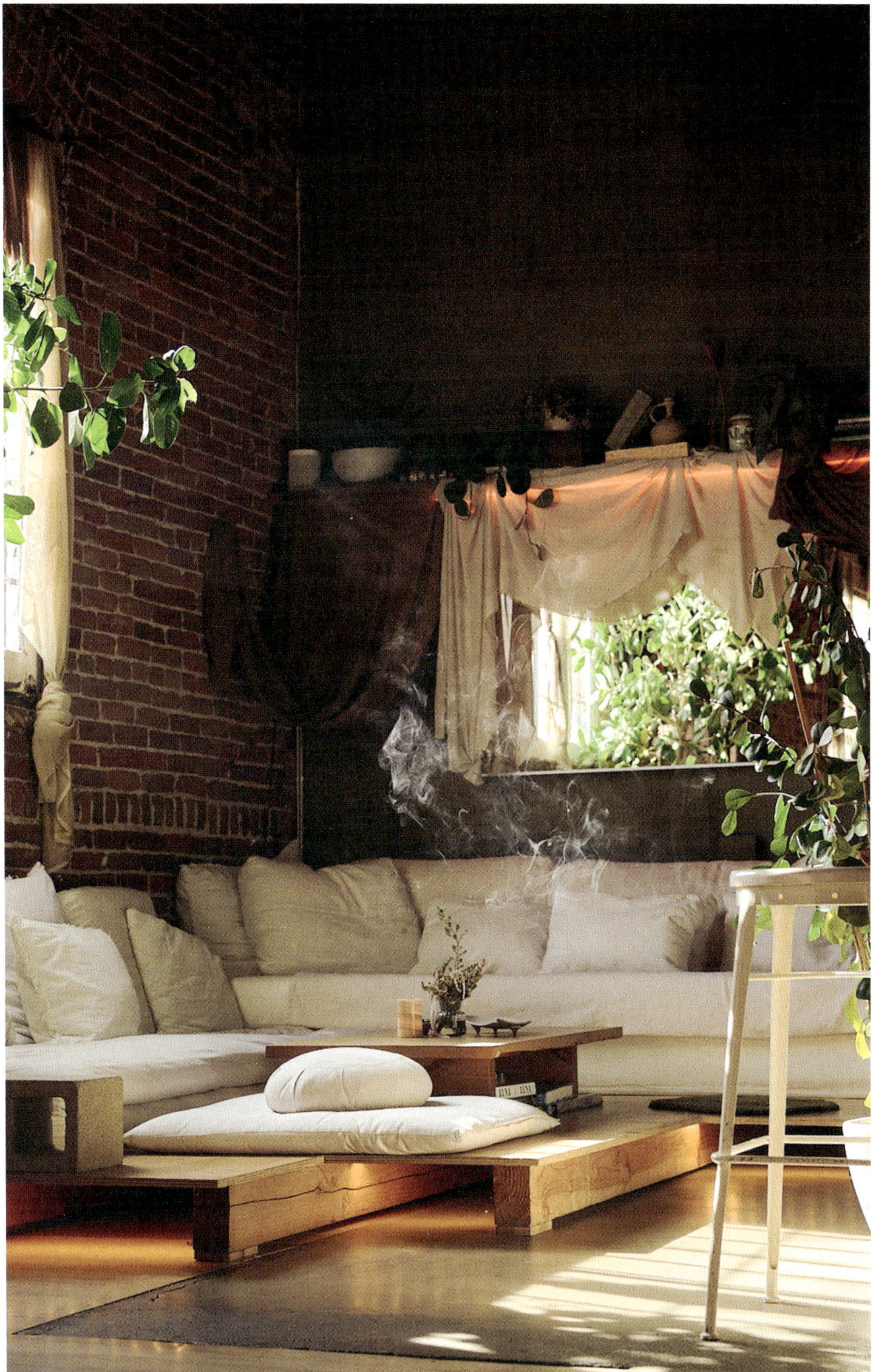

THE AMERICAS MEXICO CITY

103 CASA TASSEL

Córdoba 110, Colonia Roma, Mexico City, Mexico, 06700

TO VISIT BEFORE YOU DIE BECAUSE

A great little stop when exploring Mexico City's Roma neighbourhood, with a lovely choice of tea and tea-infused desserts.

With its cosy atmosphere, eclectic décor and mismatched tableware, this is just the kind of perfect tea spot that every neighbourhood should have. Of course, it fits right in in Mexico City's artsy Roma district, with its jazz soundtrack, bohemian furnishings and shelves lined with vintage teapots and shiny tea tins. House blends include the bestselling Romulus and Remus, a combination of black tea with honey and rosemary, as well as Indian Lady (Ceylon tea with rose petals) and Richie Rich (with lemon and strawberry). All in all, there are about 30 different types of tea, ranging from lapsang souchong and white pu-erh to Moroccan mint tea and a rooibos chai. Also on the menu are original mocktails, such as Hemingway, a mojito-style preparation with matcha from Japan, and herbal teas – a Mexican favourite – such as chamomile with lavender or a mix of anise, fennel and calendula. This is complemented by a small food menu, including savoury crêpes, Japanese sweets such as *nerikiri gato*, *alfajor* (a cookie sandwich with dulce de leche), carrot cake and matcha-infused brownies and cheesecakes.

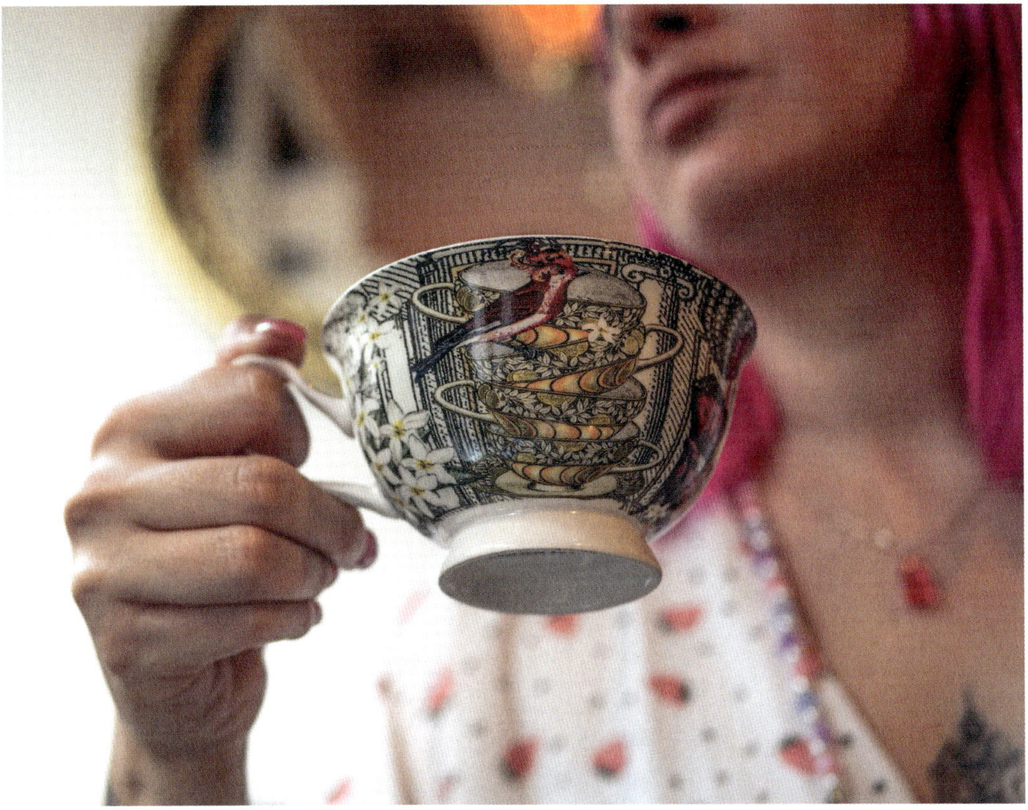

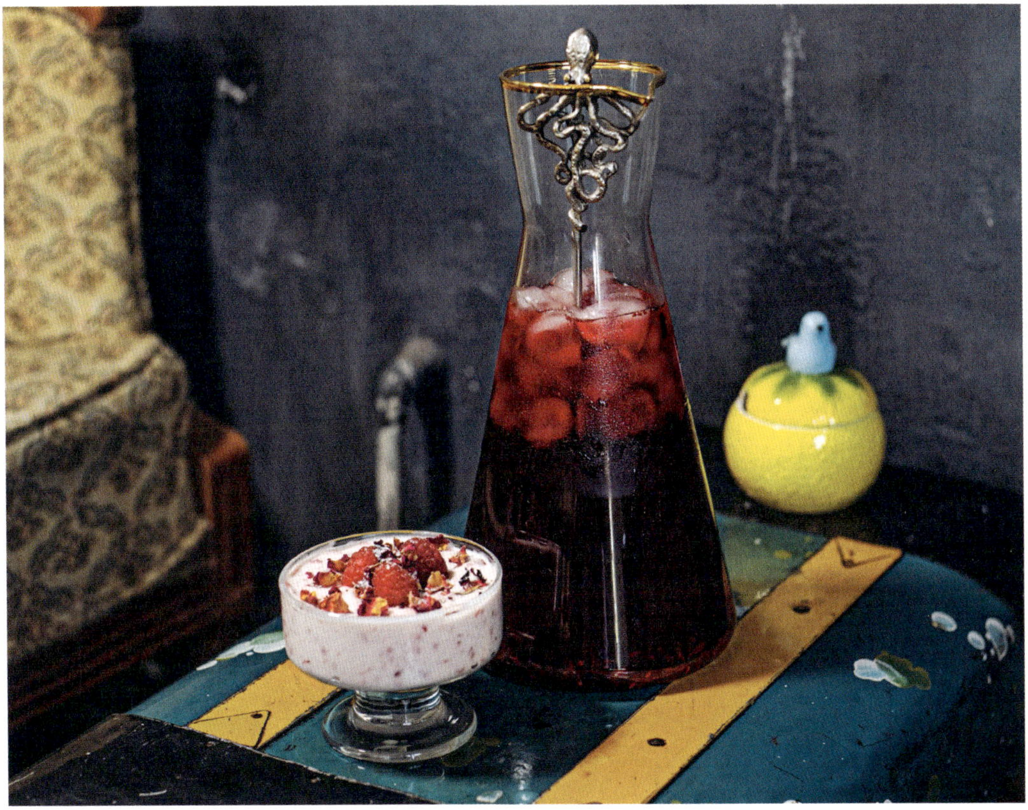

THE AMERICAS   MIAMI

104 JOJO TEA

620 NE 76th Street, Miami, Florida, 33138, United States

TO VISIT BEFORE YOU DIE BECAUSE

Why pair tea with food when you can pair it with music? Find out at this cool tea party, run by an American Tea Masters Cup winner.

Inspired by the meditative practice of gong fu cha, award-winning tea expert Mike Ortiz started JoJo Tea in 2011 to bring great tea to Miami's restaurants. His headquarters are now home to a tea party every Saturday, where you can sample the likes of Jade Mountain, a Taiwanese oolong, along with some great tunes. 'I love Madlib's *Medicine Show, Volume 3*. I would pair it with an aged raw pu-erh, our 2008 Menghai Five Mountains Blend,' says Ortiz. 'It was put together by Hong Kong tea master Vesper Chan and makes for unforgettable sips.' The most requested album is Frank Ocean's *Blond*, which they love to pair with a legendary Taiwanese oolong, Oriental Beauty. 'This was the tea that made me want to get into the business. As soon as I tasted it, I knew it was special. Years later, I learned that it comes from a cultivar that builds concentrated sugars as a defence against small insects. The result is a thick, sticky sweetness that has notes of grilled peaches and a long aromatic finish of honey.'

THE AMERICAS — MONTRÉAL

105 CARDINAL

5326 Boulevard Saint-Laurent, Montréal, Québec, H2T 1S1, Canada

TO VISIT BEFORE YOU DIE BECAUSE

Head to this weekend-only tea room for some delicious Earl Grey and homemade treats such as strawberry cheesecake.

Inspired by 1920s parlours and old English libraries, this atmospheric salon de thé in Montréal's Mile End is a great place to stop for a cup of tea and a slice of cake, served on old china cups and plates sourced from antique dealers and flea markets. On the tea menu is the bestselling London Fog, an organic fair-trade Earl Grey from local tea provider Camellia Sinensis, served with frothed milk and a homemade 'foggy sauce' with vanilla and sugar, sprinkled with pea flower to add a delicate purple dusting. Also worth a sip or two are the Earl Grey à la crème and the Special Cardinal Grey blend, from the Metropolitan Tea Company in Toronto, a full-flavoured black tea with orange pieces, cornflower petals, rose petals and lime leaves. The tea for two, with decadent chocolate squares, cranberry-orange or strawberry scones and cucumber sandwiches, is very popular, and the team is also known to make wonderful tea-infused cocktails for parties and special occasions. Since it's open only Friday to Sunday, book before you go.

thecardinaltea.com

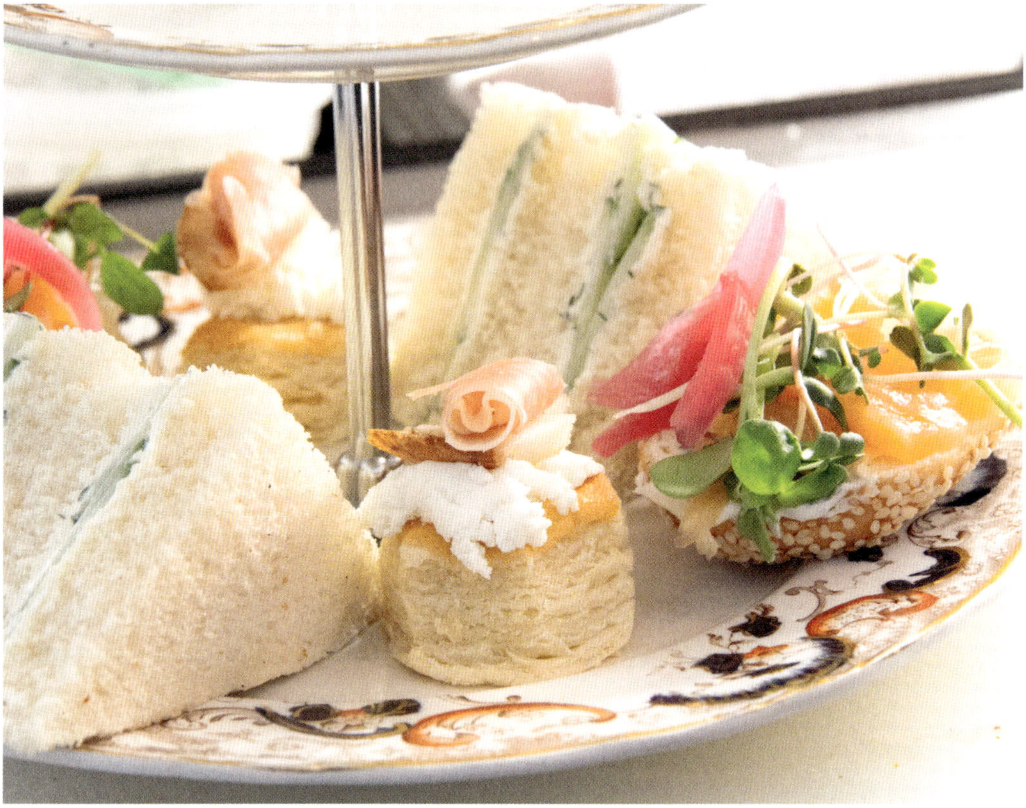

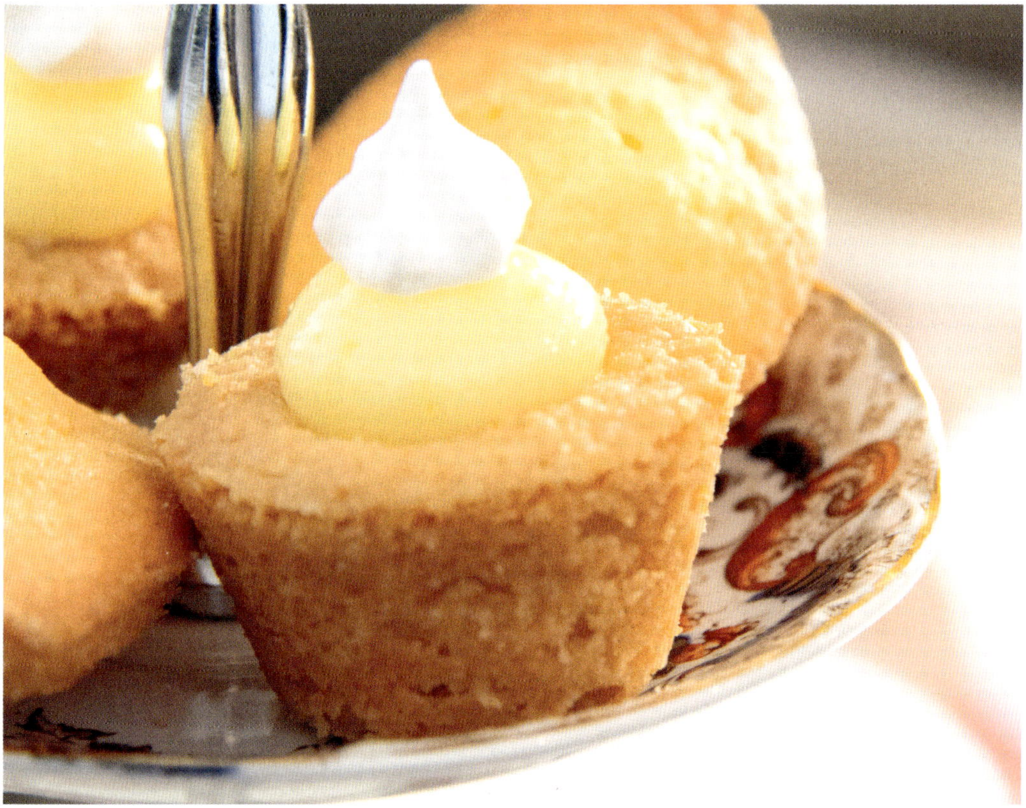

THE AMERICAS   MONTRÉAL

106 LA BRUME DANS MES LUNETTES

378 Rue Saint-Zotique, Montréal, Quebec, H2S 1L7, Canada

TO VISIT BEFORE YOU DIE BECAUSE

Freshly baked scones and Fortnum & Mason's finest blends are the highlights of this welcoming neighbourhood tea room.

The British are still debating how to pronounce the word *scone*, or which way to put the cream and jam on it, but here in Montréal, they know that the only important thing is how fresh the scone is. The little baked goods of Luc Sénéchal, founder of La Brume dans mes lunettes and self-described scone master, are now so popular that he's even started a business selling them around the city, but his tea room in Rosemont–La Petite-Patrie is the place to go for the freshest of them all. Inspired by his student days in the UK, when he couldn't afford the teas of Bettys (see page 95) or the like, La Brume is named after the steam on the eyeglasses of tea drinkers, and we can't think of a cosier place to be in the winter, when its own shopfront is all steamed up. The relaxed and affordable place serves high-quality treats and Fortnum & Mason teas (Sénéchal's favourite brand), with the most popular tea being Countess Grey, with bergamot, orange zest and calendula (but there are around 20 teas and infusions to choose from). Another crowd favourite is Her Majesty the Queen high tea, with cucumber sandwiches, strawberry financiers and, of course, a selection of the famous scones, flavoured with the likes of cranberry or lavender.

labrumedansmeslunettes.com   +1 5 143 791 178

THE AMERICAS — NEW ORLEANS

107 BOTTOM OF THE CUP TEA ROOM

327 Chartres Street, French Quarter, New Orleans, Louisiana, 70130, United States

TO VISIT BEFORE YOU DIE BECAUSE

This unique tea room in New Orleans' French Quarter has offered fine tea along with psychic readings and metaphysical gifts since 1929.

New Orleans is known for its embrace of the magical, mystical and paranormal, and nowhere is that vision clearer than at this historic teahouse. It is set in the city's French Quarter, where ladies would take a break from a shopping spree with a soothing cup of tea. As they finished their tea, a psychic would visit their table and read the tea leaves in the bottom of the cup; hence the tea room's name. Today, you can enjoy a reading of tea leaves as well as tarot cards or your palm, along with myriad teas available as loose leaf or in tea bags. Locally inspired blends sold under the brand New Orleans Tea Company include Bayou Bonfire Souchoung; Beignet, a flavoured rooibos inspired by the city's beloved dessert; and Dancing on Frenchman Street, a deep-burgundy infusion of dried fruits and herbs. There is also a private space upstairs, the Adaire Room, where you can take part in a Celestial tea experience.

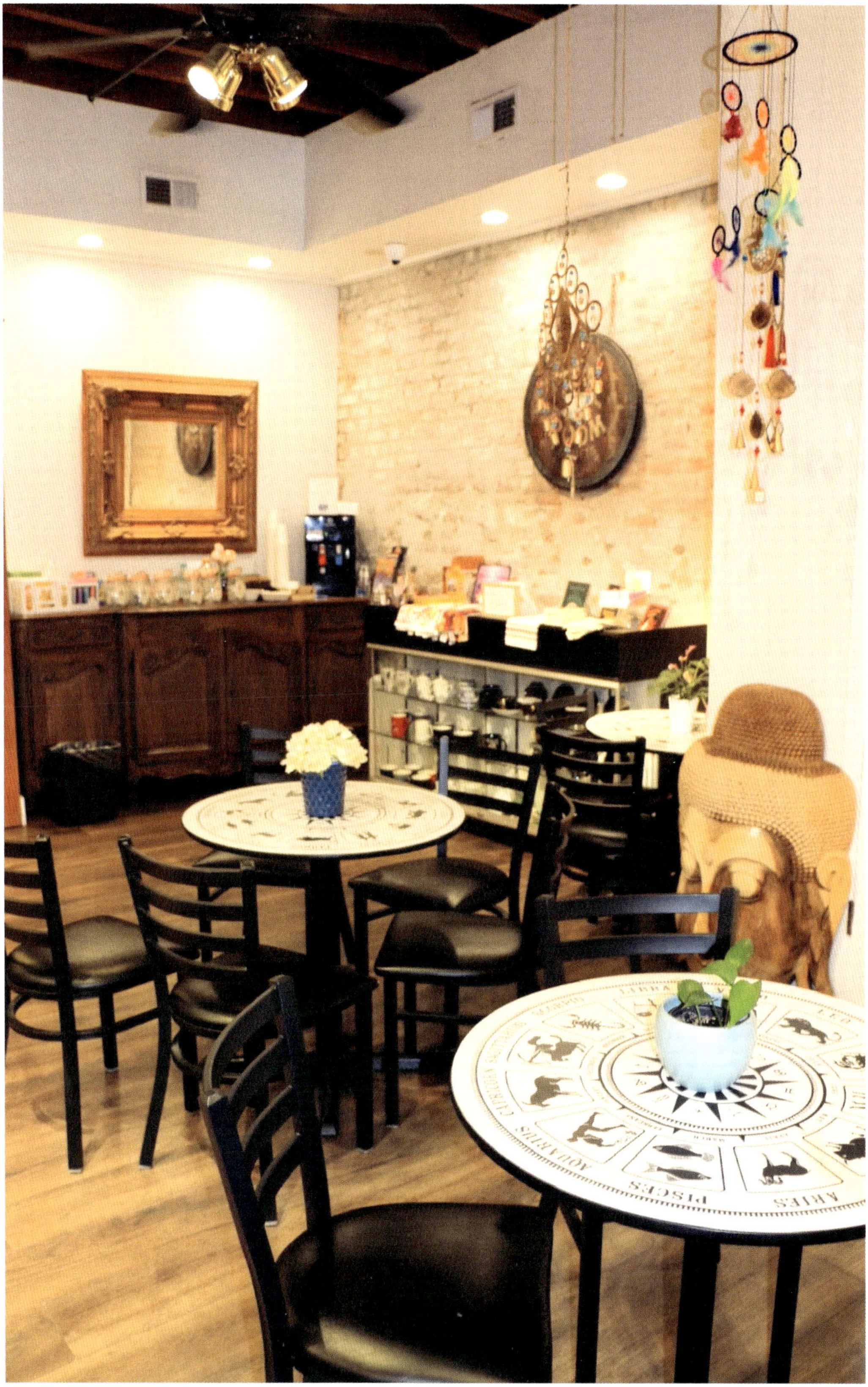
LIBRA
LEO
CAPRICORN
AQUARIUS
PISCES
ARIES

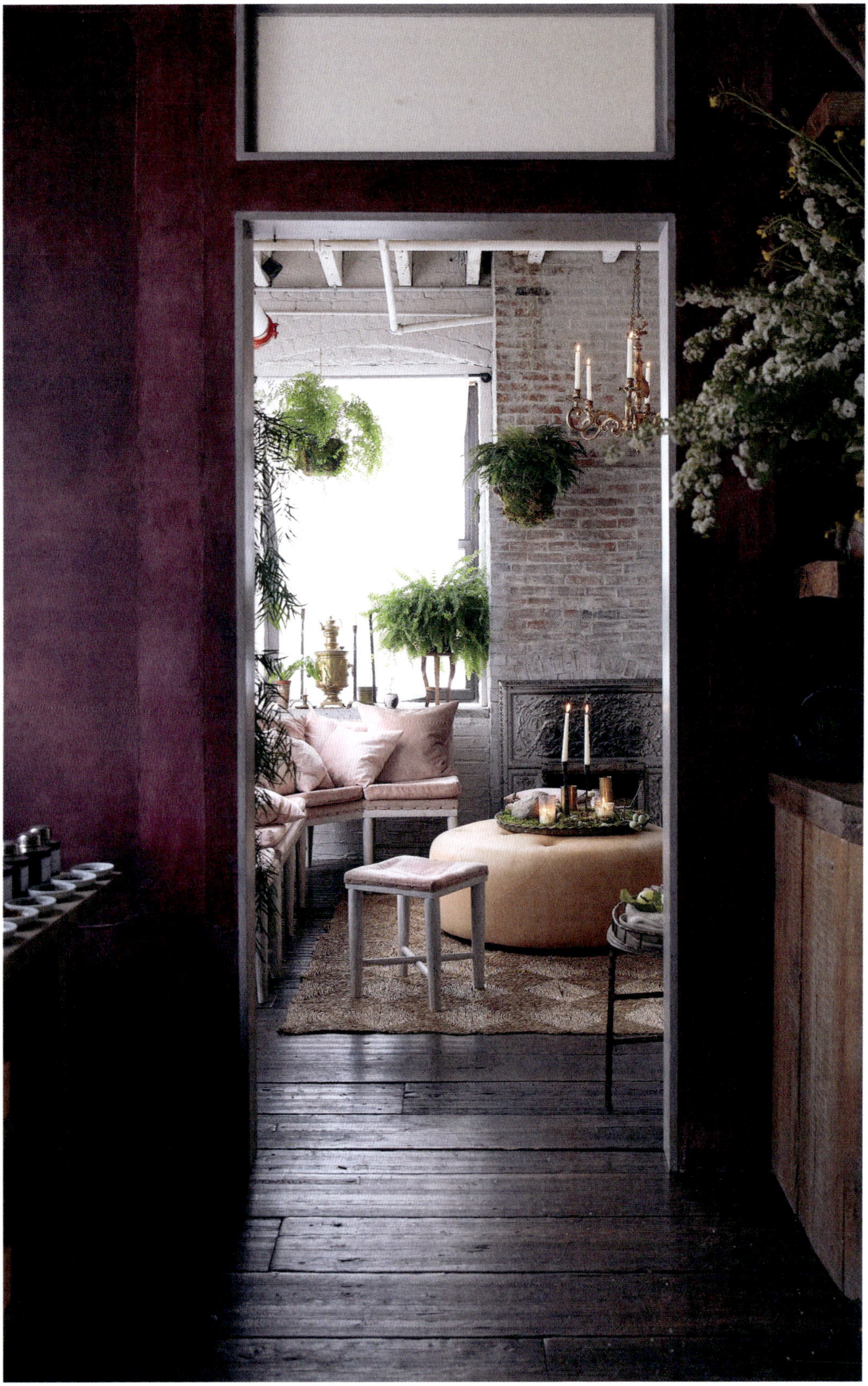

THE AMERICAS — NEW YORK

108 BELLOCQ TEA ATELIER

104 West Street, Brooklyn, New York, 11222, United States

TO VISIT BEFORE YOU DIE BECAUSE

Located in a brick warehouse in Brooklyn's Greenpoint, the tea room of leading tea company Bellocq is stocked with precious blends.

Founded by Heidi Johannsen Stewart, Bellocq is known for its single-estate full-leaf teas and signature botanical blends, as well as its famous yellow tea caddies now found in the tea rooms of some of the world's leading brands, from Tiffany & Co. to Cartier. But here in its studio in Brooklyn, a beautifully designed space with hanging ferns and artworks, it's all about the luxury of taking time to enjoy a fine cup of tea. Distilling inspiration from botanical traditions while embracing innovation and simplicity, the brand focuses on sustainable production practices, sourcing teas from exceptional gardens that reflect the unique terroirs of China, Japan, Taiwan, Nepal, Sri Lanka, India and South Africa. Its friendly team will take you through the meticulous selection process and amazing tea selection, no matter how knowledgeable you are about tea. Bellocq's Earl Grey, for example, is made with an exceptional base leaf and, uniquely, the essence of Sicilian bergamot extracted from the entire fruit. 'The leaves and botanicals are a beautiful expression of nature's endless intelligence and the devotion of many talented, hardworking people along the way,' concludes Heidi.

bellocqtea.com +1 8 004 955 416

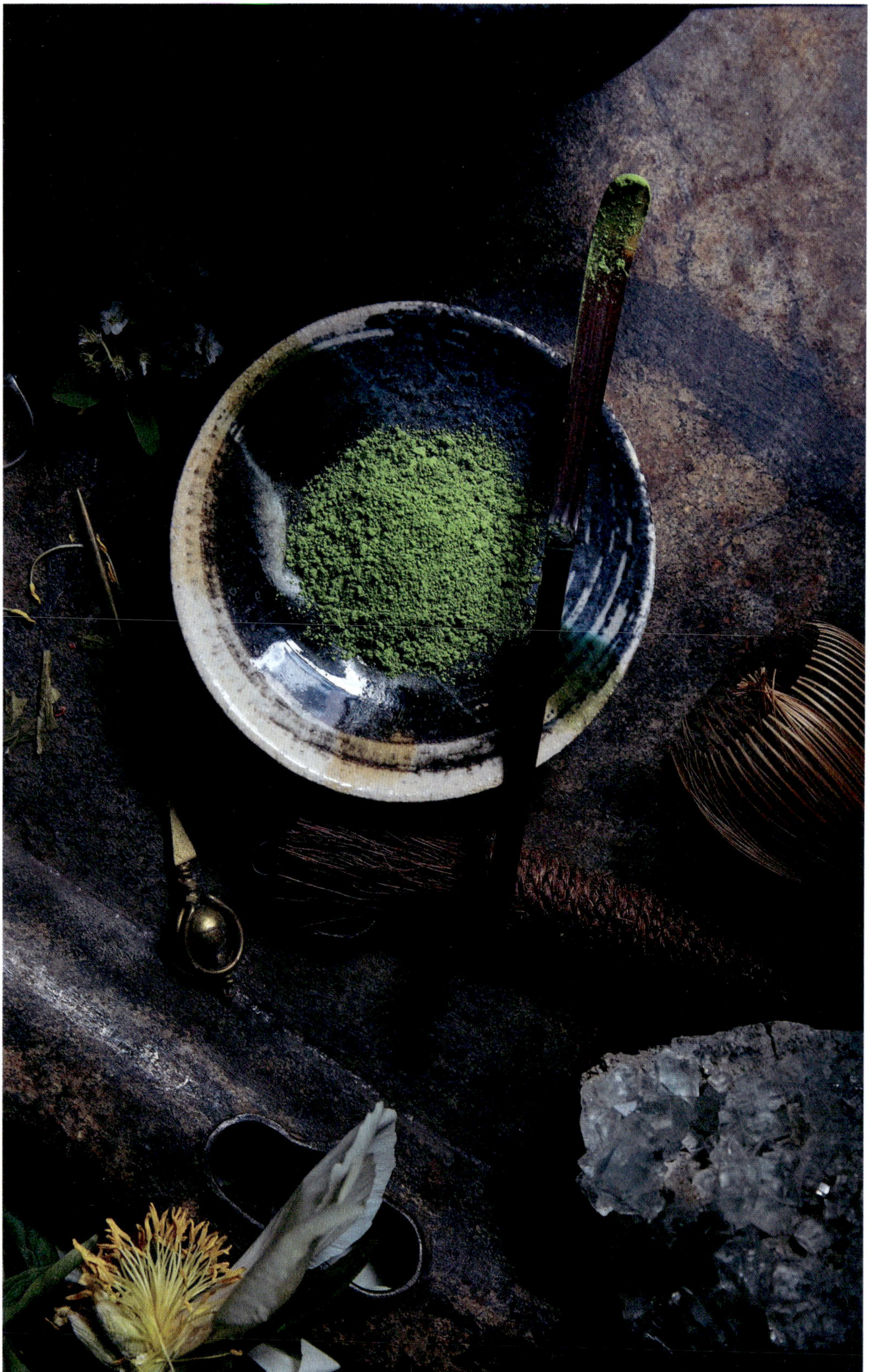

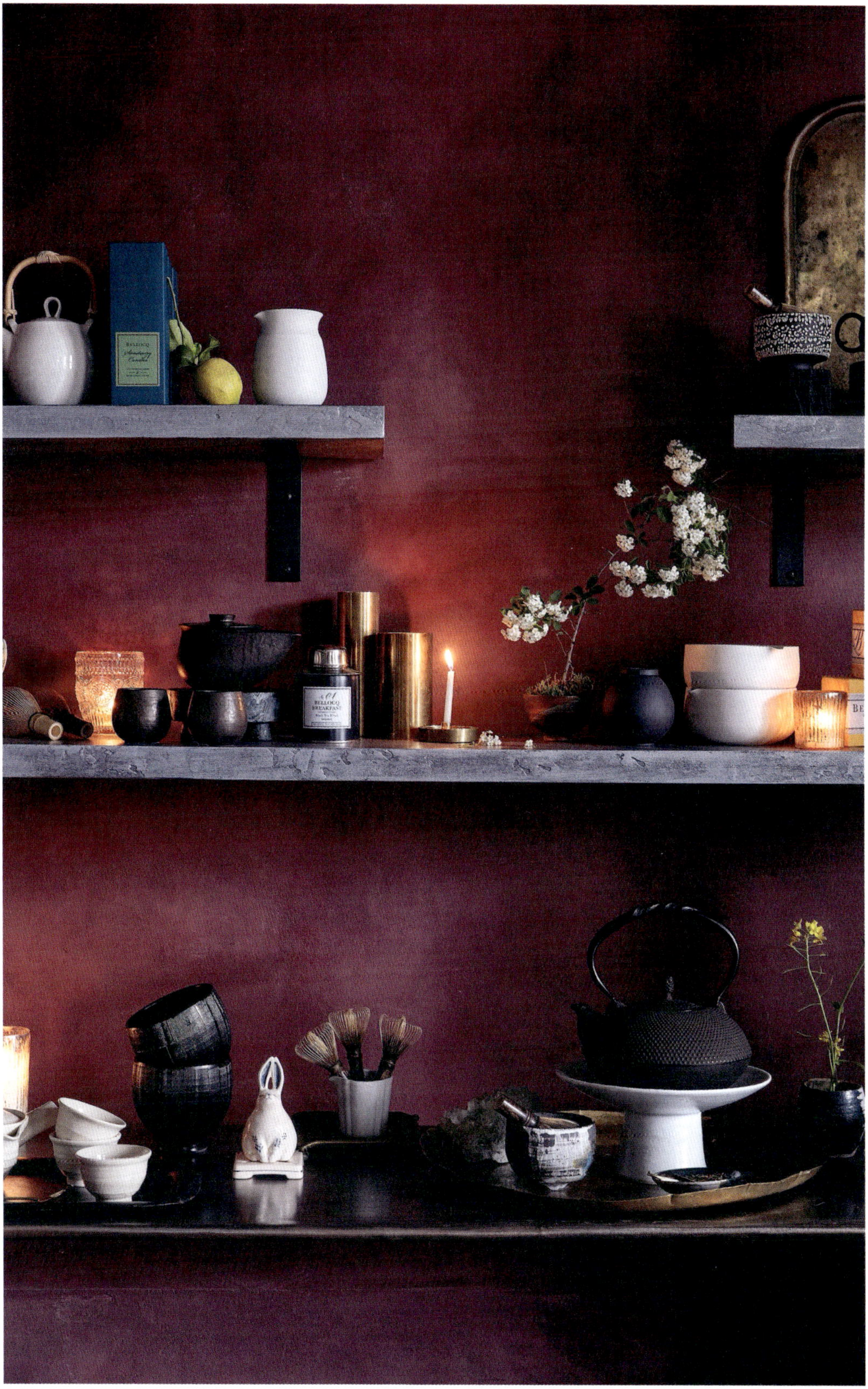
BELLOCQ
BELLOCQ BREAKFAST

THE AMERICAS NEW YORK

109 CHA-AN TEAHOUSE

230 East 9th Street, 2nd Floor, New York, New York, 10003, United States

TO VISIT BEFORE YOU DIE BECAUSE

Come to this second-floor Japanese teahouse for its green teas, and stay for its beautiful desserts and tea-infused cocktails.

Once you've found the discreet entrance of this Japanese teahouse hidden in plain sight in New York's East Village, you're in for a treat. Climb the narrow staircase, and you will enter a simple space with wooden tables and washi-paper lanterns, decorated in the style of a traditional Japanese *chashitsu*. Established in 2004 by Japanese restaurateur Tomoko Yagi with the Japanese concept of *omotenashi* (a term for whole-hearted hospitality) in mind, Cha-An Teahouse is known for its matcha teas and pretty desserts (although it also serves rice dishes topped with fried chicken or salmon). Its bestselling teas include cold matcha latte, hōjicha and sakura sencha, but the menu also includes *kanabow cha*, floral rose tea, hōjicha with rosemary and sliced oranges and tea-based cocktails such as the Matcha-tini (sake, matcha and orange liqueur). The beautifully presented afternoon teas include a matcha extravaganza starring the house speciality, the matcha tiramisu, while other eye-catching desserts range from a black sesame crème brûlée to homemade mochi, as well as harder-to-find specialities, such as *zenzai shiruko*, a hot dessert of *monaka*, chestnut mochi and red beans.

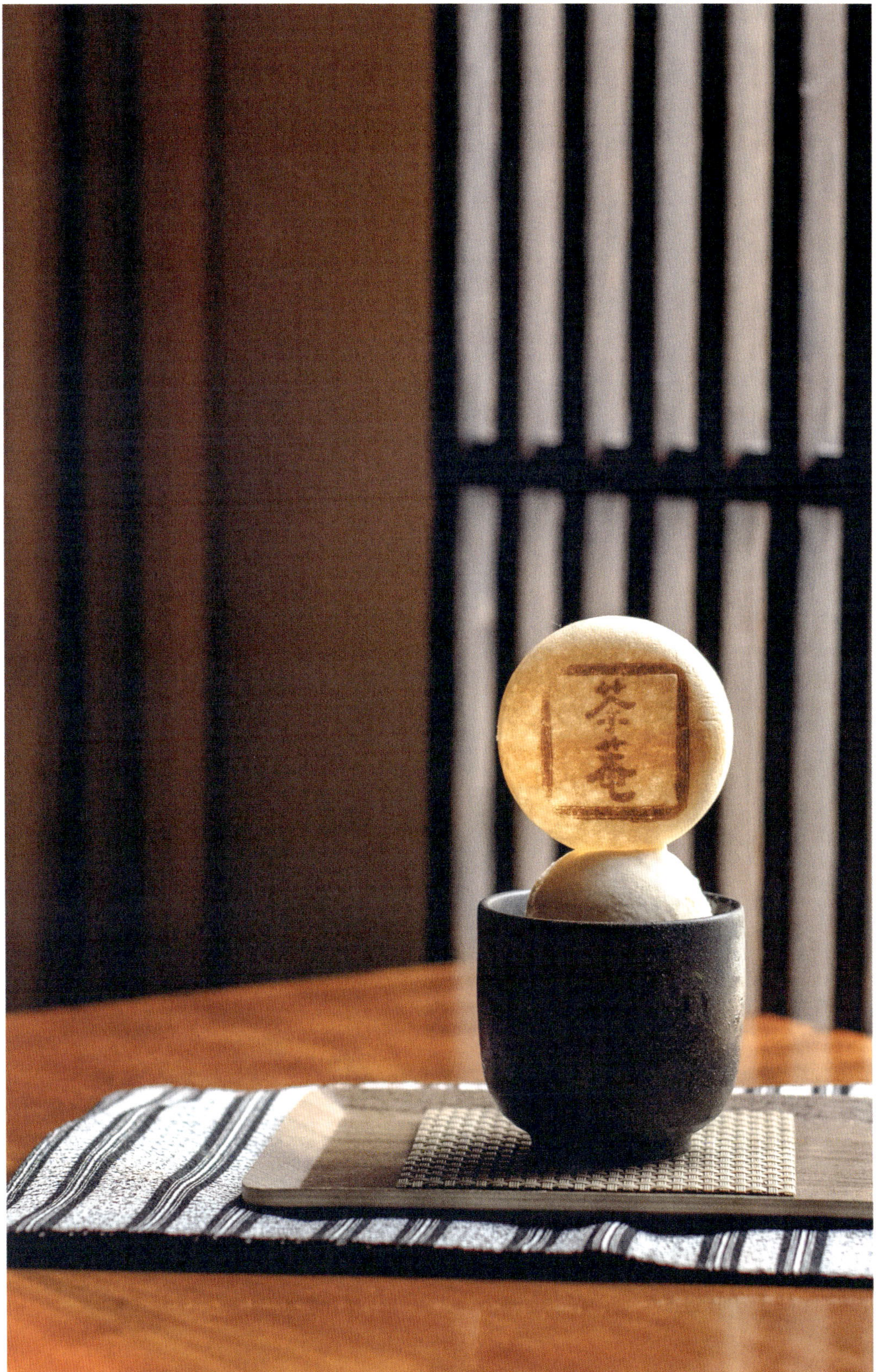
茶菴

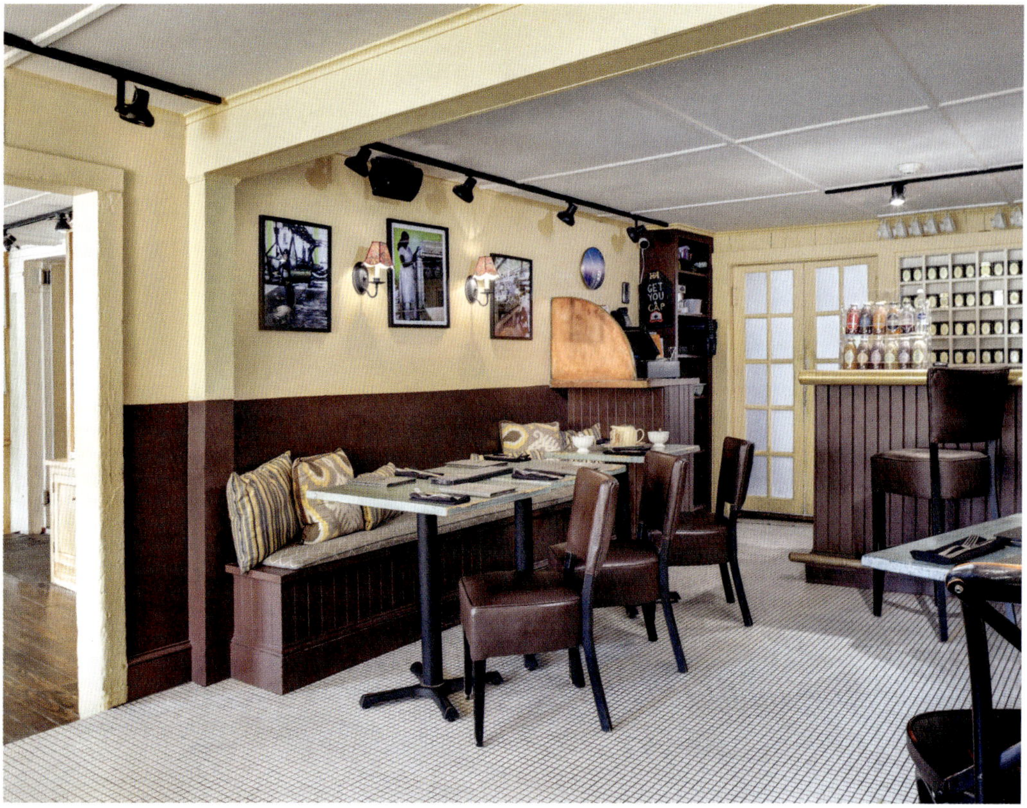

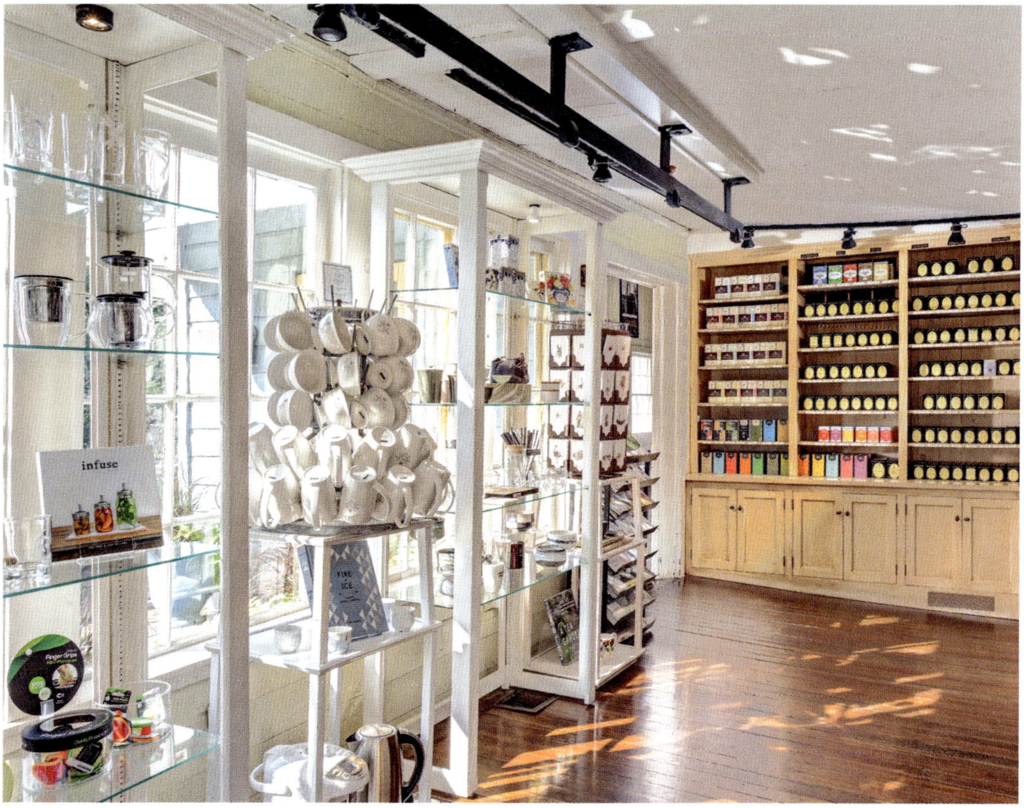
infuse

THE AMERICAS   NEW YORK

110 HARNEY & SONS

13 Main Street, Millerton, New York, 12546, United States

TO VISIT BEFORE YOU DIE BECAUSE

This wonderful tea emporium offers around 250 different high-quality teas at an affordable price, in New York's Hudson Valley.

A leading American tea company, Harney & Sons was founded in 1983 by John Harney, who started out by mastering the art of tea blending in his basement and testing his new teas on the customers of his inn. Today the family business offers over 300 varieties of the highest-quality teas, with signature flavours like Hot Cinnamon Spice and Paris (a fruity black tea with vanilla and caramel), several varieties of matcha and more adventurous infusions like bamboo and avocado leaves. Most are available to sample at the brand's tasting bar and lounge at its factory in Millerton, in the scenic Hudson Valley. As well as serving lunch, the café offers an assortment of pastries and an afternoon tea with scones, jam and clotted cream. You can also order custom-brewed iced teas or a Harney Palmer, made with fresh brewed tea and lemonade. Harney & Sons also has a shop in SoHo, which has a tea-tasting counter and a café where you can try tea flights and snack on blueberry scones.

harney.com   +1 5 187 892 121

THE AMERICAS NEW YORK

111 TÉ COMPANY

163 W 10th Street, West Village, New York, 10014, United States

---

TO VISIT BEFORE YOU DIE BECAUSE

This West Village tea room specialising in Taiwanese tea offers great oolongs and tasty tea snacks in a beautiful brownstone building.

Founded in 2012 by Elena Liao and Frederico Ribeiro, Té Company sources exquisite teas directly from small farmers in Taiwan. Named after the Taiwanese Hokkien name for tea, the company is known for both its loose-leaf teas and its delicious small bites. 'Taiwanese oolong is the darling of the tea world,' they say, noting its production requires highly skilled tea makers with centuries of experience. Frederico and Elena, who grew up in Taiwan, spent countless hours building relationships and visiting tea producers to create a selection comparable to the finest Taiwanese tea shops. There are around 25 types of oolong (available to sample with tasting flights); an infusion of wild chrysanthemum; a cold-brew green oolong iced tea with lily of the valley, almond and maple; and rare teas such as Oriental Beauty Grand and Iron Goddess. These can be paired with the beloved pineapple Linzer, a hazelnut shortbread sandwich filled with pineapple jam, or a trio of crumbly almond-and-walnut-flavoured cookies.

tecompanytea.com/pages/tea-shop

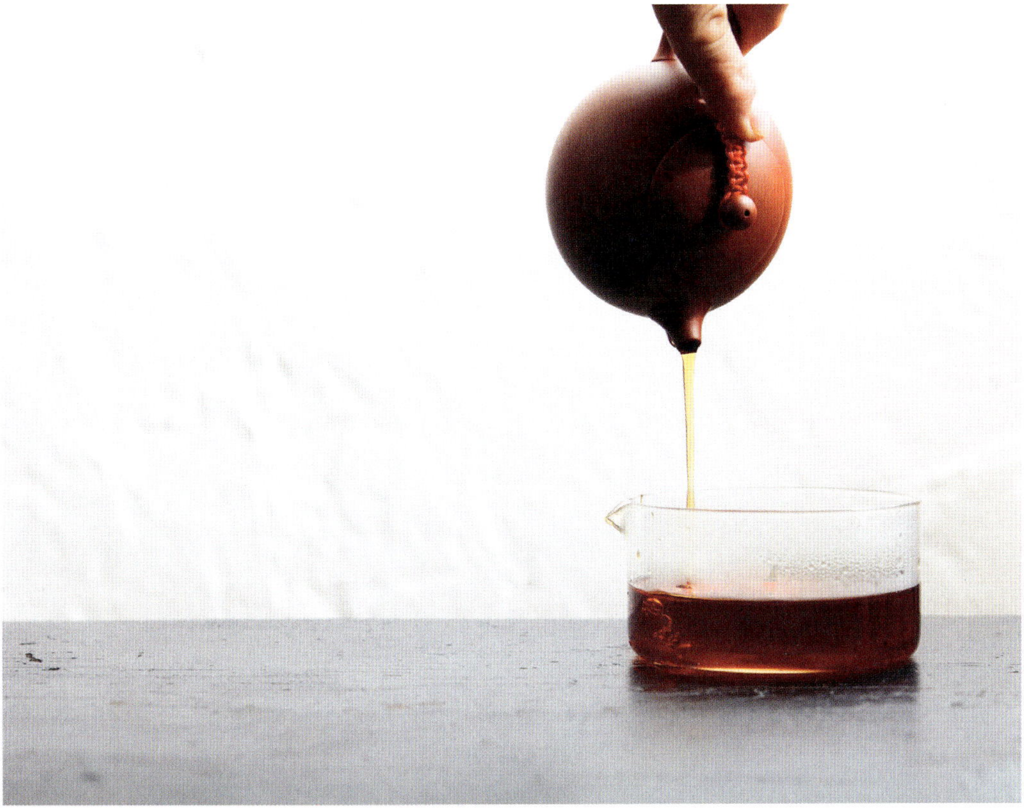

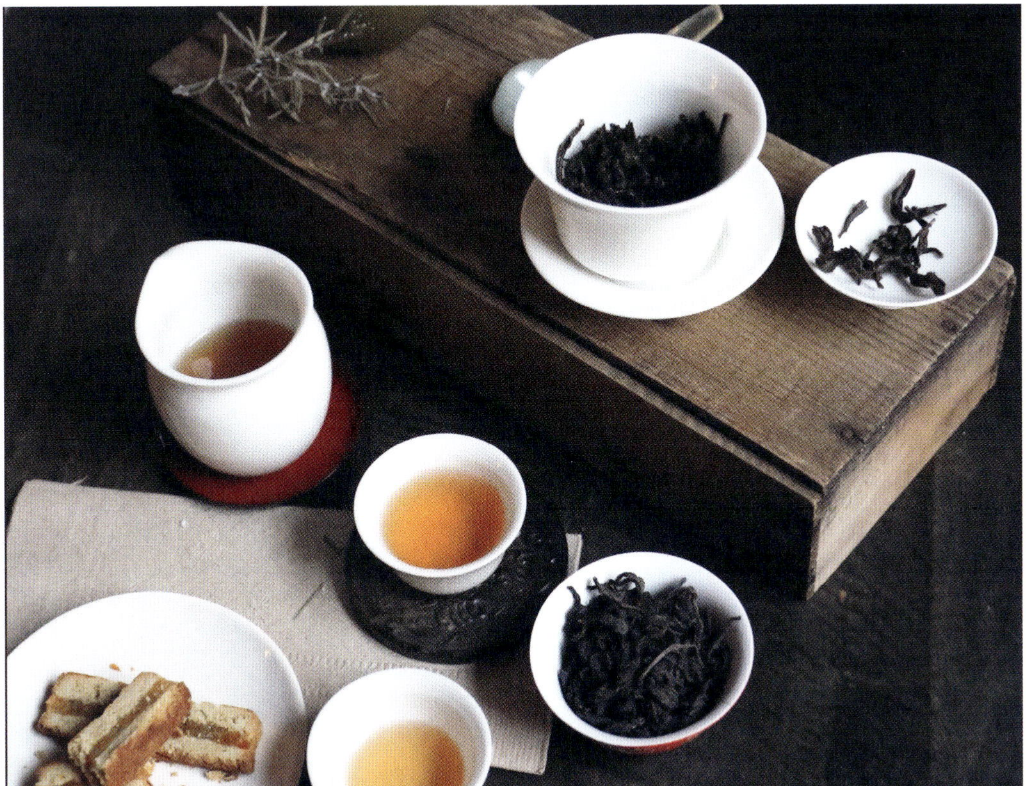

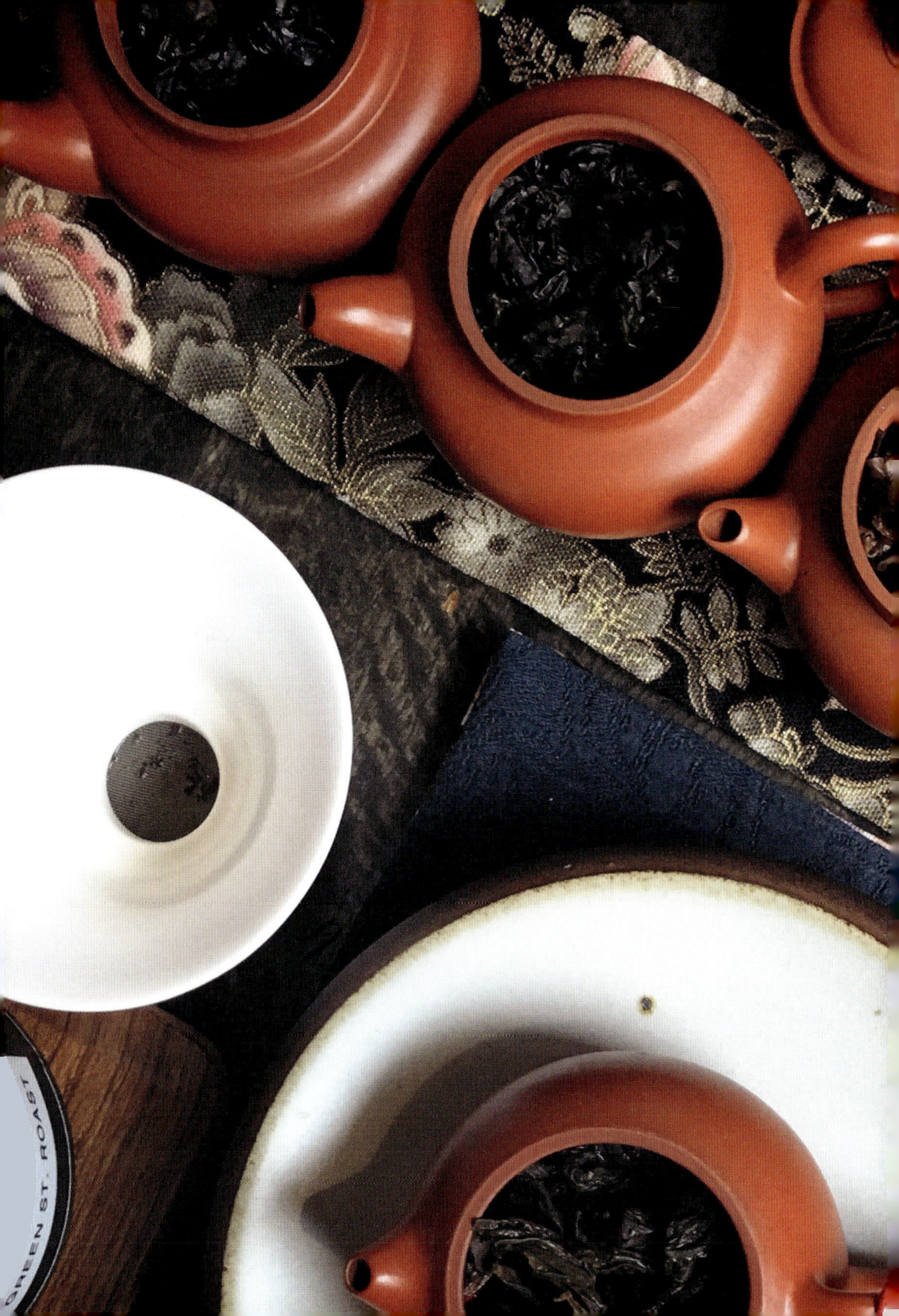
GREEN ST. ROAST

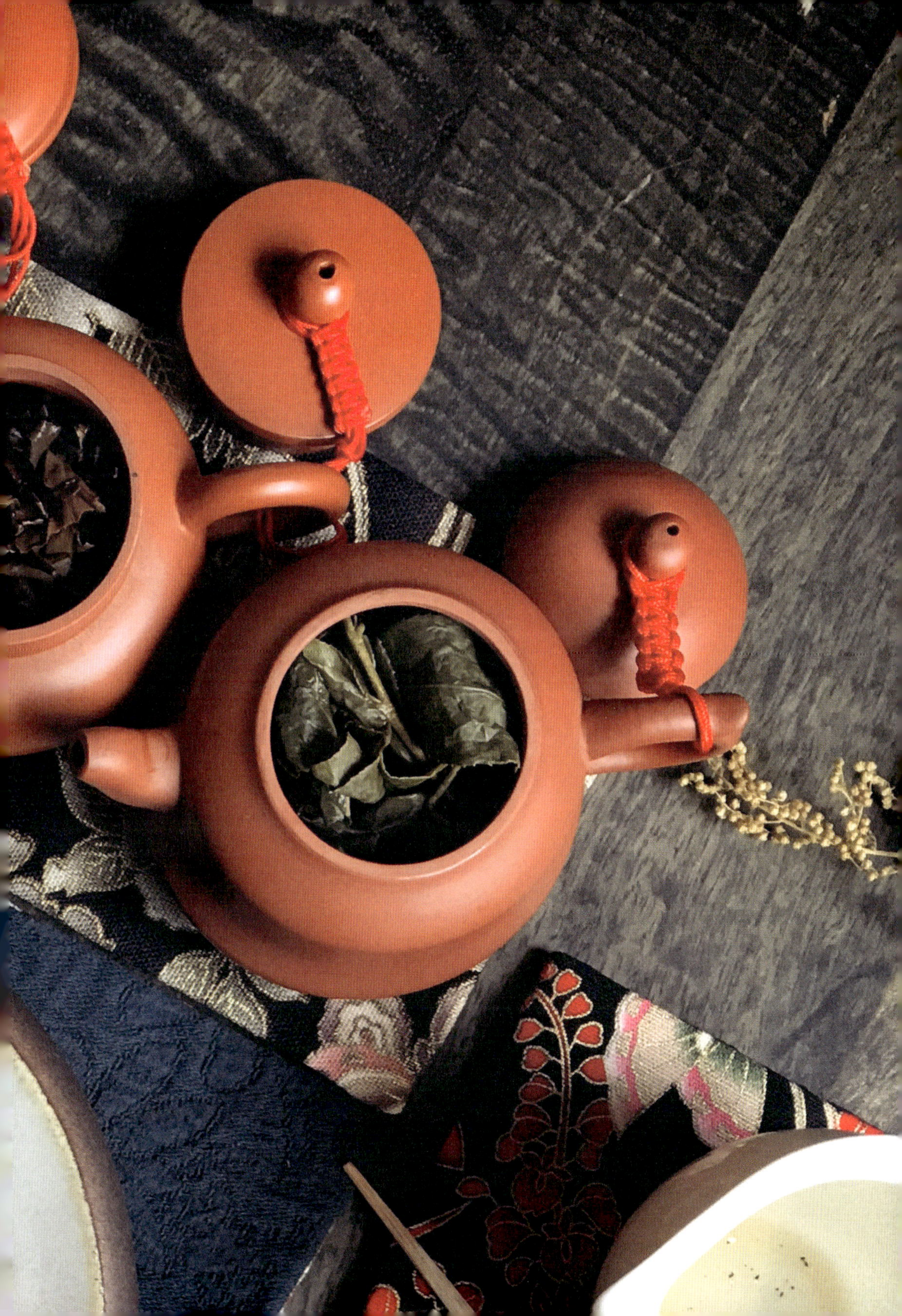

THE AMERICAS · PASADENA

112 CALLISTO TEA HOUSE

1359 N Altadena Drive, Pasadena, California, 91107, United States

TO VISIT BEFORE YOU DIE BECAUSE

East meets West for afternoon tea at this Pasadena tea room serving traditional gong fu tea accompanied by sweet and savoury snacks.

Nestled against the foothills of Mount Wilson in Altadena, this welcoming teahouse with refreshingly minimalist décor was opened by husband-and-wife team Nathan Epstein and Wendy Chen in 2022. The couple selects each single-estate tea from season to season, from Hawaii to Tanzania, and runs various tea workshops to share their passion. 'We also offer a unique afternoon tea experience, featuring flavours and ingredients drawn from tea-growing regions around the world,' explains Nathan. 'In addition, we specialise in gong fu cha, the traditional Chinese method of tea service, which teases out flavour notes and characteristics with each brew.' Small bites include mini-toasts, scones with cream and jam, black sesame toast and tea-infused macarons, while house-scented teas range from November Rain (a Darjeeling black tea with cardamom) to First Snow Jasmine (a high-grade green tea scented with jasmine flowers). Since Callisto is close to many scenic hiking trails, book ahead if you want to enjoy an afternoon tea after a walk in the San Gabriel Mountains.

THE AMERICAS   PHILADELPHIA

113 THE RANDOM TEA ROOM

713 N 4th Street, Philadelphia, Pennsylvania, 19123, United States

TO VISIT BEFORE YOU DIE BECAUSE

Serving loose-leaf tea and delicious cups of masala chai for over 17 years, this small tea room is full of personality.

'My favourite tea is our house-made masala chai. It's a bold cardamom-forward blend,' says The Random Tea Room owner Becky Goldschmidt. 'I like to joke with my customers, saying it's the only way I can manage to smile some days! They love the Philly attitude, and it usually convinces them to order the chai!' Other beloved beverages include *kaiseki* hōjicha – 'it's so warm and cosy; it is a Japanese green but has more of an autumnal flavour from the gentle roasting of the twigs and leaves' – as well as yerba maté and Bodhidharma's Eyelids. You'll find these and many more at Becky's small but cosy tea room in the city's Northern Liberties neighbourhood. The eclectic décor makes it a welcoming space – the ideal spot to play chess or read and sip tea all afternoon. Note that there is also a good selection of infusions, featuring herbs such as dandelion root, nettle and raspberry leaf. There is also a programme of events including tea-blending workshops and artist residencies focusing on community, connection, care and creativity.

therandomtearoom.com   +1 2 676 392 442

THE AMERICAS · PORTLAND

114 SMITH TEAMAKER

110 SE Washington Street, Portland, Oregon, 97214, United States

TO VISIT BEFORE YOU DIE BECAUSE

Try carefully sourced, imaginative tea blends at the tasting room of this Portland tea factory known for its handcrafted small batches.

This 'haute couture' tea company was founded by Steven Smith. Having sold his large tea business and moved to France, Steven was inspired by the nation's small luxury artisans and chocolatiers to create a speciality operation with the best tea on the market. The resulting outfit, Smith Teamaker, offers a wide variety of fine teas at its tasting room in the hip, industrial Central Eastside District. There is outdoor seating and the opportunity to spy on the packing and production through a glass panel, as well as smell samples and tea flights accompanied by educational cards. There's a short but sweet selection of snacks such as macarons and pastries, but of course the main event is the tea and herbal infusions from around the world. Among the bestselling blends are Portland Breakfast, a strong blend of organic second-flush Assam, and a Hibiscus Mango iced tea with orange peel and rooibos. The company is completely transparent on provenance – thanks to the batch numbers, they can tell you exactly where your tea was harvested.

smithtea.com · +1 5 037 198 752

THE AMERICAS RIO DE JANEIRO

115 COPACABANA BEACH

Avenida Atlântica, Copacabana, Rio de Janeiro, Brazil

TO VISIT
BEFORE YOU DIE
BECAUSE

There's no better place to enjoy a glass of iced yerba maté with lemon and a biscuit than on the city's most famous beach.

There's no point recommending somewhere inside in Rio, when the whole city basically lives on the beach. As any Carioca will tell you, the best tea room is in actual fact Copacabana Beach, where you can set up your towel with a view of Sugarloaf Mountain and wait for a maté gelado seller to wake you from your daydreaming with a cry of 'Olha o mate! Mate gelado!' The beach sellers, also known as *ambulantes*, carry two gallons, one filled with cold yerba maté, often the Matte Leão brand, the other filled with lemon juice, and mix both to taste. What's more, they come with snacks, too: they usually also sell the famous *Biscoito Globo*, a doughnut-shaped biscuit made from manioc flour, coconut and eggs, which comes in sweet and savoury flavours and has become a symbol of Rio. This perfect combination of crispy biscuit and ice-cold yerba maté has become the unmistakable aroma of the beach – locals missed it so much during the pandemic lockdowns that they got it delivered to their homes.

THE AMERICAS SAN FRANCISCO

116 IMPERIAL TEA COURT

1 Ferry Building, San Francisco, CA 94111, United States

TO VISIT BEFORE YOU DIE BECAUSE

Located in San Francisco's landmark Ferry Building Marketplace, this family-run establishment is the first traditional Chinese teahouse in the US.

Founded by Hong Kong-born tea master Roy Fong in 1993, Imperial Tea Court serves over 100 teas, sourced directly from tea farms around the world, including in China, Taiwan and Japan. 'Our bestsellers include Imperial Jasmine Pearls, Monkey Picked Tieguanyin and a large collection of pu-erh teas, which can be aged like wines. Well-aged pu-erh tea is known for its complexity, its ability to grow, and will continue to amaze you over the years,' says Roy. 'It's a tea that can be humbling and noble at the same time.' An ordained Daoist priest and the author of the book *The Great Teas of China*, Roy has also built close ties with the historic pottery workshops of Yixing in Jiangsu, and sells stunning 'purple sand' teapots as well as bespoke designs. His wife and co-founder Grace Fong, originally from Beijing, has devised a menu featuring tea-infused shrimp dumplings, tea shortbread cookies as well as the house favourite, hand-pulled noodles.

imperialtea.com/pages/our-teahouse +1 4 155 449 830

YUNNAN
PU-ERH TEA CAKE
裕隆
茶莊
Imperial Tea Court
San Francisco, CA USA

THE AMERICAS · SAN FRANCISCO

117 JAPANESE TEA GARDEN

75 Hagiwara Tea Garden Drive, San Francisco, California, 94118, United States

TO VISIT BEFORE YOU DIE BECAUSE

Enjoy a green tea and Japanese snack at this traditional teahouse in the heart of San Francisco's Golden Gate Park.

Originally created as a Japanese village for the 1894 California Midwinter Fair, San Francisco's beautiful Japanese Tea Garden attracts visitors in droves. For a more zen experience, visit in the early morning when you can wander in the peaceful gardens, scattered with stone lanterns and pagodas, before heading to the teahouse by the koi-filled pond. Sample green teas, including matcha served with wagashi, while reflecting on the site's fascinating history. Its landscape architect, Makoto Hagiwara, poured all his money and creativity into the site, only to lose everything in 1942, when he and his family were sent to internment camps. He is said to have made his fortune by selling fortune cookies in the early 1900s, adding vanilla flavour and sugar to the plain classic version. The tradition of serving fortune cookies to visitors continues today. Other snacks available include *dorayaki* pancakes and mochi, best enjoyed with a cup of bright and sweet sencha or nutty genmaicha, a green tea with roasted rice.

japaneseteagardensf.com/tea-house

THE AMERICAS · SAN JUAN CAPISTRANO

118 THE TEA HOUSE ON LOS RIOS

31731 Los Rios Street, San Juan Capistrano, California, 92675, United States

TO VISIT BEFORE YOU DIE BECAUSE

Enjoy delicious afternoon tea and signature blends at this lovely cottage in the oldest residential neighbourhood in all of California.

Surrounded by yucca and birch trees in the historic Los Rios district of Orange County, this charming teahouse was opened in 1998 by Allan and Claudia Niccola. Today, their grandson Damian is at the helm. The teahouse is a firm favourite for celebrations, with loose-leaf teas served in mismatched china and currant scones with raspberry preserves and Early California Cream. This being an afternoon tea hotspot, black teas such as Cream of Earl Grey or Margaret's Hope Darjeeling are great options, but everyone's favourite is the teahouse's signature Private Reserve, a Ceylon black tea with vanilla and grenadine. The menu has something for everyone, from Formosa Oolong, Jasmine, Cucumber Melon and Sencha Kyoto Cherry Rose, to a good selection of herbal teas, such as Romance of the Mission, a blend of cinnamon, almonds, rooibos and hibiscus. The team has really thought about every customer: there is PG Tips for their British guests and a cute bubble gum infusion with strawberry, apple and rose hips for the little ones.

theteahouseonlosrios.com · +1 9 494 433 914

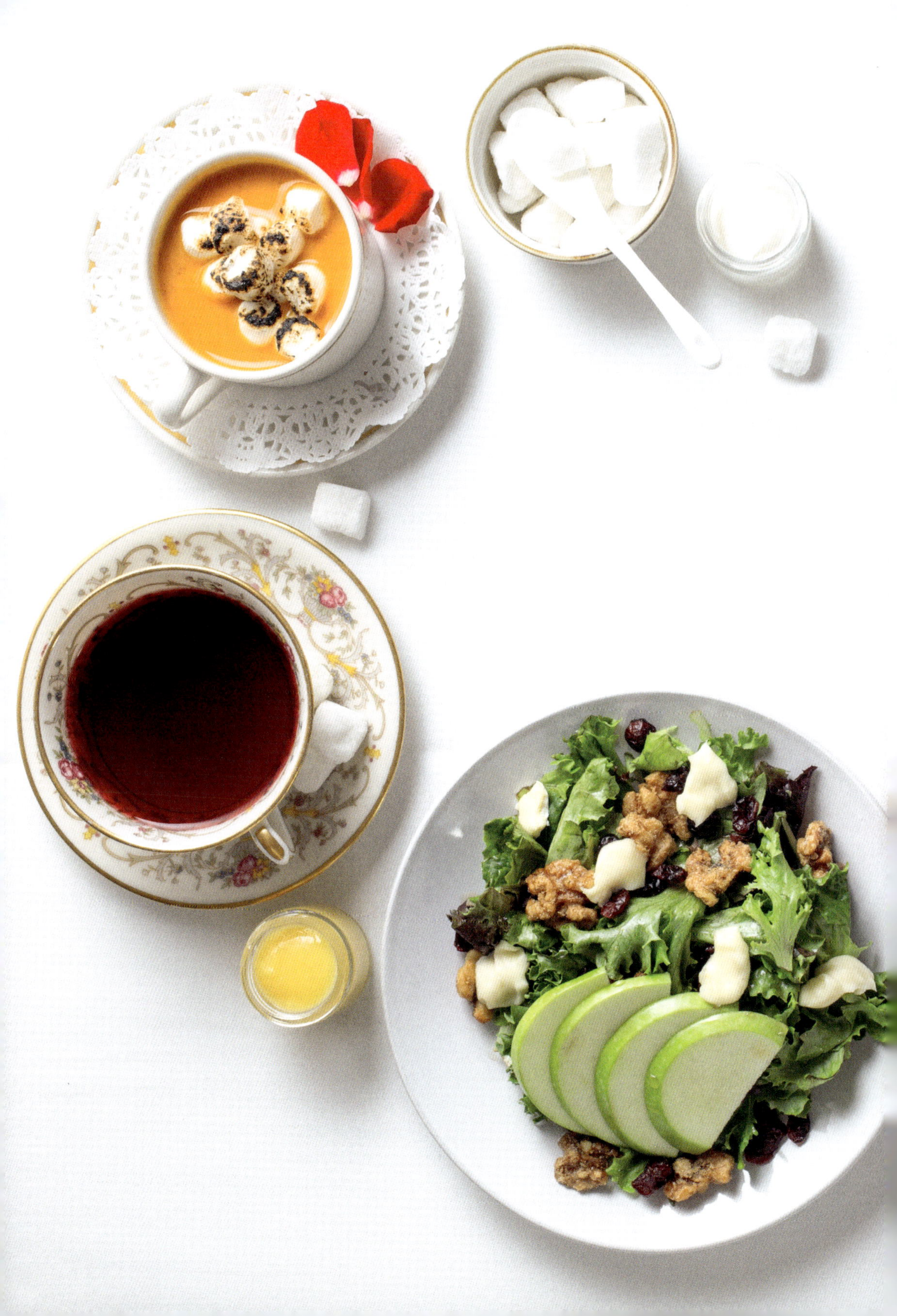

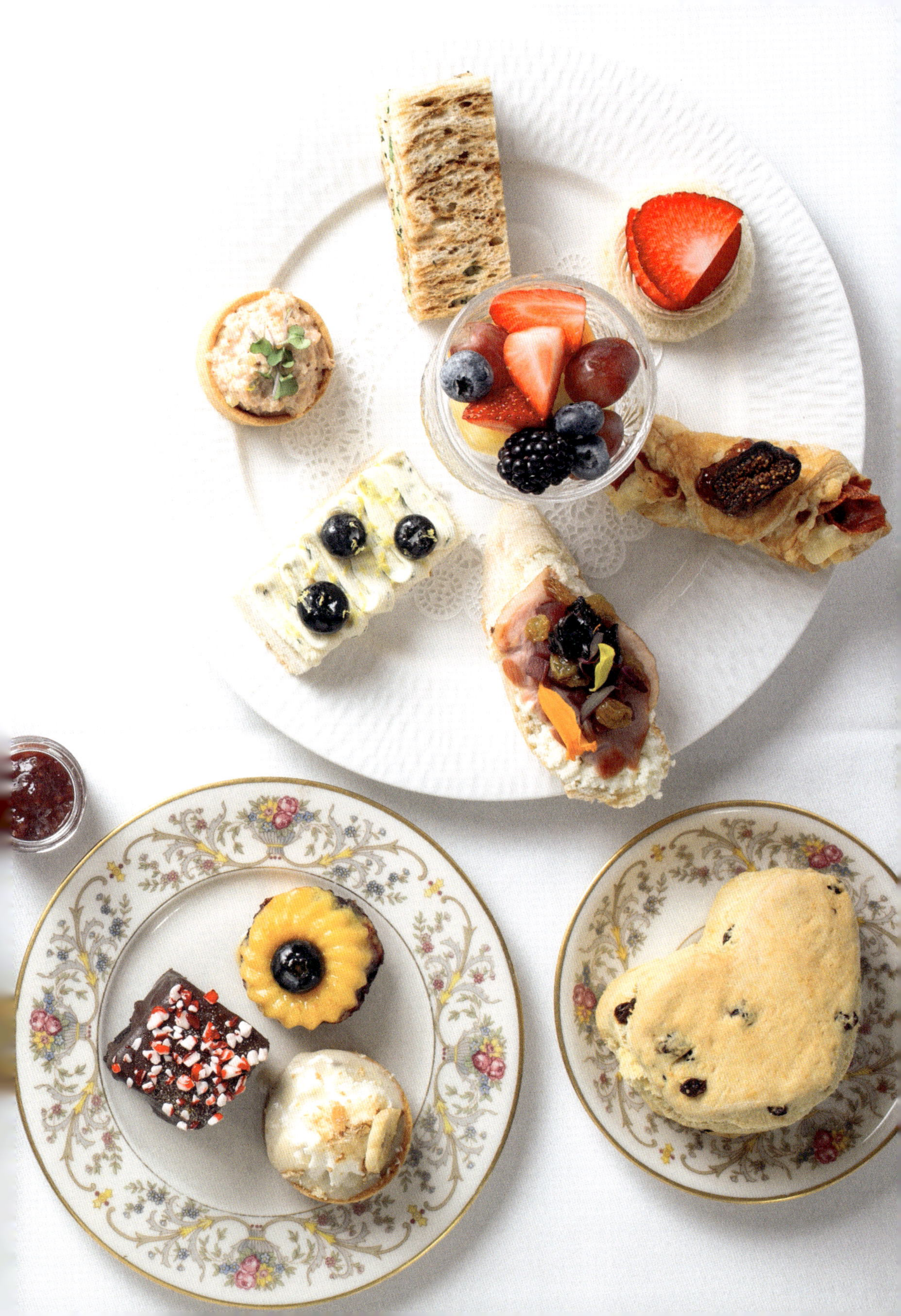

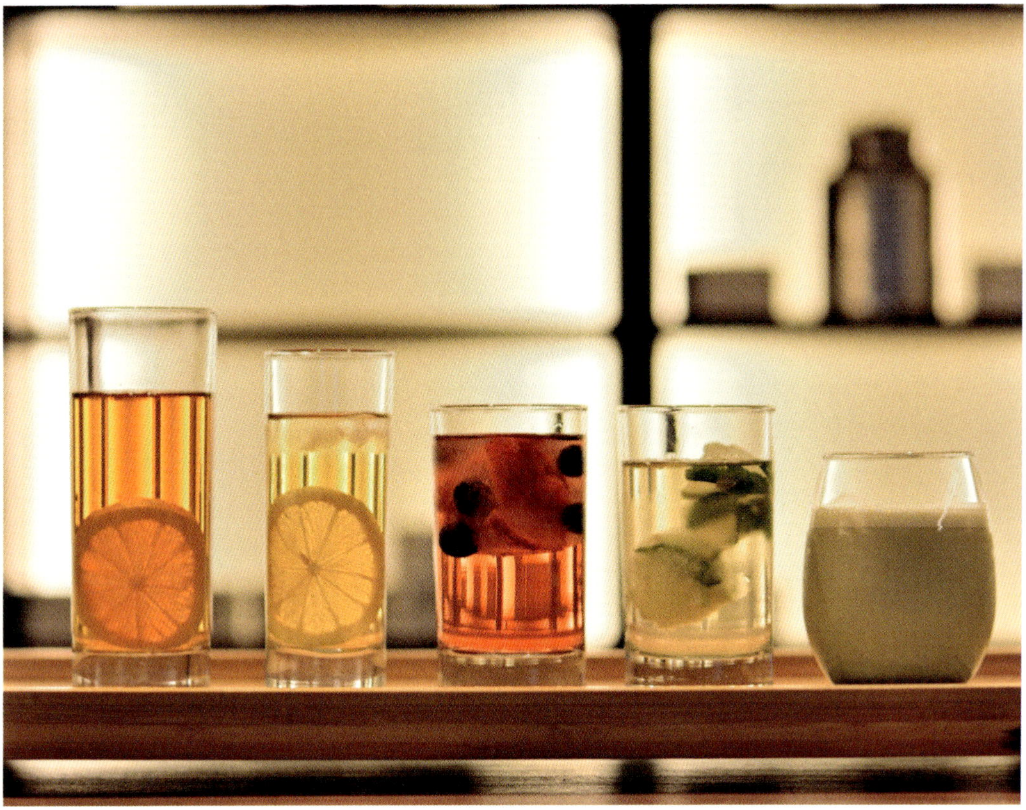

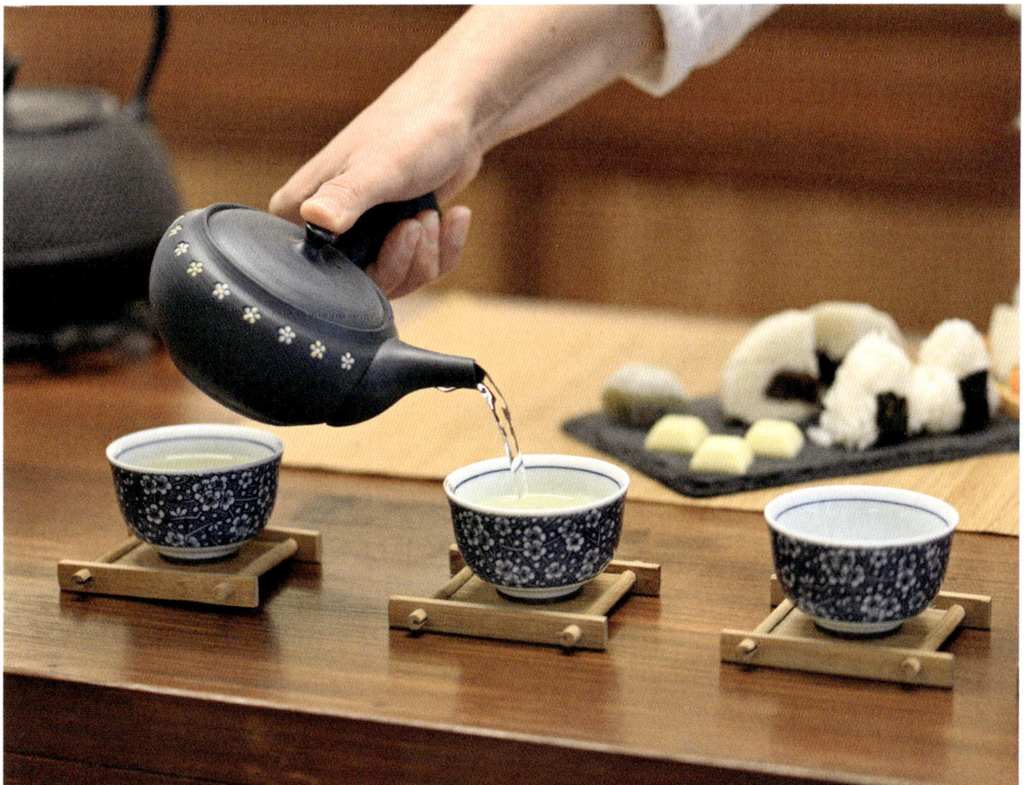

THE AMERICAS   SANTIAGO

119   LA TETERÍA

Santa Magdalena 86, Providencia, Santiago, Chile, 7510057

TO VISIT BEFORE YOU DIE BECAUSE

Deepen your knowledge of the world of tea with wonderful tasting sessions and courses led by tea enthusiasts.

After a visit to Santiago's hilltop botanical or Japanese gardens, we can't think of anything better to do than cross the Mapocho River and head to La Tetería, the Chilean capital's tea specialist since 2007. Although this is primarily a shop rather than a tea room, it does offer some incredible tea tastings and experiences, run by tea master Patricio Hurtado. A session on the colours of tea, for example, is a tasting experience of the six different types of tea, featuring an all-star cast including Yellow Sun and Shui Xian Ban Yan. Each is paired with a variety of snacks, fresh fruit and nuts. Another option is the session focusing on iced teas and herbal infusions, such as cold brews and bubble teas, which are accompanied by edible flowers and cookies. For those wanting a long-haul journey of discovery, an 'Around the world in 100 teas' course, comprising 22 sessions, is also available. Make sure to also try some local herbal infusions, such as boldo or lemon verbena, which are both native to South America.

THE AMERICAS TAMPA

120 TEBELLA TEA COMPANY

Oxford Exchange, 420 W Kennedy Boulevard, Tampa, Florida, 33602, United States

TO VISIT BEFORE YOU DIE BECAUSE

Sample a refreshing iced tea at this outpost of Florida tea specialists TeBella, in the lobby of a historic building in Tampa.

Located in Tampa's beautiful Oxford Exchange, a 1920s building that also houses a bookstore, a gift shop and a workspace, TeBella offers several options for tea lovers: enjoy a cup of something special at the tea bar or with a meal at the adjoining restaurant, or simply buy one of the 40 loose teas for sale by the ounce. Particular favourites include White Coconut Dulce white tea, Blueberry Pomegranate green tea and Carrot Cake rooibos, as well as masala chai latte and seasonal drinks such as Honey Lavender Matcha and Autumn Hōjicha Latte. The star of the show, though, is the Strawberry Mint Julep, sold only at this location. 'It's a Mint Julep white tea which we steep with freshly muddled strawberries, basil, mint and a touch of sugar to create a refreshing iced tea. It's a crowd-pleaser for sure!' says TeBella's Erin Dickerson. Also worth a visit is the company's flagship store on Davis Islands; its tea bar serves any tea from a collection of nearly 100 teas, either hot or iced.

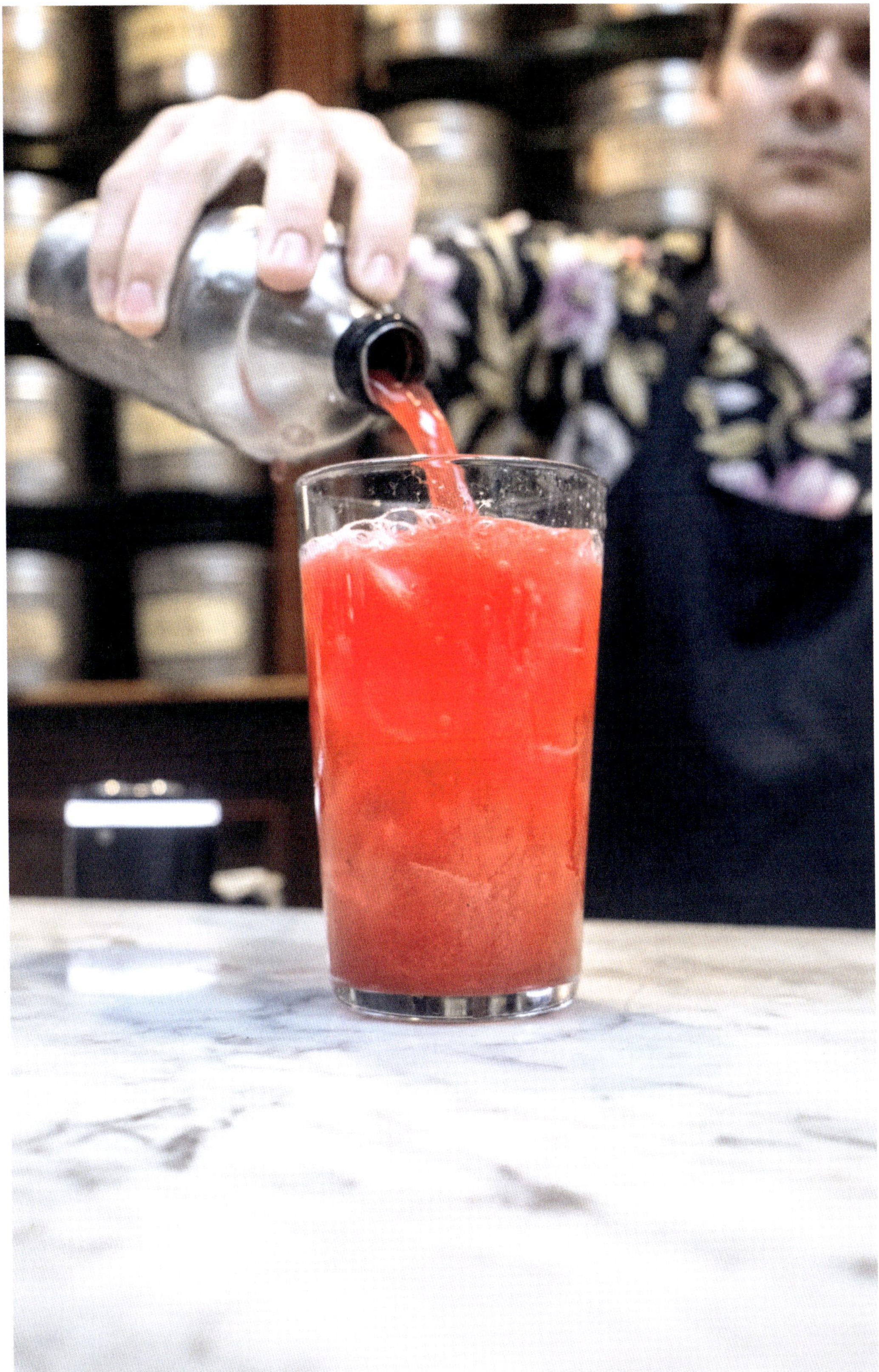

KUKICHA
FESTIVAL BLEND
THE BEE'S KNEES
MADAM APRICOT
OOLONG ROSE
RASPBERRY NOIRE
GEORGIA PEACH
PEACH OOLONG
EARL GREY LAVENDER
MOROCCAN MINT
OOLONG NIRVANA
EARL GREY
MINT JULEP
MATE BRIO
MASALA CHAI
TROPICAL BREEZE
BREAKFAST BLEND
STRAWBERRY MANGO
DARJEELING

TeBella
TEA COMPANY

Classic Cuppa hot or iced $3.75
from our Reserve Collection $4.75

SPECIALTY BEVERAGES

London Fog hot or iced $4.20
Lavender Fog hot or iced $4.20
Chai Latte hot or iced $4.20
Salted Caramel Latte hot or iced $4.20
Earl Grey Lavender Lemonade iced $4.20
Matcha Lemonade iced $4.20
Strawberry Mint Julep iced $4.20

TAKE HOME SOME TEA!
All of our Teas are available by the ounce

THE AMERICAS • TUCSON

121 SEVEN CUPS FINE CHINESE TEAS

2510 E Fort Lowell Road, Tucson, Arizona, 85716, United States

TO VISIT BEFORE YOU DIE BECAUSE

Known for offering China's freshest harvest, this Tucson teahouse was the first in the US to offer Anji white tea and purple bamboo shoot tea.

Named after Lu Tong's famous poem describing the various effects of tea, Seven Cups Fine Chinese Teas was founded by Austin and Zhuping Hodge, who started by selling at Tucson farmers' markets before opening their own tea room in 2002. The husband-and-wife team has earned a great reputation for their high-quality organic teas, sourced directly from 32 producers across China, and now supplies a number of cafés and restaurants around the world. Come in for a cup of da hong pao, or purple bamboo shoot tea, made by a woman tea maker in Zhejiang, or delight in a flowering jasmine tea. There are pastries and homemade Chinese snacks, and the infusions are unique (the Eight Treasures, with jujube date, goji and ginseng, was made for Seven Cups by a master Sichuan herbalist). You can also take part in tasting sessions, Chinese tea ceremonies or private tea lessons. Lu Tong's seventh cup is meant to transport us to a sacred island – quite a thought in the middle of the Arizona desert, but if anyone can find the right tea to achieve this, it's Austin and Zhuping.

sevencups.com +1 5 208 814 072

THE AMERICAS — VALPARAÍSO

122 SKI PORTILLO

Ruta 60 420, Portillo, Los Andes, Valparaíso, Chile

TO VISIT BEFORE YOU DIE BECAUSE

Experience Chile's *onces* tradition and the magic of the snowy Andes at this high-altitude resort, famous for its après-ski teatime.

A true melting pot fringed by the Andes and the Pacific Ocean, Chile is full of surprising traditions. One unique custom is *onces*, the local teatime, a gift from the British who settled in the country in the 1800s. Every day from 5pm, cafés around the country fill up with friends and families sharing tea, toasts, cheese and charcuterie, as well as *sopaipillas*, toffees and cakes. It's an evening brunch, really, and sometimes involves German *kuchen*, especially in the south near Frutillar, where bakeries set up by German settlers are still going strong. However, we suggest that the best place to enjoy such a copious meal is after a nice day spent skiing in the Andes, at Ski Portillo near Valparaíso. Perched at an altitude of 2,800 metres, the resort is famous for both its *onces* and its friendly atmosphere. Enjoy a cup of après-ski tea, including a range of local infusions such as *boldo* and *cedron*, served with Chilean *alfajor* (two cookies sandwiched with dulce de leche), and take in the views of the slopes and the legendary Lake of the Inca through the panoramic windows. Just remember, this being the southern hemisphere, the ski season runs from June to September, but the resort is open in the summer, too, for kayaking, trekking, wine tastings, live music and more tea, of course.

skiportillo.com — +56 223 617 000

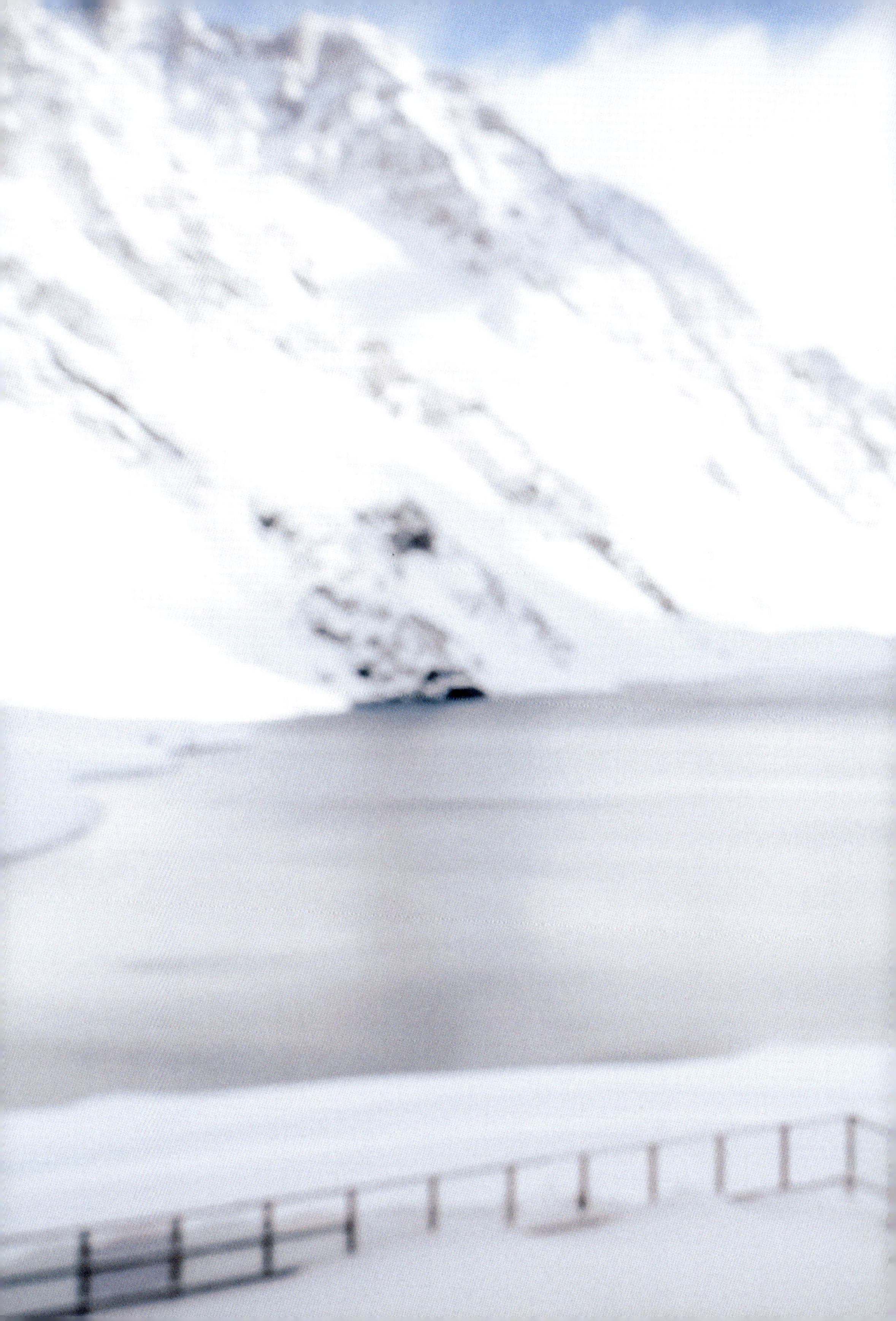

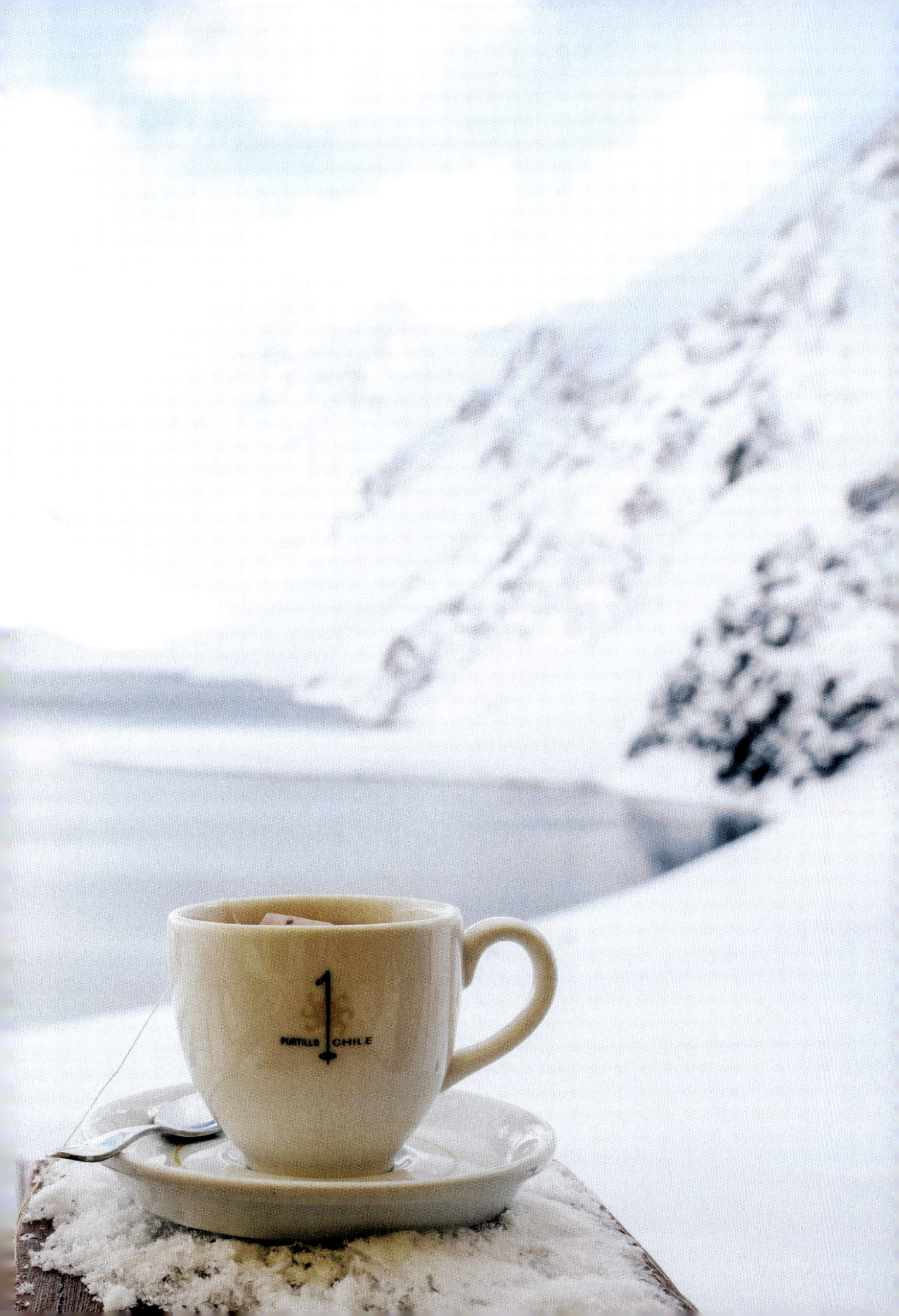
PORTILLO CHILE

THE AMERICAS — VANCOUVER

123 THE SECRET GARDEN TEA COMPANY

2138 W 40th Avenue, Vancouver, British Columbia, V6M 3W7, Canada

TO VISIT BEFORE YOU DIE BECAUSE

This cosy little teahouse knows the power of staying small and has been offering delightful afternoon tea since 1995.

Sisters-in-law Kathy and Erin Wyder were inspired to open The Secret Garden Tea Company by their grandmothers' love for tea. Erin has fond memories of telling her nana all about her day over a big pot of steaming tea after school, while Kathy's gammy held 'beautiful tea parties with lovely ladies dressed up in wonderful hats'. The pair combined this sense of occasion and focus on the details that count in their award-winning tea room. Banquette seating, books and crockery line the walls of the welcoming space, with the menu offering loose-leaf black teas such as Gammy's Darjeeling and the bestselling Creamy Earl Grey with bergamot and vanilla. All are served in teapots wrapped in branded tea cosies, while the seasonal high tea, served on vintage tiered stands, includes lemon tarts, pumpkin spice cupcakes with maple icing and chai scones. There are special gluten-free, vegetarian, vegan and children's menus, too, and you can order high tea to go to enjoy at the nearby Queen Elizabeth Park.

secretgardentea.com +1 6 042 613 070

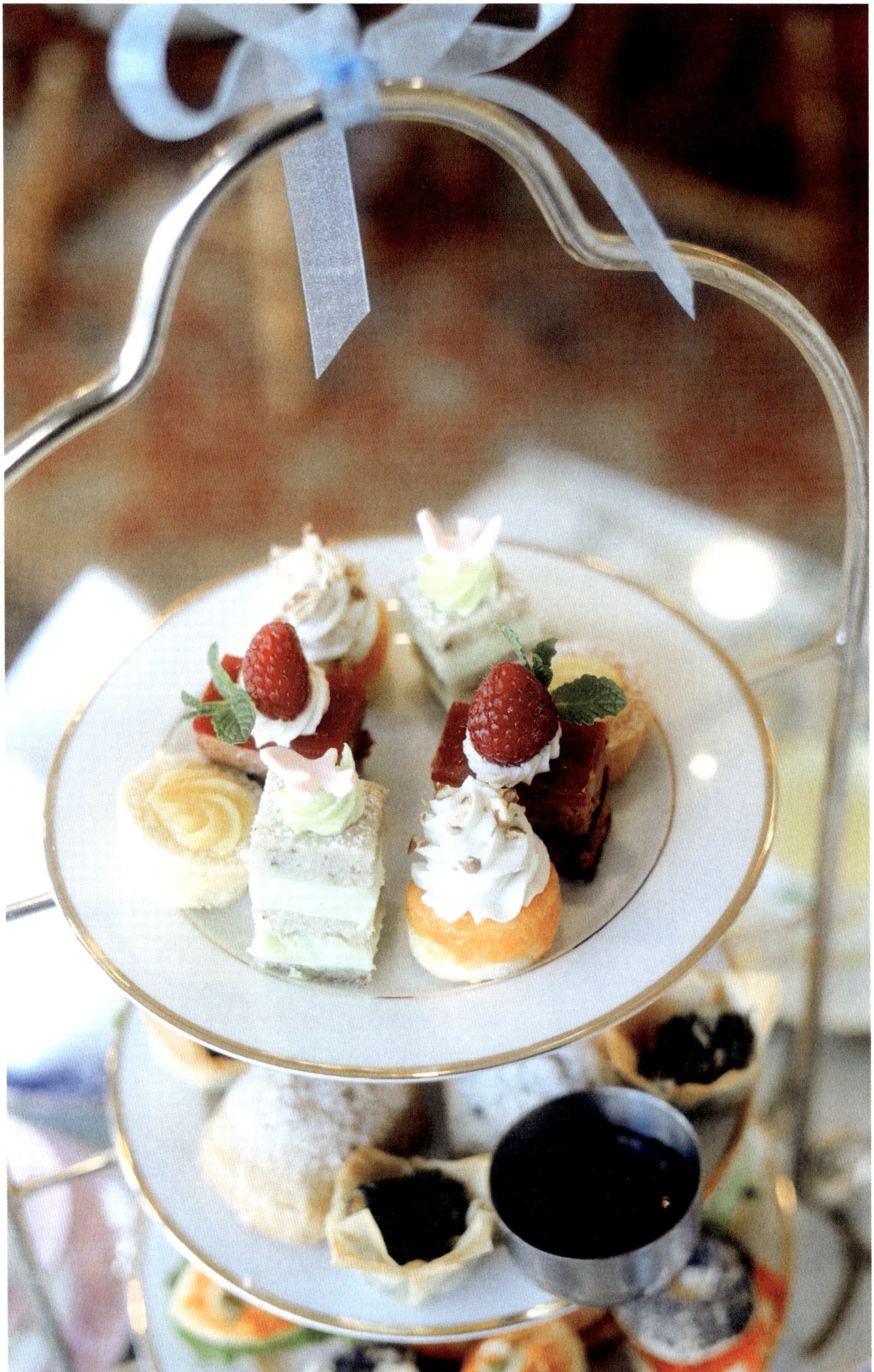

AFRICA AND THE MIDDLE EAST

ABIDJAN

124 AFRICAFÉ

Avenue Franchet d'Esperey, Plateau, Abidjan, Côte d'Ivoire

TO VISIT BEFORE YOU DIE BECAUSE

It's the perfect space to enjoy the all-important local tradition of ataya in a chic but welcoming contemporary setting.

Founded by Djeneba Keita from her kitchen as a lunch box delivery service, Africafé has quickly become known for its contemporary twist on West African classics. Most interesting for us is its wide range of local drinks, including the ever-popular *bissap*, a refreshing hibiscus infusion enjoyed hot or cold and popular across Africa, as well as the bestselling citronnelle, or lemongrass iced tea. After its first location in the Ivoire Trade Center shopping mall, Africafé opened a new outpost in the Plateau neighbourhood, designed by Nikita de Oliveira of Nomads Architecture. Stylish yet cosy, the café is a great spot to enjoy *ataya*, a bittersweet brew of gunpowder green tea, sugar and mint served in a teapot called a *barada*. A key symbol of hospitality throughout sub-Saharan Africa, this informal ritual is an integral part of daily life in the region. It includes tea being poured into small glasses from a height to create foam and is shared with friends and family in three rounds, each with a different taste.

AFRICA AND THE MIDDLE EAST

AGAFAY DESERT

125 INARA CAMP

Commune d'Agafay, Douar Ifrane N° 806, Agafay, 40272, Morocco

---

TO VISIT BEFORE YOU DIE BECAUSE

Your tea room here is the stunning rocky desert of Agafay, where mint tea is served with ancestral traditions and stories.

For the nomadic people of North Africa who once travelled the trade routes through the Sahara from Egypt to Morocco, the precious tea leaves were both a commodity and part of a simple ceremony that underpinned all friendly chats and business deals. They still are today, and here at Inara Camp, you can sample the strong mint tea, which is served as a welcome drink and as part of excursions in the desert landscape. A key symbol of the Amazighs' famed hospitality, the tea is prepared in a metal teapot over a fire using green tea and mint and served in small glasses. Rather than one tea, it is actually three teas, as the leaves are boiled in three rounds, with sugar added at each step. The first tea is called 'bitter like death', symbolising a first step into the unknown when meeting strangers. The second is 'strong like life', when relationships deepen with trust and shared understanding. The third and last is 'sweet like love', representing new friendship and mutual respect.

AFRICA AND THE MIDDLE EAST — AL BUSTAN

126 THE ATRIUM TEA LOUNGE AT AL BUSTAN PALACE

Al Bustan Street, Muscat, 114, Oman

TO VISIT BEFORE YOU DIE BECAUSE

The majestic atrium of this modern beachside palace is a very special place to sip on a *karak* chai, the local spiced tea.

Opened in 1985, the Al Bustan Palace, now a Ritz-Carlton Hotel, was designed to represent Omani culture and hospitality. At its heart is a 38 metre-high domed lounge – the grandest setting imaginable for an afternoon tea, served on bespoke tableware decorated with the same traditional gold-and-maroon Islamic fretwork that appears on the atrium's walls. Snack on an Umm Ali pastry while sipping a *karak* chai (the local spiced tea, a mix of black tea, cardamom and condensed milk found on every street corner). Or go for the full Omani Delight afternoon tea: sweets include pistachio kunafa tiramisu, date and cardamom cake and baklava, while savouries range from a za'atar and cucumber éclairs to a muhammara wrap. To round this out, there are also scones and a selection of teas from Dammann Frères, such as Anichaï, a black tea with cardamom, pink pepper, clove and ginger. The signature Al Bustan blend is a black tea with pineapple, passion fruit, bush peach and wild strawberry, and the Palace Iced Tea is a rooibos with lemon and orange juice.

AFRICA AND THE MIDDLE EAST — AMMAN

127 RUMI CAFE

14 Kulliyat Al Sharee'ah Street, Amman, Jordan

TO VISIT BEFORE YOU DIE BECAUSE

The Middle East has endless variations on black tea with spices and herbs; try them all in this welcoming café in the heart of Amman.

Most visitors come to Jordan to visit Petra and Wadi Rum. While there, they are bound to be asked *Tashrab shay*? ('Would you like to drink tea?') and enjoy Bedouin hospitality in the desert. For a more urban experience, try this beautiful café founded in 2013 and located near Amman's Darat al Funun museum. It is a great place to sample some of the region's spiced teas, made with the finest loose-leaf Ceylon tea. Sit down inside to admire the handcrafted tiles, or outside under the jasmine trees. On the menu are the popular black tea with mint, as well as Yemeni tea (with cardamom and cloves), Iraqi tea (with cardamom only) and Iranian tea (with rose water). Jordan is known for its sweet black tea flavoured with *maremiah*, or sage, so make sure to try that too. Caffeine-free highlights include cinnamon tea; Yellow Daze, a mix of lemongrass, chamomile, anise and dried rose; and iced teas flavoured with lime powder. Enjoy with a slice of cardamom cake.

AFRICA AND THE MIDDLE EAST — ASWAN

128 SOFITEL LEGEND OLD CATARACT HOTEL

Abtal El Tahrir Street, 81511, Aswan, Egypt

TO VISIT BEFORE YOU DIE BECAUSE

This classic afternoon tea with stunning views of the Nile will remind you of how the entire British Empire was built on cups of tea.

The Old Cataract Hotel is a grand remnant of Egypt's British colonial era, a legacy of the golden age of travel to Egypt by wealthy Victorians, who discovered the Nile by following in the footsteps of Thomas Cook & Son, pioneering travel agents and hotel builders. The hotel is famous both for its plethora of VIP guests and for inspiring Agatha Christie's *Death on the Nile* novel in the 1930s. It's an atmospheric building, but the best spot is outside, on the terrace overlooking the Nile and Elephantine Island. There, you can enjoy a cup of tea by luxury French specialists Dammann Frères, as well as an afternoon tea inspired by the great crime novelist herself. Sample a velvety Early Grey Fleurs with Calabrian bergamot, or cool down with an iced tea flavoured with lemon and mint, before tucking into an assortment of light bites including scones, muffins, sandwiches and patisseries. It's a truly magical spot at sunset, with the golden light reflected by the sails of the *dahabiyas* dotted on the river.

sofitel.accor.com — +20 1 022 229 071

AFRICA AND THE MIDDLE EAST

BOIS CHÉRI

129 DOMAINE DE BOIS CHÉRI

Bois Chéri, Mauritius

TO VISIT BEFORE YOU DIE BECAUSE

This historic plantation dating from 1892 is a lovely place to sample local teas, whether as hot beverages, as iced drinks or even in sauces and jellies.

Most people come to Mauritius for its beaches, but the island's real treasure lies in its creole gastronomy and culture. Its delicious samosas and dumplings are best paired with the country's favourite drink, vanilla tea. Particularly popular is Trois Pavillions, a mild black tea flavoured with real vanilla (an Indian Ocean speciality, of course) made by Domaine de Bois Chéri, the island's largest producer. Located in the mountainous southern region, its plantation is one of the oldest on the island. Its *Zistwar dité*, or 'Tea stories experience', will take you from the tea fields (where you'll try your hand at tea plucking) to the factory, museum and restaurant, for blind tea tastings. Lunch is a series of tea-infused dishes in a dining room overlooking a small picturesque lake. The salad is served with a tea dressing, the chicken is in a green tea sauce and the dessert is a tea-flavoured panna cotta. If you like your tea sweet, a visit to the sugar cane museum on the other side of the island is also recommended.

AFRICA AND THE MIDDLE EAST · CAIRO

130 EL-FISHAWY CAFÉ

27X6+5XQ, Haret Khan Al Khalili, El Gamaliya, Cairo, Egypt

TO VISIT BEFORE YOU DIE BECAUSE

Follow in the footsteps of kings, artists and intellectuals at the oldest café in the heart of Cairo's Khan el-Khalili market.

Egypt's national beverage is, of course, *shai*, mostly served black and sugared to taste. Also popular are *karkade* (known as bissap in West Africa), a deep-red infusion of hibiscus flower enjoyed hot or cold, and *yansoon*, anise tea, with roots tracing back to Ancient Egypt. You can sample them all on a walk around Cairo's Khan el-Khalili bazaar, where you might stumble across a tea vendor carrying an ornate samovar on their back, or, even better, the entrance to the historic El-Fishawy Café, which opened its doors in 1797 – the year before Napoleon invaded Egypt. Family-run for generations, it has welcomed many Egyptian intellectuals, including the writer Naguib Mahfouz. Its tables line the narrow alleyway, while inside, the aroma of shisha wafts past its huge iconic oval mirrors, handmade dark wooden screens and old copper chandeliers. Fittingly for a country known for its dunes and deserts, the house speciality is *shai barad*, tea boiled in a metal teapot in a heated basin of sand.

AFRICA AND THE MIDDLE EAST   CAPE TOWN

131 MOUNT NELSON, A BELMOND HOTEL

76 Orange Street, Gardens, Cape Town, 8001, South Africa

TO VISIT BEFORE YOU DIE BECAUSE

Sample a carefully curated tea menu by an expert tea sommelier at Cape Town's bubblegum-pink landmark, the Mount Nelson Hotel.

Also known as the Nellie, Mount Nelson is home to South Africa's first expert-trained tea sommelier, Craig Cupido. 'I have always felt that tea is about connections, to the people you are enjoying it with and the places it comes from,' he says. 'I love sharing its many positive properties with the guests and helping them choose the ideal tea to pair with a chosen dish.' In partnership with Mingwei Tsai of Nigiro Tea Merchants, Cupido has carefully selected over 60 premium loose-leaf and flowering teas, as well as local infusions such as *buchu*. Make sure to try the signature Mount Nelson Tea, a blend of Darjeeling, Kenya, Assam, Keemun, Yunnan and Ceylon with pink rose petals and a blush colour that complements the hotel's famously pink walls, or the caffeine-free 125 Year Blend, a mix of local rooibos and honeybush with more rose petals, baked mesquite sourced from the Great Karoo and apples from the Cederberg Mountains. For afternoon tea, Cupido's teas are paired with pastry chef Vicky Gurovich's creations, including naartjie and chocolate tart and roasted strawberry choux.

AFRICA AND THE MIDDLE EAST

CITRUSDAL

132 CARMIÉN TEA SHOP AT DE TOL FARM DELI

Piekenierskloofpass N7, Citrusdal, 7435, South Africa

TO VISIT BEFORE YOU DIE BECAUSE

Perched on a mountain pass with splendid views of rooibos fields, this is the ideal place to discover South Africa's national drink.

Located on the foothills of the Western Cape's splendid Cederberg Mountains, Carmién Tea Shop is right in the heart of rooibos-growing country. It has been producing herbal tea, or bush tea, since 1998 and has recently opened a tea shop at the De Tol Farm Deli near Citrusdal. This charming outpost is the place to learn all about rooibos, which grows only in South Africa's *fynbos* biome, and sample an impressive variety of drinks – rooibos is used here to make 'cappuccino', gin cocktails and cordials, and is paired with chocolate truffles or local wines in special tasting sessions. The tea and nibbles pairing is particularly popular and can be combined with tours of the factory and fields. Make sure to try the sparkling iced teas or the cold brew teas, which come in flavours such as berry hibiscus and apple mint. It's also a popular stop on the way to the wildflower spectacle of Namaqualand, a desert that blooms once a year – combine both for a true celebration of South Africa's native plants.

carmientea.co.za

+27 674 103 315

AFRICA AND THE MIDDLE EAST

DUBAI

133 TANIA'S TEAHOUSE

Dubai Hills Estate Business Park 3, GF, Dubai, United Arab Emirates

TO VISIT BEFORE YOU DIE BECAUSE

It has gained fame as one of the world's most Instagrammable cafés, but this colourful spot also has plenty of great teas up its – very chic – sleeves.

Initially a pink teahouse by the beach, this self-described 'sanctuary blending wellness and creativity' was founded by Tania Lodi, a local who discovered the healing power of tea and mindfulness after being diagnosed with an autoimmune disorder as a student. It has been such a success with Dubaites that it recently moved into a larger, airier location in Dubai Hills, with three distinct event spaces and a range of tea-infused cocktails. Combining neutral shades with fun touches, plants and artworks, the teahouse serves carefully crafted dishes and a collection of soothing teas, sourced ethically from around the globe, each custom blended and selected by Tania herself. Behind a secret door is not a speakeasy but a tea room – an intimate lounge with jewel-toned finishes. It's the perfect place to enjoy a cup of flavoured black teas such as Cherry Cheesecake and Dat Cookie, Dough; a herbal tea such as Golden Glow, made with ginger, turmeric, carrot, beet and pineapple; or Detox, Tea-tox, made with lemongrass, liquorice, chamomile and jiaogulan.

taniasteahouse.com

+971 42 824 606

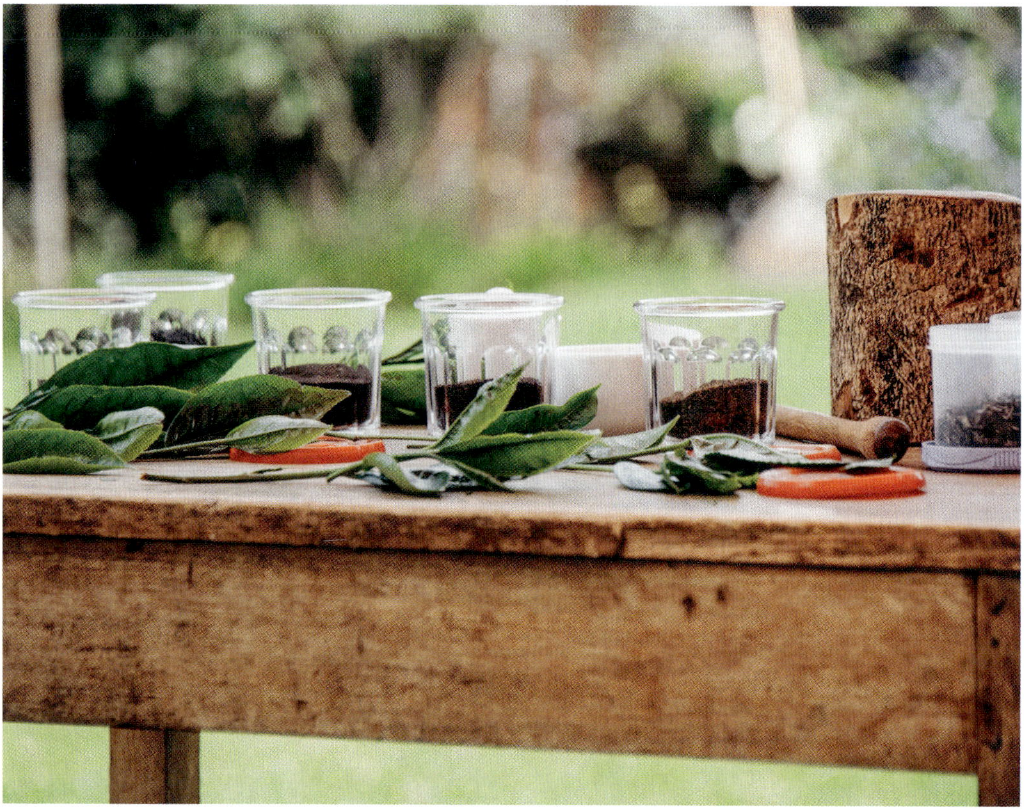

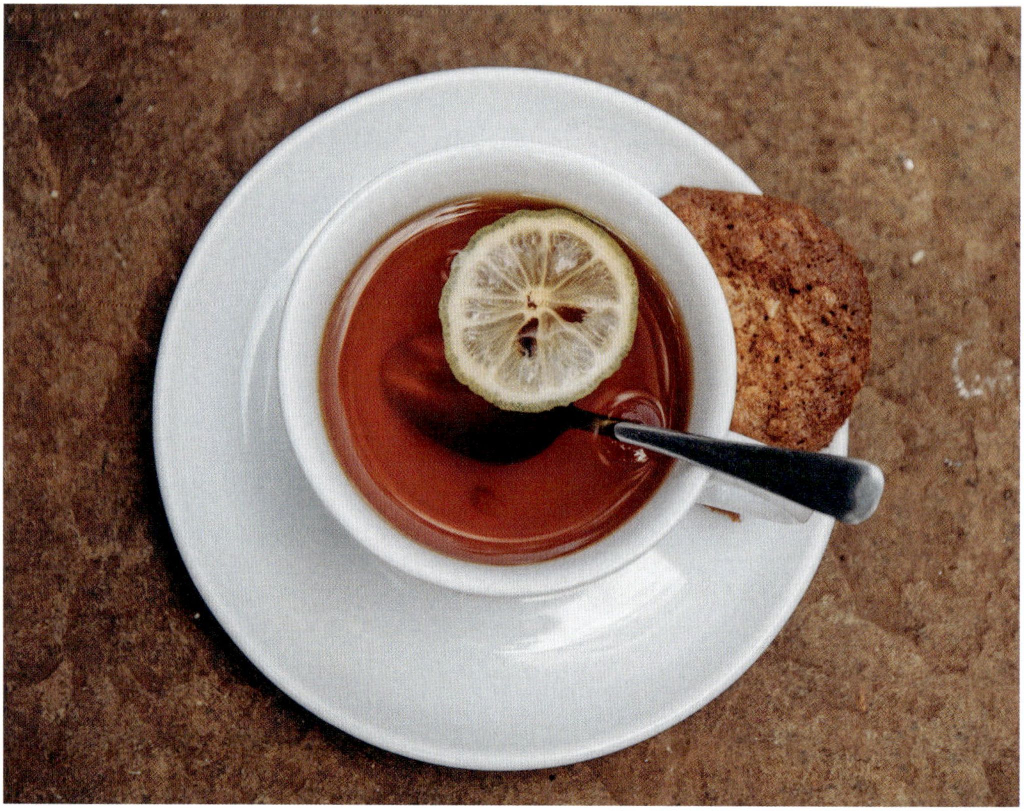

AFRICA AND THE MIDDLE EAST

LIMURU

134 KIAMBETHU TEA FARM

Girls School Road, Limuru, Kenya

TO VISIT BEFORE YOU DIE BECAUSE

Taste first-rate Kenyan tea on the veranda of this historic farm, with sweeping views across the tea fields and the Ngong Hills.

Where better to enjoy the magic of a fresh cup of tea than surrounded by rows of tea bushes stretching to the horizon? Kiambethu Farm, set in lush gardens just a short drive from Nairobi, was founded in 1910 by A.B. McDonell, one of the first in Kenya to make and sell tea – now one of the country's largest exports. Five generations later, his granddaughter Fiona Vernon is at the helm, offering tea experiences and tours of the plantation and the surrounding forest, where a local guide will focus on native plants and how they are used. Guests are treated to tea and homemade cookies in the morning, followed by lunch in the farm building or on the terrace. The delicious dishes are prepared with produce from the kitchen garden; desserts are topped with cream from the herd of Channel Island cows; and cups are filled with the estate's unblended, top-quality PF1 tea, straight from the local factory.

kiambethufarm.com

+254 729 290 894

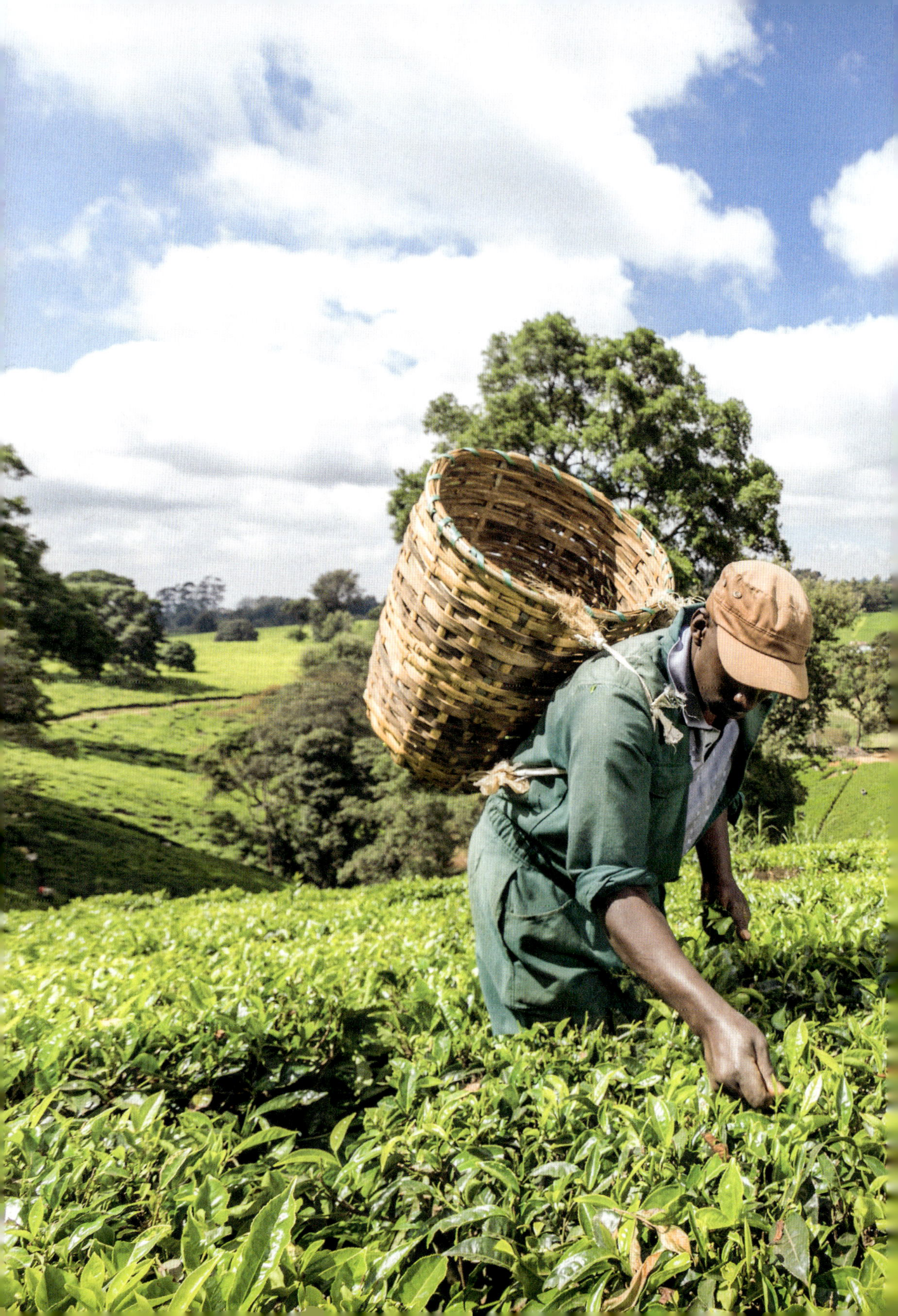

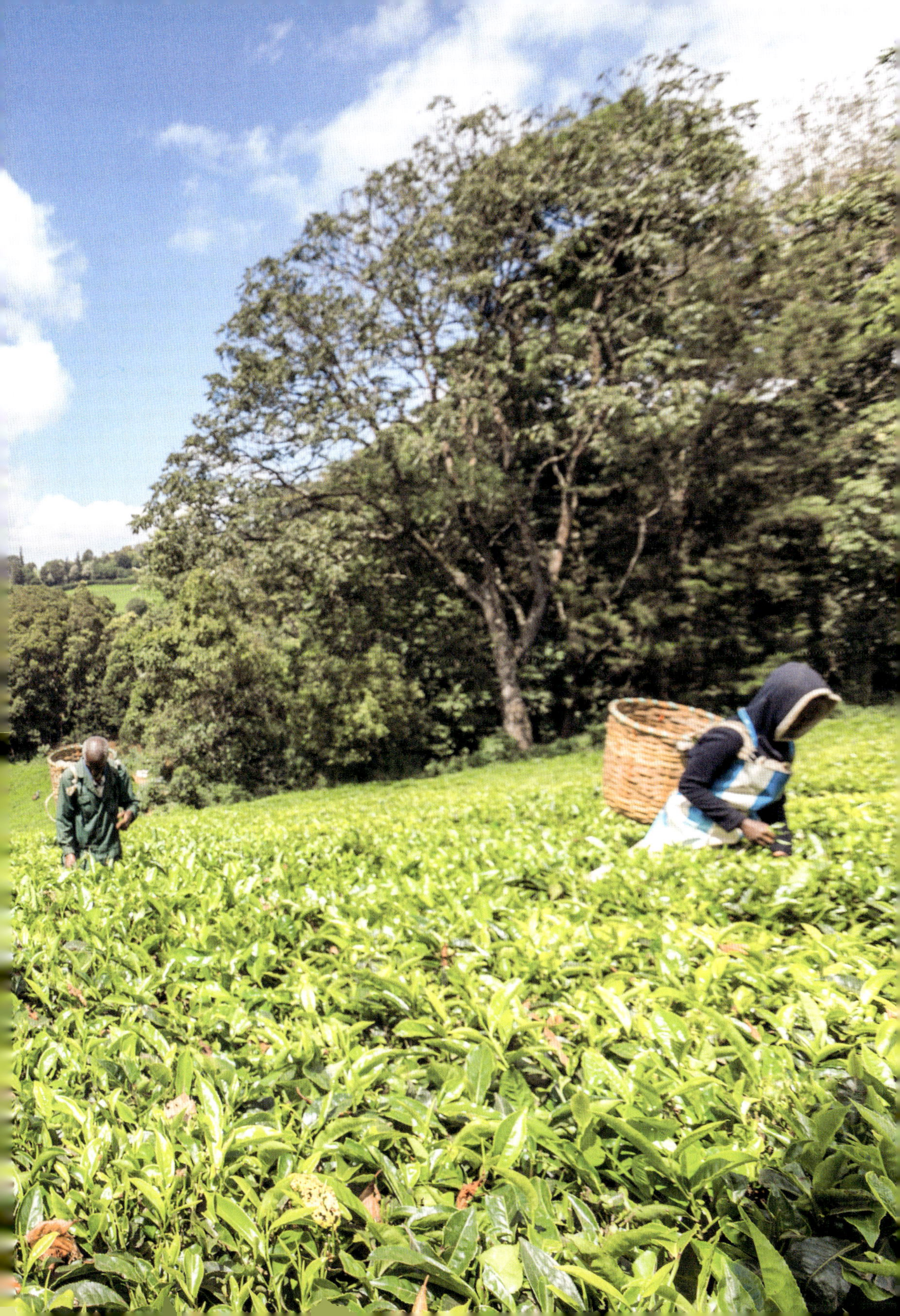

AFRICA AND THE MIDDLE EAST

MARRAKESH

135 CAFÉ GUERRAB

39 Souk Ablouh Jemma el Fna, Marrakesh, Morocco

TO VISIT BEFORE YOU DIE BECAUSE

Offering great views of the medina from its rooftop terrace, this is the perfect spot to enjoy a Moroccan mint tea before braving the souk.

Marrakesh's famed Jemma el Fna square is known for its snake charmers, orange juice sellers, henna artists, storytellers and street performers, but it is of course also home to various spiced tea and pastry stalls, herbalists and dried mint sellers. We suggest you brave the evening crowds to soak up its magical atmosphere – then retreat to Café Guerrab and its rooftop terraces in time for sunset. It is just around the corner from the square, past the souk's spice sellers, but a whole different world. From the peaceful top terrace, you can admire the entire medina, the Koutoubia Mosque and the Atlas Mountains on the horizon, while sipping freshly brewed tea. Options include traditional mint, ginger, cinnamon, spiced, orange blossom and verbena, served with Moroccan pastries or delicious savouries, including meatball tagine, harira soup and aubergine salad. Painted in bright colours and furnished with handmade chairs, the café's cosy lounge is also a great spot to take a break from the bustle of the surrounding souk.

cafe-guerrab.com

+212 524 378 330

AFRICA AND THE MIDDLE EAST — MARRAKESH

136 LE MENZEH AT LA MAMOUNIA

Avenue Bad Jdid, Medina, Marrakesh, 40040, Morocco

TO VISIT BEFORE YOU DIE BECAUSE

This Marrakesh grande dame's secret garden is a tranquil spot to enjoy teas and patisserie by celebrated French pastry chef Pierre Hermé.

La Mamounia's story started in the 18th century, when Prince Al-Mamoun turned his vast estate into a venue renowned for its magnificent open-air receptions. Two centuries later, and the luxury hotel still boasts stunning grounds, with ancient olive and palm trees mixing with Aleppo pines, lemon trees and blossoming jacarandas to create a peaceful haven just a stone's throw from the Koutoubia Mosque. In this urban oasis, you will find Le Menzeh by Pierre Hermé, one of the hotel's two tea rooms (the other is Le Salon de Thé par Pierre Hermé, on the equally beautiful Andalusian patio). Try the renowned French pâtissier's own blends, such as the popular Ispahan (black tea with rose, raspberry and lychee), and delicate creations, including a macaron filled with rose petal cream and a Moroccan corne de gazelle with local almonds and marmalade. In addition to the classic Moroccan mint tea, drinks include an iced tea with citrus, rose, jasmine and violet flowers, and a surprising Moroccan cola made from a syrup of chai, orange and garden geranium.

AFRICA AND THE MIDDLE EAST — NAIROBI

137 MUTHAIGA TEA COMPANY

156 Whispers Avenue, Gigiri Nairobi, Kenya

TO VISIT BEFORE YOU DIE BECAUSE

The tea workshops by one of the first tea sommeliers of East Africa will help you discover fine teas from Kenya and beyond.

Kenya is the world's third-largest exporter of tea, and Kenyans love a cup of black tea with ginger, spices and milk – funnily enough, it is one of the most popular drinks at the nation's largest coffee chain. For an expert deep dive into the world of African tea, book a tea alchemy experience at Muthaiga Tea Company, led by tea sommelier Tehmeena Manji. With a passion for tea inspired by the secret tea blends of her grandmother, Tehmeena set up her company in 2020 after studying in the UK and Japan, with the aim to showcase the artistry of African tea making with carefully selected products, such as Mawimbi Dance, a tropical blend with mango and baobab bark inspired by the Swahili coast. It regularly organises tasting sessions featuring fine teas from small African farms dedicated to sustainable practices. 'The experience pairs tea and food, and you'll also learn about the stories behind our artisanal teas, the crafting process and what makes our blends so unique,' says Tehmeena.

muthaigatea.com

AFRICA AND THE MIDDLE EAST

TANGIER

138 CAFÉ HAFA

Rue Hafa, Tangier, Morocco

TO VISIT BEFORE YOU DIE BECAUSE

Sip on a glass or two of Moroccan mint tea and watch the boats go by at this historic café overlooking the Bay of Tangier.

Located on a clifftop just outside the old town of Tangier, Café Hafa opened in the 1920s, when its owners had to bring water from the well on a cart to prepare their tea. Dotted with greenery and home to quite a few well-fed cats, it's a very simple place, with colourful plastic chairs and mosaic tables spread across a series of narrow terraces on multiple levels. But it offers jaw-dropping views of the Mediterranean Sea and the Strait of Gibraltar, where the Atlantic meets the Mediterranean. This unique setting once made the humble café a favourite hangout of the Beat Generation, with famous patrons such as William Burroughs, Jack Kerouac, Allen Ginsberg and the Rolling Stones. Today, people still come for the view and the Moroccan mint tea, a special Tangier brew with orange blossom flowers. Brought to the tables in metal carriers holding up to 15 glasses, tea is served every afternoon, along with simple snacks such as msemen flatbread with honey, to crowds of families and friends.

@cafehafa

AFRICA AND THE MIDDLE EAST

THYOLO

139 HUNTINGDON HOUSE

Satemwa Tea Estate, Box 6, Thyolo, Malawi

TO VISIT BEFORE YOU DIE BECAUSE

This pioneering farm in Malawi's Shire Highlands is a truly magical place, with rolling green tea fields and the mighty Mount Mulanje on the horizon.

Founded in 1923 by a Scotsman, Maclean Kay, Satemwa is a third-generation family-owned tea and coffee estate in southern Malawi, the first country in Africa where tea was planted commercially. Today, its teas – a wide range of black, green, oolong and white, including the rare Satemwa Antlers – are sold to large brands such as Pickwick and Starbucks, while its artisanal range is on offer in high-end restaurants. Tea professionals from around the world come here for the team's sought-after expertise, but, thankfully, the farm – which is Rainforest Alliance certified and community minded – is also open to the general public. The 1930s farmhouse, Huntingdon House, welcomes guests for lunch, high tea, walks, pairings and tastings. Sample fresh trial lots straight from the factory; delicious iced teas; and dishes such as tea-marinated fillet steak, dumplings steamed with Satemwa Zomba green tea and homemade Earl Grey buns. Plus there's no need to rush: it is possible to spend the night on the estate and enjoy a sundowner of Satemwa G&Tea on the terrace.

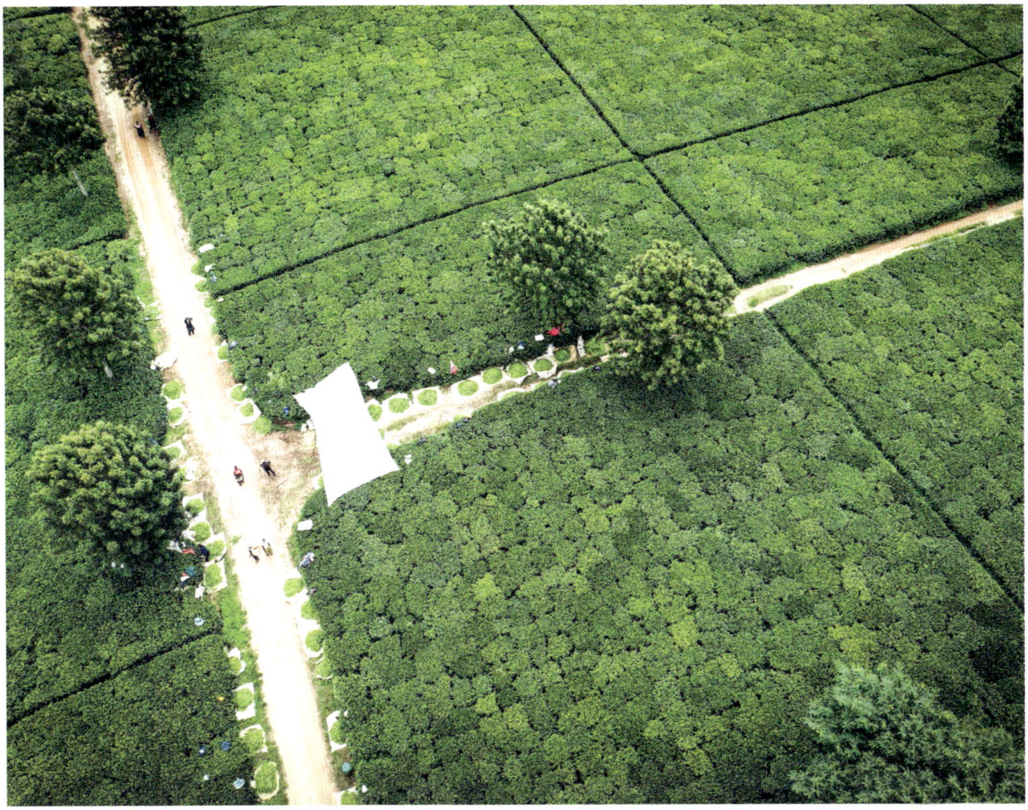
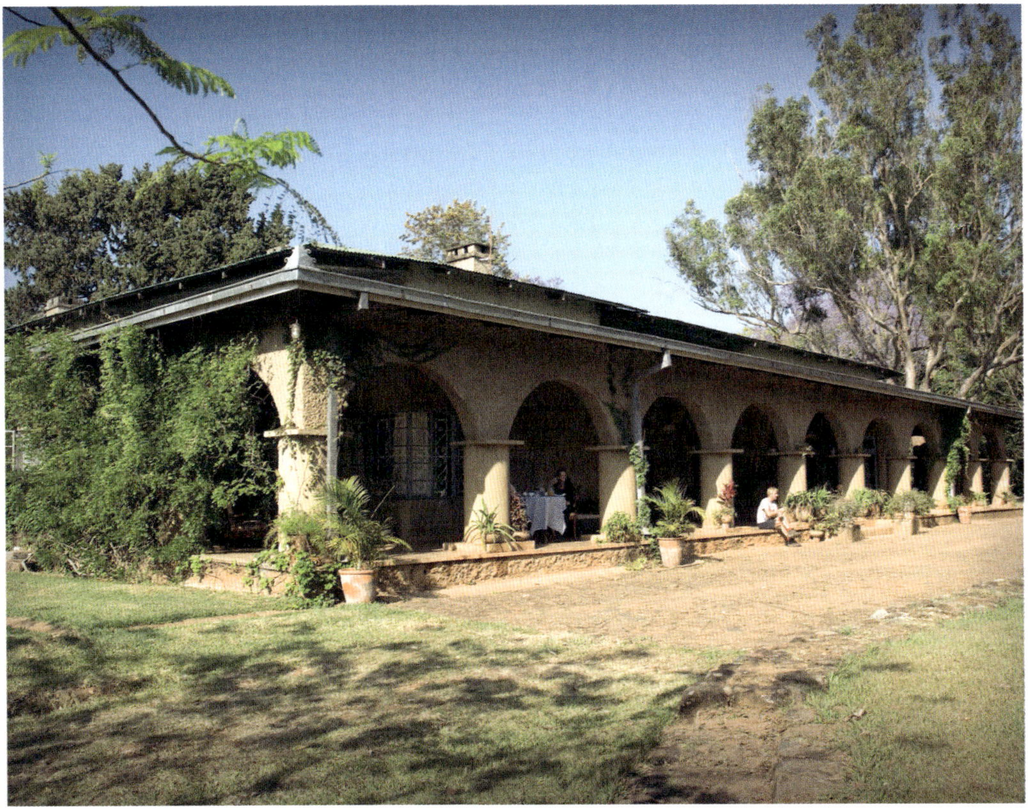

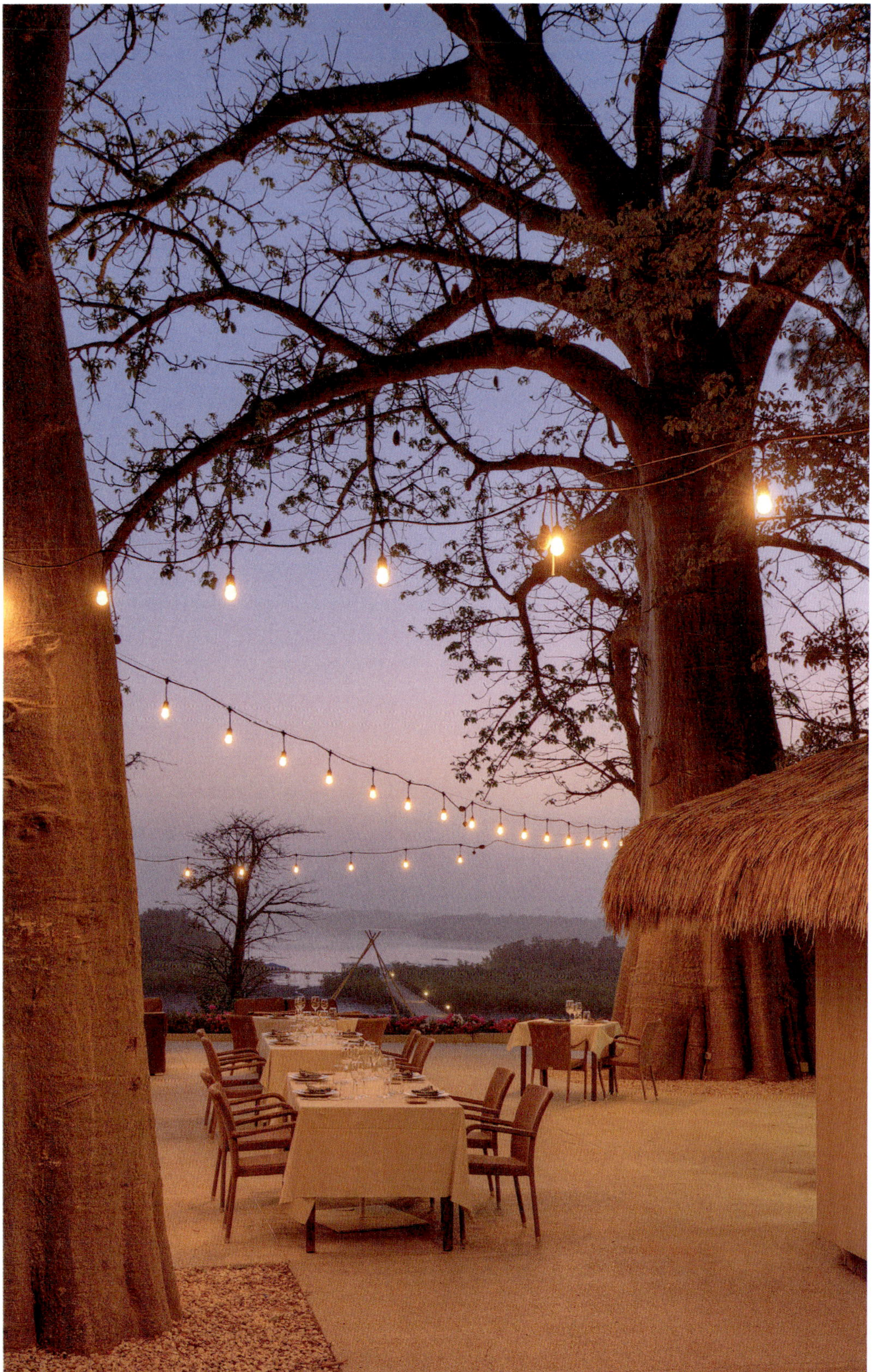

AFRICA AND THE MIDDLE EAST — TOUBAKOUTA

140 LES PALÉTUVIERS

Toubakouta, Senegal

TO VISIT BEFORE YOU DIE BECAUSE

Find peace and tranquillity with a cup of strong mint tea on Senegal's beautiful Sine-Saloum Delta.

Typically offered to friends and visitors, tea is at the centre of the Senegalese tea ritual ataya, which takes place daily on doorsteps and in village squares around the country. Although the beverage – gunpowder tea with mint and sugar – is important, what is so powerful about this humble ceremony is the sense of community and well-being it creates, as the host pours the tea back and forth between the teapot and the glass to create a thick foam, while friends chat away for hours. It is the wellness aspect of ataya that is explored at Les Palétuviers, a hotel on the lush Sine-Saloum Delta, where you can experience traditional *teranga* – classic Senegalese hospitality. Ataya here forms part of the healing experience, which includes barefoot mud walks and massages on the jetty. Time really slows down as you watch the sun set over the mangroves while sipping a strong cup of green tea – which, of course, is a powerful antioxidant. Other rejuvenating beverages here include cold-pressed drinks featuring baobab, moringa leaves and hibiscus flowers.

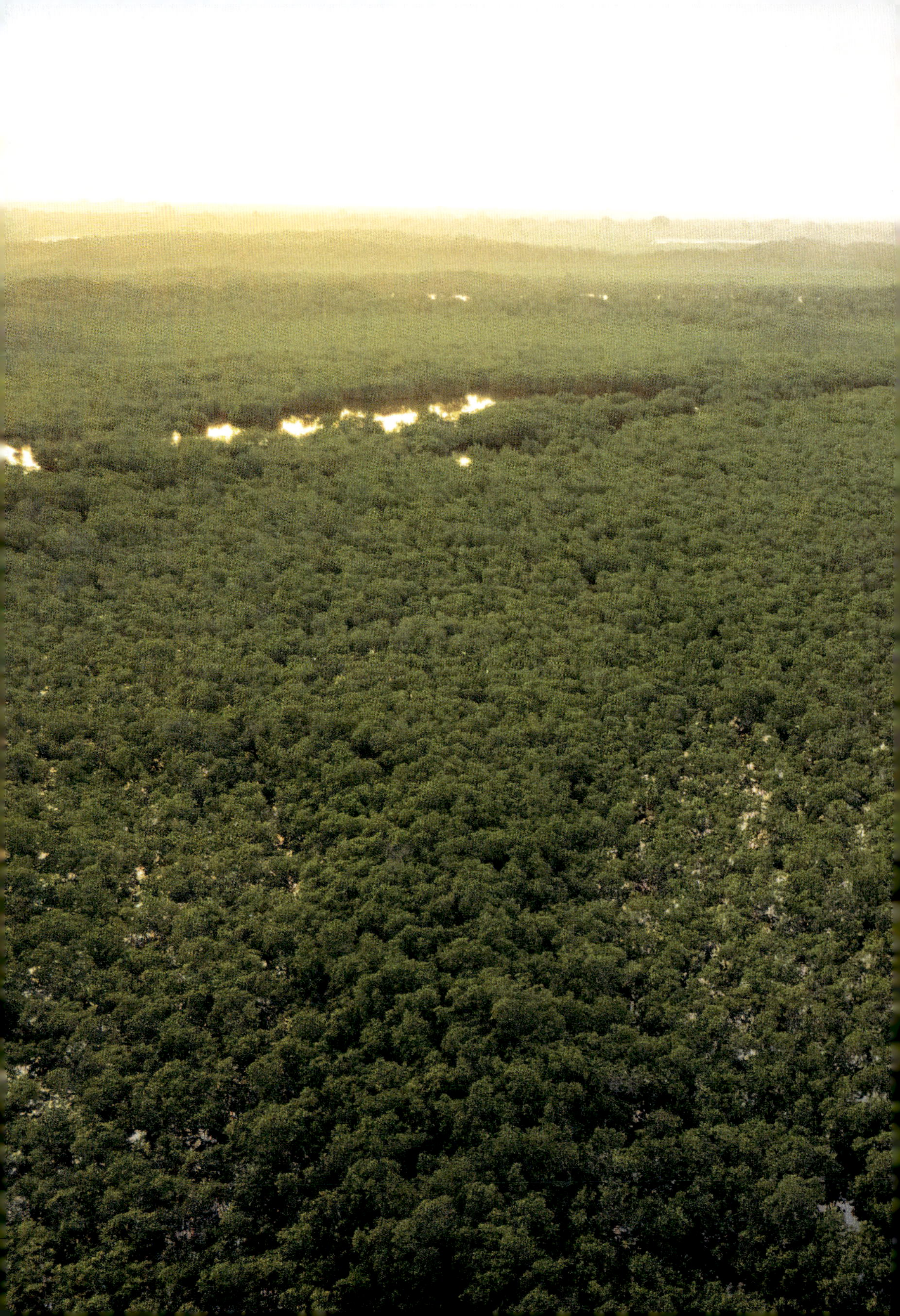

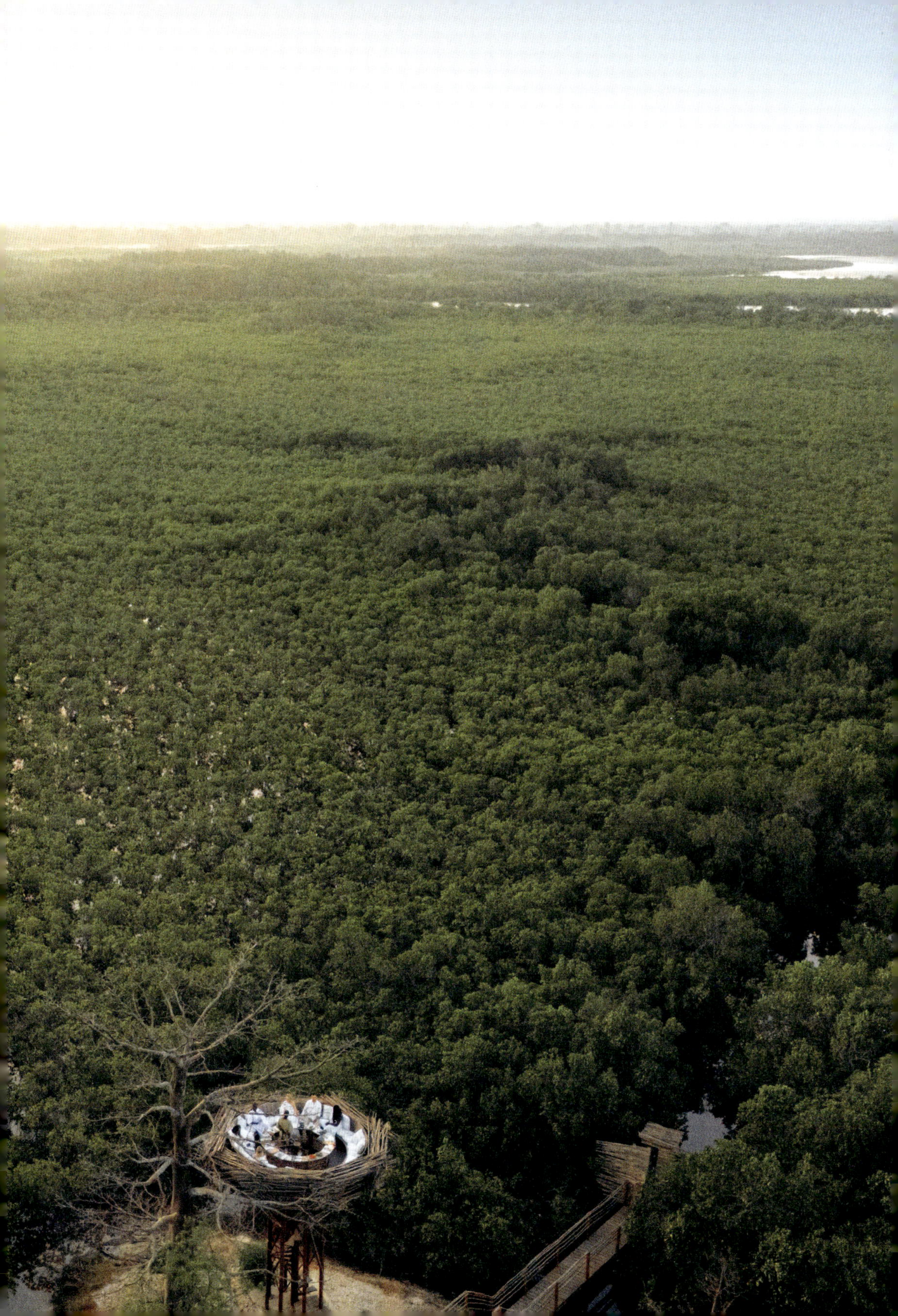

AFRICA AND THE MIDDLE EAST — UMHLANGA

141 THE PALM COURT AT THE OYSTER BOX

2 Lighthouse Road, Umhlanga, KwaZulu-Natal, South Africa

TO VISIT BEFORE YOU DIE BECAUSE

This five-star hotel on South Africa's Indian Ocean coast has it all: a historic setting, a delicious high tea and plenty of personality.

Perched on Umhlanga's beachfront, the Oyster Box is known for its chic terrace overlooking a landmark lighthouse. But the grand colonial-era property has plenty of wow factor inside, too: at its heart is The Palm Court, a majestic room filled with light and greenery and adorned with a Vladimir Tretchikoff painting of a cat (fittingly, as the court is home to a local star, resident cat Skabenga). Here, under chandeliers once hanging at the Savoy in London, high tea is served in colourful Royal Albert tableware and comprises a selection of small bites including macarons, Yorkshire puddings and lemon tarts, with eight Dilmah teas from Sri Lanka to choose from. The hotel is part of the Red Carnation Hotel Collection, whose founder, Beatrice Tollman, is a keen baker herself – on the menu are some of her signature items, including a delicious cheesecake. And the team is not resting on its laurels: new offerings this year include a curated loose-tea experience, food and tea pairing sessions, themed evening teas and an intriguing tea journey around the world.

oysterboxhotel.com +27 315 145 000

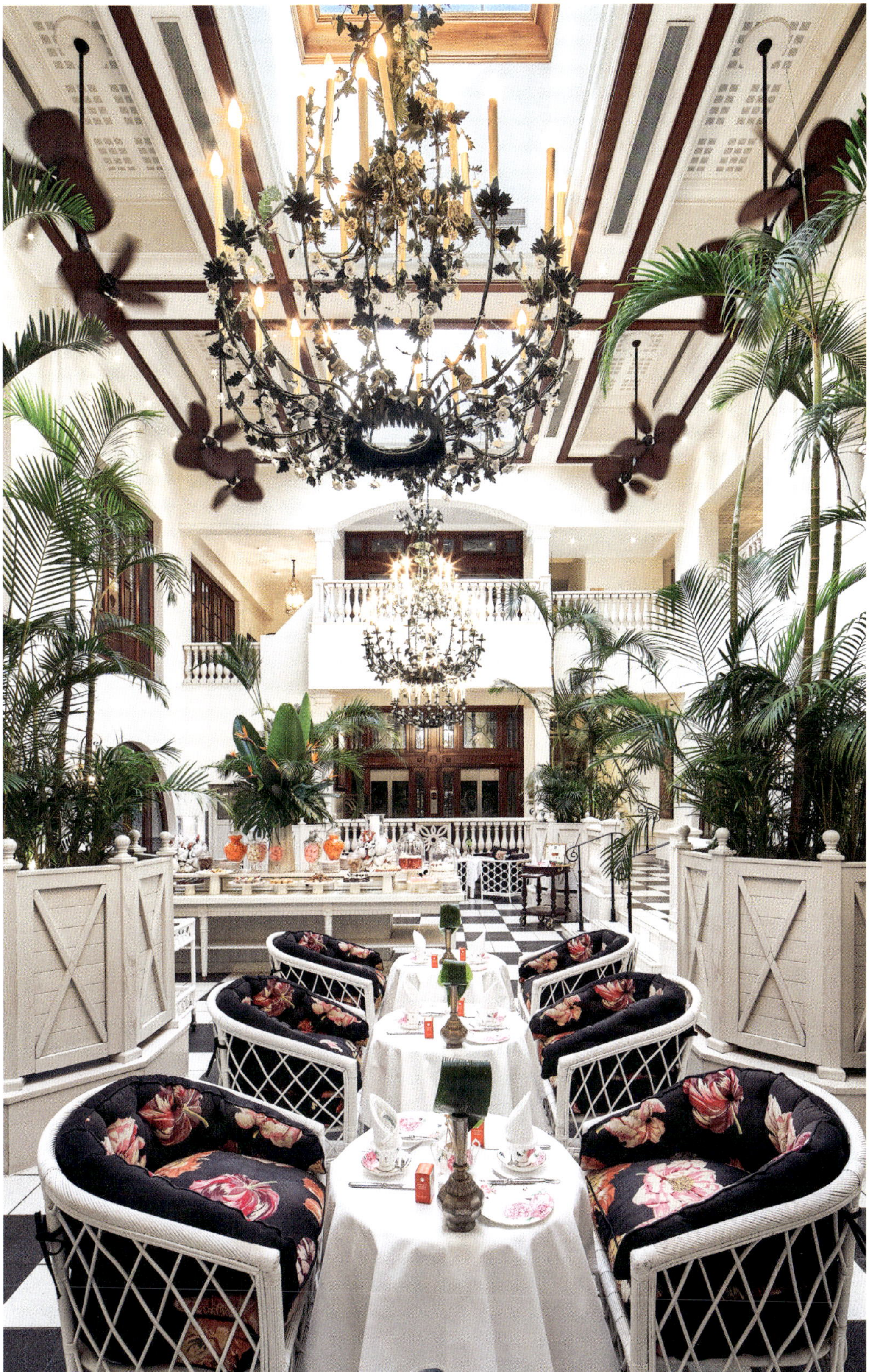

OCEANIA AUCKLAND

142 CHAPTER BOOK & TEA SHOP

442 Mount Eden Road, Mount Eden, Auckland, New Zealand

TO VISIT BEFORE YOU DIE BECAUSE

Fall in love with the tea selection and romance novels of this cosy neighbourhood spot, the longest-established speciality tea store in Auckland.

In the suburbs of Auckland is the dormant volcano Maungawhau, or Mount Eden, a great vantage point to take in spectacular views over the harbour city. On the way there, make sure to stop at another heavenly place: the Chapter Book & Tea Shop, which has been selling tea for over 15 years. The small café stocks over 300 teas, with the most popular being Earl Grey Blue Star and lapsang souchong. 'We are happy to do custom blends,' explains owner Frances Loo, 'and we include native herbs such as *kawakawa* and *manuka* in our range, both as pure teas and in blends.' Try teas from local labels Zealong (see opposite page), Kerikeri Organic and ŌKU, while browsing one of Chapter's 2,500 romance novels and snacking on a slice of ginger loaf or a rhubarb and raspberry tart. As well as crowd-pleasers such as Turkish apple tea and chai lattes, the menu includes premium teas such as Izu green matcha, artisan teas like dragon pearls and blends such as honeybush with golden kiwi fruit.

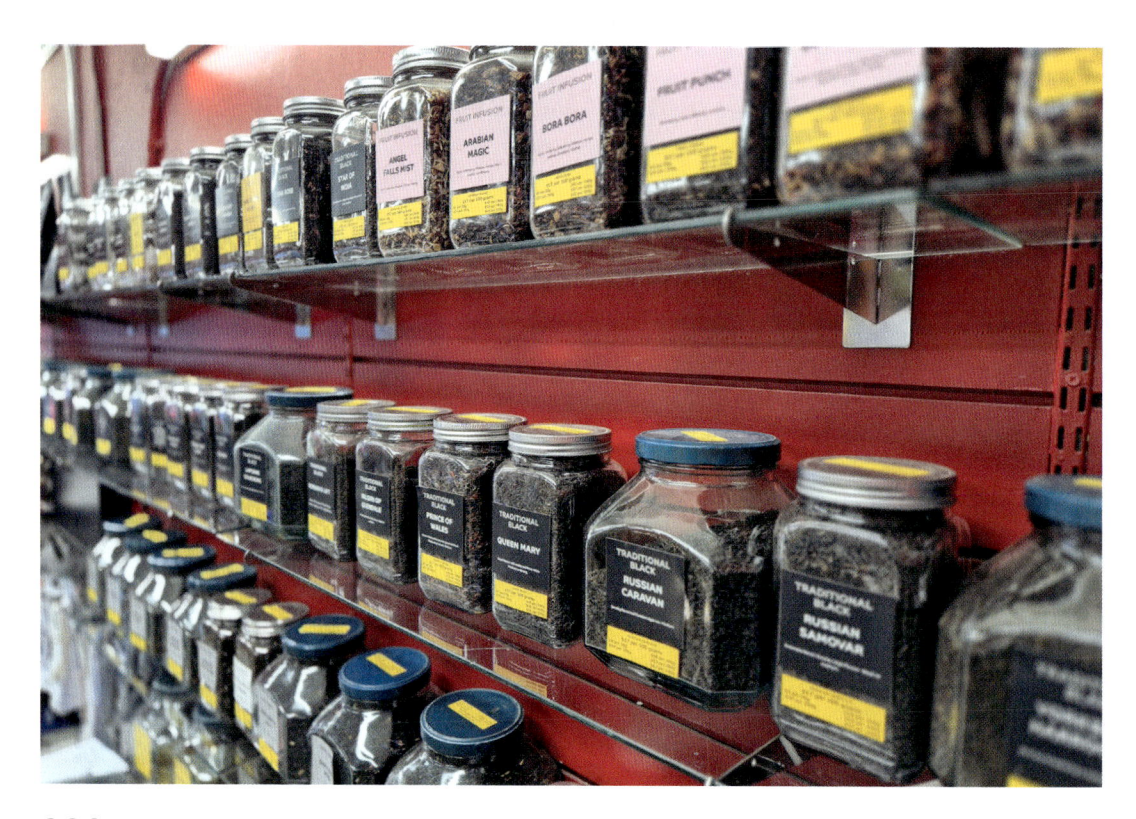

chapter.co.nz +64 96 232 319

OCEANIA HAMILTON

143 ZEALONG TEA ROOM

495 Gordonton Road, Gordonton, Hamilton, 3281, New Zealand

TO VISIT BEFORE YOU DIE BECAUSE

Take in the stunning views and award-winning organic teas at the Zealong Tea Estate, New Zealand's only tea producer.

Located near Hamilton, the Zealong Tea Estate was founded in the 1990s by Vincent Chen, who came across a flowering camellia in the Waikato region and thought, 'Tea is a kind of camellia… maybe tea could grow here too.' Many years and 1,500 tea cuttings later, his dream has come true. Only 130 of the original plants survived, but that was plenty: the estate's 1.2 million tea bushes now spread over 48 hectares, thanks to the team's careful caretaking and the region's unique climate and rich soil. Its teas are sought after for their smooth taste and sweet character, and the selection includes award-winning highly oxidised and aged oolongs. Sample them all at the Zealong Tea Room, a former farmhouse with a large deck overlooking the tea terraces. Accompanied by a Zealong tea or the iced tea of the day, the signature high tea includes items such as a truffle croque monsieur, chocolate tart and Chantilly bavarois. The estate is also home to the fine-dining Camellia Restaurant and a guesthouse.

zealong.com/tea-room +64 78 533 018

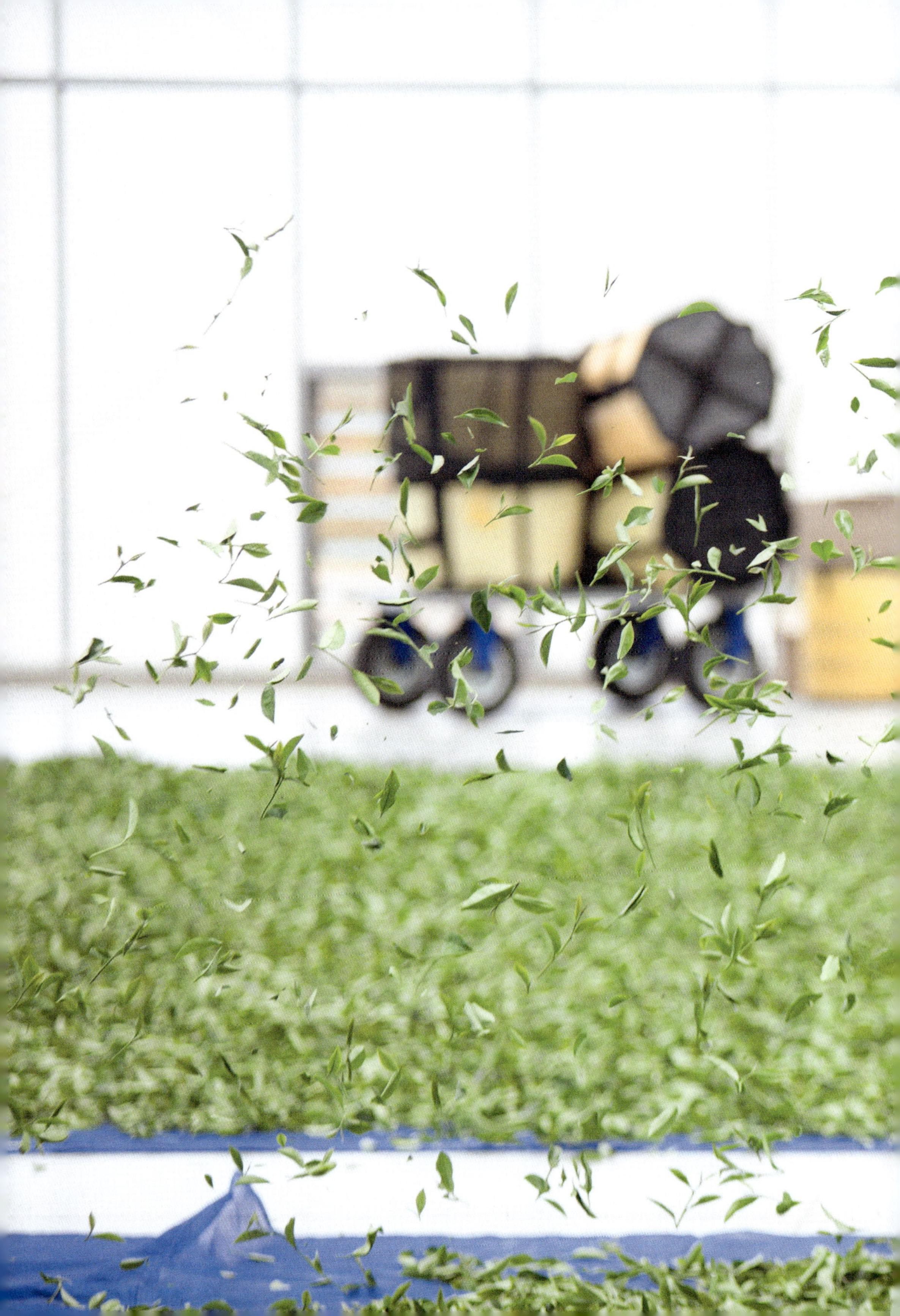

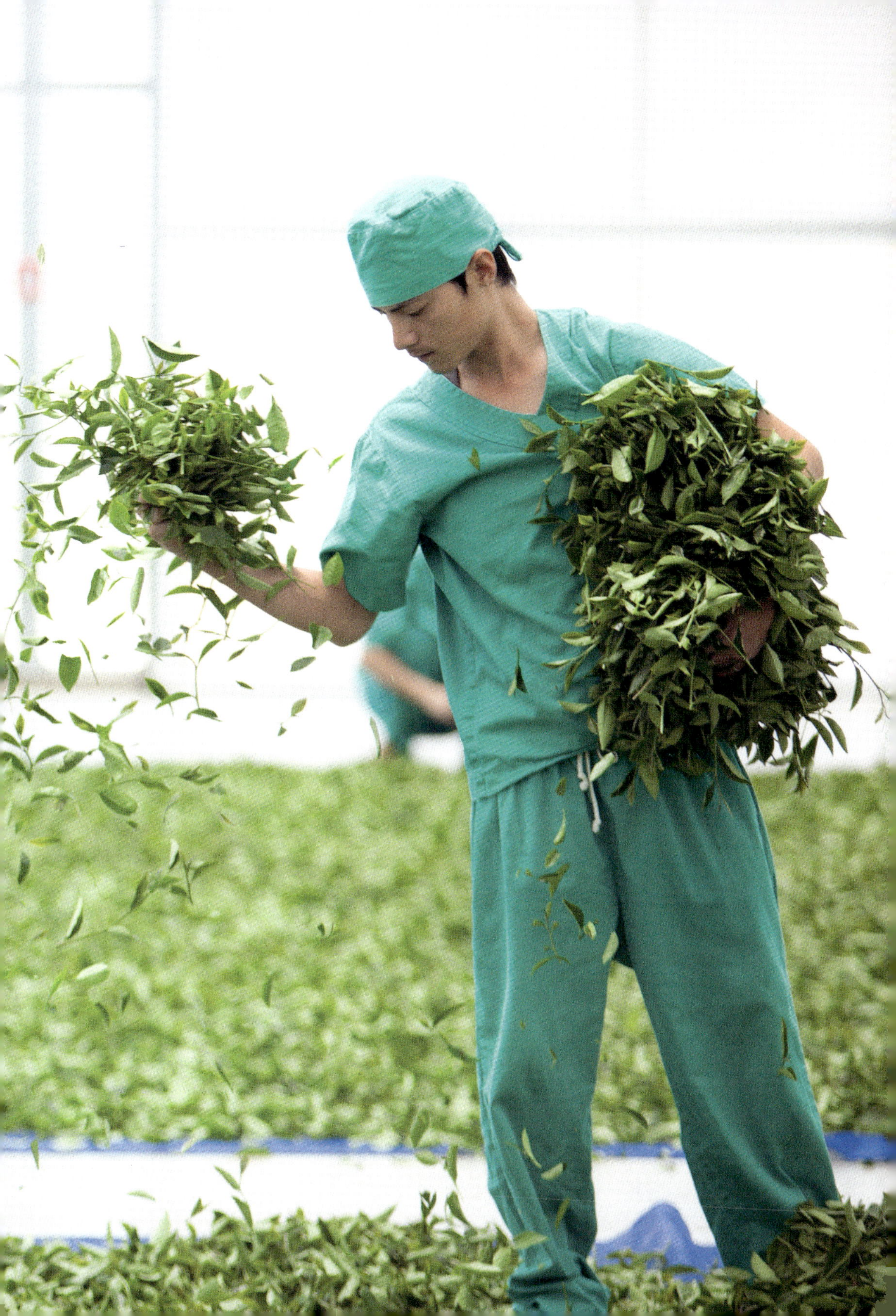

OCEANIA · MELBOURNE

144 OXI TEA ROOM

T4/158 Victoria Street, Carlton, Melbourne, Victoria, 3053, Australia

TO VISIT BEFORE YOU DIE BECAUSE

Known for its exquisitely detailed themed afternoon teas, this Afro-Asian tea room reflects its owners' unique heritage.

This serene, contemporary tea room in downtown Melbourne celebrates the tea terroirs of Kenya and Taiwan, the home countries of owners Mehboob and Andy. 'We offer a delightful fusion of cultures with a deep-rooted passion for black and oolong teas,' they explain. From Kenya come teas such as Nandi Gold, a fruity black tea with hints of roasted hazelnuts, while from Taiwan are sourced crisp Alishan and delicate dong ding oolongs. The 33 premium whole-leaf teas are paired with 'meticulously crafted menus designed around seasonal ingredients and unexpected flavour combinations', and an interactive app guides diners through a culinary journey, revealing the stories behind each dish and including engaging puzzles. Oxi Tea Room is well known for its themed afternoon teas, which change every four months, with past inspirations ranging from Australian honeys, spring greenhouses and fairy tales to artists such as Vincent van Gogh and Yayoi Kusama. All feature pastry chef Johnny Ping's eye-catching savoury and sweet bites, including surprising bites such as cheesecake with plum, blueberry and tofu.

145 THE TEA ROOMS 1892

The Block Arcade, 282 Collins Street, Melbourne, Victoria, Australia

TO VISIT BEFORE YOU DIE BECAUSE

The oldest tea room in Australia combines a historic setting, freshly baked treats and a forward-thinking tea menu.

The organic tea menu at this historic tea room in central Melbourne includes unusual finds such as Colonille, a Vietnamese black tea with French vanilla, and Fiji, a green tea with papaya and wild pineapple. Particularly interesting are blends showcasing First Nations ingredients, such as an Earl Grey infused with *gumbi gumbi*; a lemon myrtle and ginger infusion; and RiverMint, blended with chamomile. So, settle in with an English Breakfast tea with wattleseed and take in the stunning surroundings, from the emerald wallpaper and chandelier to the Block Arcade just outside, inspired by Milan's Galleria Vittorio Emanuele II and featuring a magnificent etched-glass roof and mosaic floors. The Tea Rooms 1892 actually started out as the Victorian ladies' work association, a fashionable spot for lunch or afternoon tea in the 1890s, and you can still enjoy both today here. Served on a three-tiered stand, the high tea includes pinwheels with Tasmanian smoked salmon and a signature chicken liver pâté, as well as scones and an assortment of petit fours.

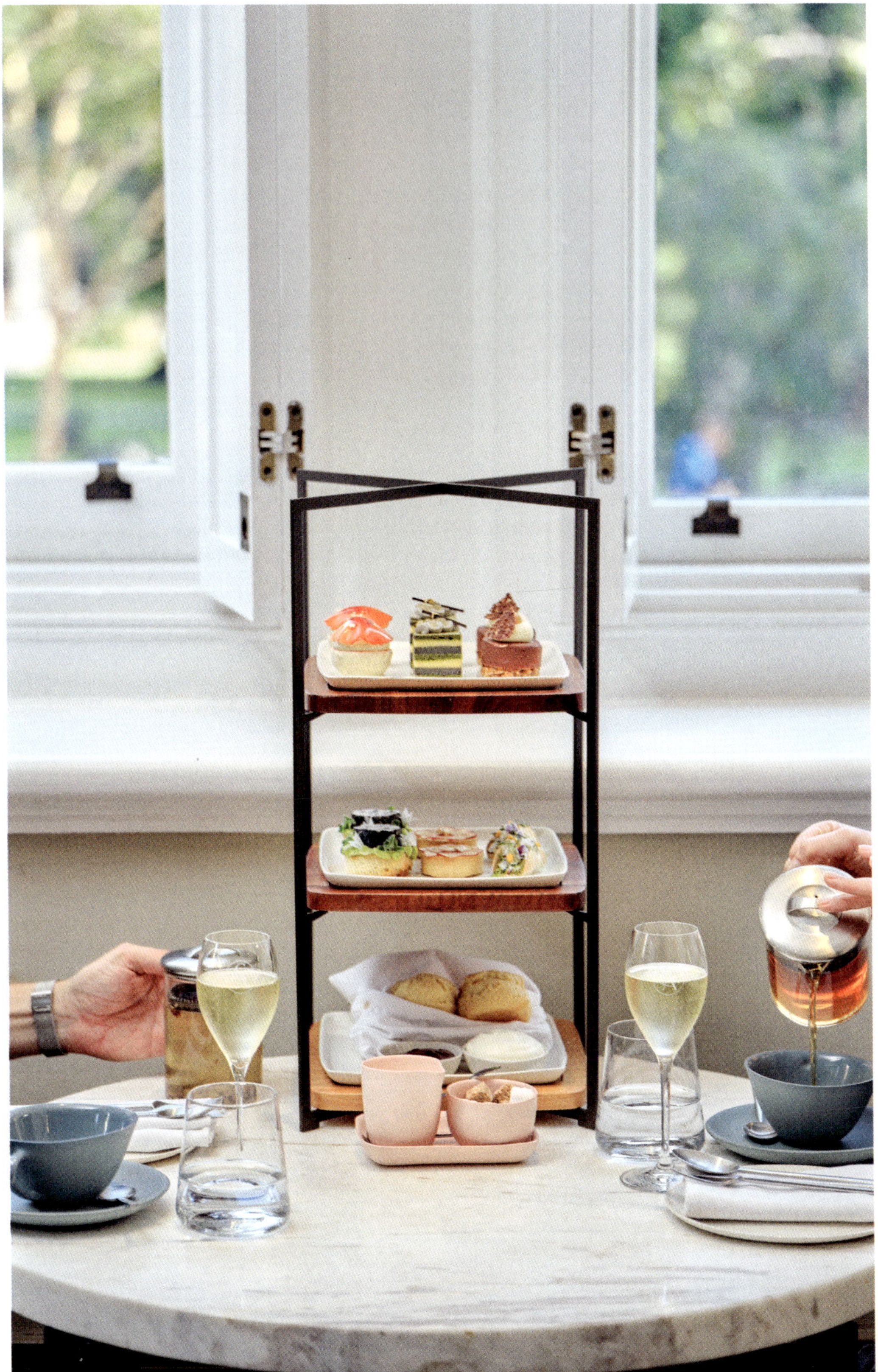

OCEANIA   PERTH

146 CAPE ARID ROOMS

COMO The Treasury, 1 Cathedral Avenue, Perth, Western Australia, 6000, Australia

---

TO VISIT BEFORE YOU DIE BECAUSE

This is a perfect blend of nature-inspired art and tea in a series of elegant rooms in the heart of Perth.

Is there anything better than an afternoon spent in the company of great tea and art? Head to COMO The Treasury, a luxury hotel in the southeastern wing of Perth's historic State Buildings, to find out. A series of three interconnected rooms with high ceilings and wooden shutters, its tea lounge is named after the collection of beautifully detailed watercolour and ink paintings that line its wall. The work of renowned West Australian artists Alex and Philippa Nikulinsky, it is inspired by the couple's adventures to the nearby Cape Arid National Park. And what adorns the walls has translated into what is on the table, with a menu featuring the best of local ingredients, from Shark Bay crab to Carnarvon banana. All tea blends have been curated in collaboration with Teassential, a Western Australian tea company located within the State Buildings. They include an Australian-grown Arakai Estate premium black tea; Cape Arid Breakfast tea blended with native strawberry gum; and the rare gyokuro green tea, grown in Japan and shaded with bamboo mats before harvest.

OCEANIA   SYDNEY

147   G&TEA AT THE STAR

Hotel Lobby, The Star, 80 Pyrmont Street, Pyrmont, Sydney, New South Wales, 2009, Australia

TO VISIT BEFORE YOU DIE BECAUSE

More than just a hotel lobby bar, G&Tea celebrates the power of tea leaves through both hot drinks and exquisite cocktails.

With its floating glass terrariums, turquoise walls and art deco-inspired furniture, G&Tea certainly has the wow factor. But it's definitely not a case of style over substance, with the bar and tea lounge serving a great choice of tea, breakfasts such as baked eggs and avocado toast, and sweet treats including a deliciously light pandan cake. The tea menu spans various brands and styles, from Golden Wattle oolong with osmanthus petals and apple pieces, to Tea Craft hōjicha with hints of roasted hazelnut and caramel, and a Dilmah black tea with orange, lemon, spice and eucalyptus. They are displayed in a cabinet behind the bar, but come 5pm and it all changes: the team swaps the teas out for spirits in a daily ritual, although tea doesn't quite disappear from the menu. As its name implies, in the evenings, G&Tea serves excellent tea- and gin-based cocktails, including an Earl Grey iced tea with vodka and a Beefeater gin cocktail with sencha, grapefruit, angelica seed and orris.

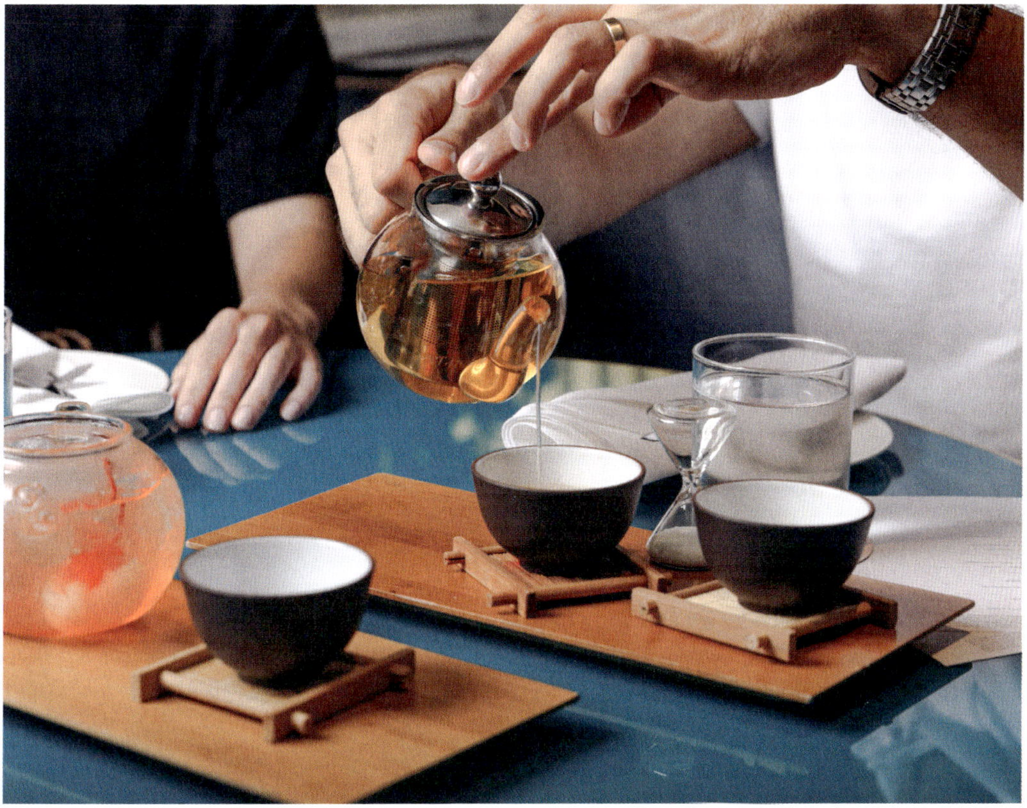

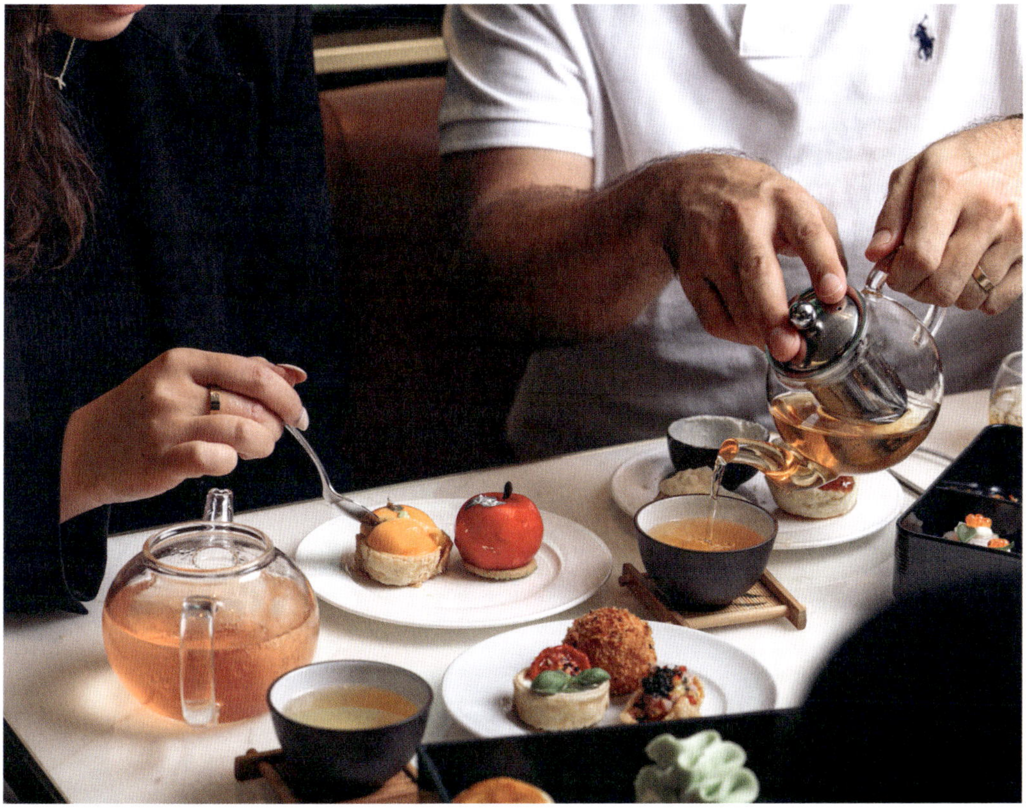

OCEANIA   SYDNEY

148 GUNNERS' BARRACKS

End of Suakin Drive, Mosman, Sydney, New South Wales, 2088, Australia

TO VISIT BEFORE YOU DIE BECAUSE

The stunning views of Gunners' Barracks are complemented by an extensive menu of teas, infusions and iced teas.

Surrounded by bushland but only a short drive away from central Sydney, this former barracks dating from 1873 is perched on Georges Head and offers jaw-dropping views across Sydney Harbour to Rose Bay and Watsons Bay. It has turned away from its military past to become a popular wedding venue and a peaceful spot for a luxurious afternoon tea. Originally designed by colonial architect James Barnet, its interiors feature hand-printed wallpaper and crystal chandeliers, but it is the terrace that is the main attraction. Enjoy Asia-Pacific's largest selection of teas by German specialist Ronnefeldt, from Sri Lankan Orange Pekoe to Indian Assam Mokalbari. Flavoured teas come with pieces of vanilla or strawberry, while green teas include a premium large-leafed sencha. There is also a great choice of infusions, mocktails and iced teas, including a cold-brew rose petal iced tea. Last but not least, the high tea is an assortment of savoury bites, such as egg and chive sandwiches, and sweet treats, including apple crumble choux.

gunnersbarracks.com.au   +61 289 625 900

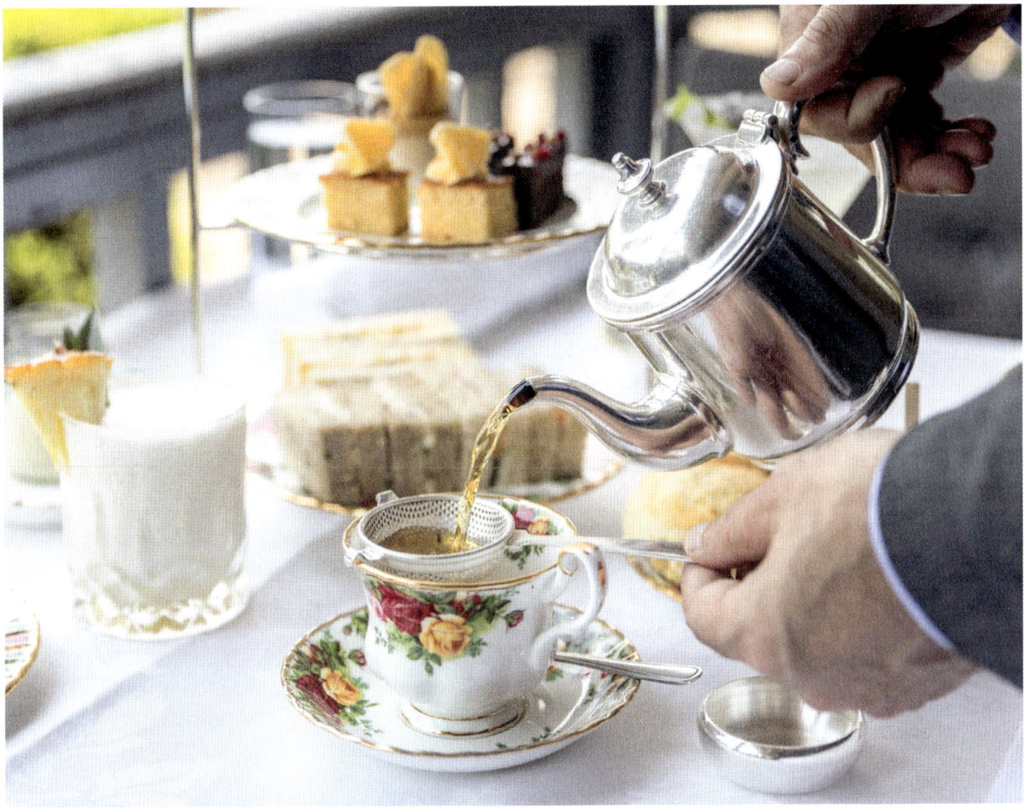

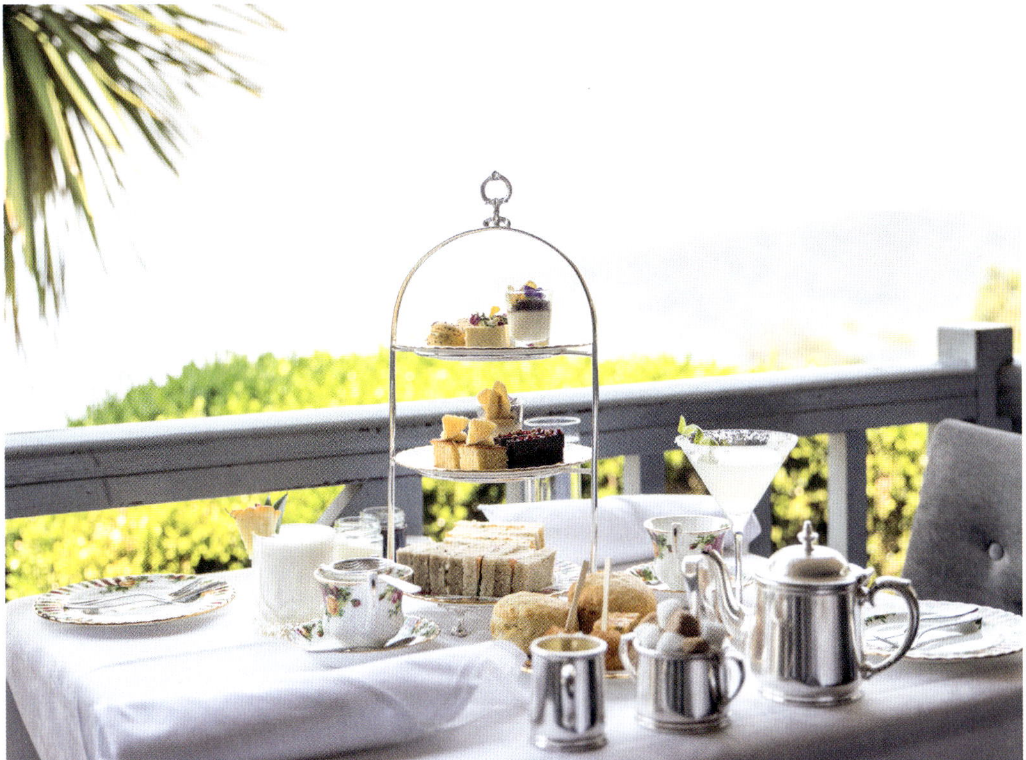

149 STRANGERS' RESTAURANT

6 Macquarie Street, Sydney, New South Wales, 2000, Australia

TO VISIT BEFORE YOU DIE BECAUSE

Parliament House's contemporary restaurant serves a wonderful weekly afternoon tea with the greenery of The Domain as a backdrop.

As well as public tours and art exhibitions, the historic New South Wales Parliament House is also home to Strangers' Restaurant, where high tea is served every Friday afternoon. It is worth a visit for its lush backdrop, comprising large windows overlooking The Domain and the Royal Botanic Garden Sydney, as well as a stunning wool tapestry, *Country Tree*, by artist Fahy Bottrell. Inspired by the Moreton Bay figs on the edge of The Domain, the 1981 artwork takes over an entire wall and represents the Parliament, the heat and drought of the Australian Outback, and the First Nations people. The tea selection – from classic Earl Grey and English Breakfast, to an Immunity Tea with eucalyptus, echinacea and lemon myrtle – is by New South Wales' Byron Bay Tea Company. Accompanying the teas are a series of sweet and savoury treats, such as lamingtons and Coronation chicken sandwiches presented on Parliamentary-crested Wedgwood plates. Thanks to its seasonal menu and occasional themed afternoon teas, this Friday treat is very popular, so book well in advance.

OCEANIA   SYDNEY

150 WHITE RABBIT GALLERY TEA HOUSE

30 Balfour Street, Chippendale, Sydney, New South Wales, 2008, Australia

TO VISIT BEFORE YOU DIE BECAUSE

Sample a thoughtfully curated tea selection alongside Chinese contemporary art at this small gallery in the heart of Sydney.

When White Rabbit Gallery founder Judith Neilson opened her art gallery in 2009, she knew she had to include a space to foster conversations and start new friendships. 'I imagined a space where we could recreate the salons I'd seen in China, where artists and their friends hung out, chatting, swapping stories and discussing art.' Today, her street-level teahouse is the perfect place to catch up with friends over a cup of the finest Chinese and Taiwanese teas. These include *jin xuan* and ginseng-flavoured oolongs; Princess Flower tea, its jasmine and amaranth flowers wrapped in white tea leaves, slowly unfurling in hot water; the prized Bamboo Leaf green tea, from Mount Emei in Sichuan; and refreshing Lychee Red iced tea. Chinese teas often taste best on the second or third steeping, and your teapot will be topped up with hot water as often as needed here – in fact, you will want to linger until you're hungry enough to sample the handmade dumplings.

whiterabbitcollection.org/tea-house   +61 283 992 867

Index 150 Tea Houses

A.C. Perch's Thehandel............ 88
Abigail's Tea Room & Terrace......151
Africafé..........................212
Aman Summer Palace 17
Araksa Tea Garden 25
Basao Tea 70
Bellocq Tea Atelier 179
Betjeman & Barton's Tea Bar 127
Bettys...........................95
Bontemps 'Le Jardin Secret'...... 128
Bottom of the cup Tea Room.......176
Boulder Dushanbe Tea House......152
Café Guerrab 226
Café Hafa 229
Café Svenskt Tenn................139
Čaj Chai.........................81
Callisto Tea House............... 190
Cape Arid Rooms................. 245
Cardinal........................173
Carmién Tea Shop
  at De Tol Farm Deli 220
Casa de Chá 154
Casa Tassel......................170
Ceylon Tea Trails.................34
Cha'ya Moda..................... 99
Cha-An Teahouse 182
Chaiiwala Fosse Park 106
Chalet da Tia Mercês.............138
Chapter Book & Tea Shop 238
Ching Shin Fu Chuan 64
Claridge's...................... 109
Confiserie Sprüngli..............147
Copacabana Beach 193
Dem Moda........................101
Dobrá čajovna 135
Domaine de Bois Chéri............217
Du Côté de chez Swann 143
El-Fishawy Café 218
Fortnum & Mason.................110
Four Seasons Hotel Hangzhou
  at West Lake 32
G&Tea at The Star................ 246
Gardens of the World 83
Glass Tea House 'Mondrian' 56
Glenburn Tea Estate.............. 28
Green Ginkgo Tea 39
Gunners' Barracks................ 248
Haas&Haas.......................144
Harney & Sons...................185
Heming Teahouse 24
Housel Bay Hotel 108
Huntingdon House 230
Imperial Tea Court 194
Inara Camp......................213
Ippodo Tea 50
Japanese Tea Garden 196
Jojo Tea........................172
Jugetsudo Ginza Kabukiza 67
Just Add Honey..................149
Ksana Matcha....................16
Kiambethu Tea Farm 223
La Brume dans mes lunettes......175
La Tetería 201
Lake Agnes Tea House............165
Lao She Teahouse 18

Latitude at Banyan Tree Anji 10
Le Luminarium 123
Le Menzeh at La Mamounia.......227
Le Nélie........................130
Le Thé des Muses 140
Leman Tea Room 87
Les Palétuviers................. 233
Mackintosh at the Willow 94
Madulkelle Tea & Eco Lodge 44
Mandarin Oriental
  Qianmen Beijing 19
Mariage Frères..................131
Matea Aromas y Sabores 157
Melez Tea Lab 102
MingCha Tea House 40
Monsoon Tea Wat Ket.............27
Mount Nelson, a Belmond Hotel ..219
Moychay 74
Muthaiga Tea Company.......... 228
Ostfriesisches Teemuseum 125
Osulloc Tea Museum 42
Oxi Tea Room 242
Pages & Sips....................93
Palm Court at The Langham.......118
Paper & Tea..................... 84
Petersham Nurseries Teahouse 111
Pink Velvet 79
Postcard Teas 113
Raju Ki Chai 54
Rangoon Tea House 73
Royal Deck Tearoom............. 92
Rumi Cafe.......................215
Russian Tea Time 158
Same Fusy......................145
Sengan-en Matcha Café (Saryo)....43
Seven Cups Fine Chinese Teas 206
Shaman Tearoom 49
Silk Road Tea House.............23
Sindhorn Kempinski
  Hotel Bangkok 13
Ski Portillo 207
Smith Teamaker................. 192
Socha 68
Sofitel Legend Old
  Cataract Hotel................ 216
Stargazing Tea Houses...........22
Steep La........................167
Strangers' Restaurant........... 250
T.nomad 57
T9 Premium tea..................59
Tadshikische Teestube 86
Tania's Teahouse 221
Tarihi Çınaraltı 105
Té Company 186
Tea at Shiloh.................. 168
Tea Bar by Nepal Tea Collective.... 48
Tea Chapter 62
Cafe Tea Trunk 31
Teapots 124
Tebella Tea Company 202
Tējo Tea House.................136
Tell Camellia 41
Templo Té......................150
The Atrium Tea Lounge
  at Al Bustan Palace 214

The French Room
  at The Adolphus 160
The Gallery at Sketch 114
The Palm Court
  at The Oyster Box............. 236
The Pump Room 82
The Random Tea Room 191
The Secret Garden Tea Company...210
The Shinmonzen..................51
The Tea House on Los Rios.......197
The Tea Room
  from Blossom Kochhar..........29
The Tea Rooms 1892 243
Théhuone 96
Thưởng Trà.....................33
TĪNG at The Shard 119
To Søstre 126
To Tsai 80
Twinings – The Strand..........122
Ty Gwyn 164
Wah Tea Estate 47
Wall & Keogh 91
Wan Ling Tea House............. 60
White Rabbit Gallery Tea House ...251
Windermere Estate...............55
Woods Bali 12
Yam'tcha 134
Yaoyue Teahouse.................65
Zealong Tea Room............... 239

© Photos

Tea house 01: Banyan Tree Hotels & Resorts / Tea house 02: Woods Bali / Tea house 03: Kempinski Hotels / Tea house 04: Ksana Matcha / Tea house 05: Aman Hotels / Tea house 06: zhaojiankang, iStock / Tea house 07: Mandarin Oriental Qianmen, Beijing / Tea house 08: Fumio Araki, Moriyuki Ochiai Architects / Tea house 09: Silk Road Tea House / Tea house 10: plej92, iStock / Tea house 11: Araksa Tea / Tea house 12: William Persson for Monteaco / Tea house 13: Glenburn Tea Estate / Tea house 14: The Tea Room / Tea house 15: Cafe Tea Trunk / Tea house 16: Ken Seet for Four Seasons / Tea house 17: Thưởng Trà / Tea house 18: Ceylon Tea Trails / Tea house 19: Green Ginkgo Tea / Tea house 20: MingCha Tea House / Tea house 21: Tell Camellia / Tea house 22: Osulloc Tea Museum / Tea house 23: Sengan-en Matcha Café (Saryo) / Tea house 24: Madulkelle Hotel / Tea house 25: Wah Tea Estate / Tea house 26: Nepal Tea Collective / Tea house 27: courtesy of the artist / Tea house 28: Ippodo Tea / Tea house 29: The Shinmonzen / Tea house 30: Dev Sanghvi / Tea house 31: Windermere Estate / Tea house 32: 2014 Sugimoto Studio – Benesse / Tea house 33: Kim Sanghee & Kim Jongwon / Tea house 34: T9 Premium Tea / Tea house 35: Linfeng Li / Tea house 36: Tea Chapter / Tea house 37: Moment Capsule Photography, iStock / Tea house 38: KC/YaoYue Teahouse / Tea house 39: Jugetsudo Ginza Kabukiza / Tea house 40: Shuhei Tonami / Tea house 41: Jonathan Leijonhufvud, Norm Architects / Tea house 42: Rangoon Tea House / Tea house 43: Moychay / Tea house 44: Pink Velvet / Tea house 45: To Tsai / Tea house 46: Mariana Stankevych / Tea house 47: Searcys / Tea house 48: Visit Berlin / Tea house 49: Schnepp Renou for Paper & Tea / Tea house 50: Visit Berlin / Tea house 51: Leman Tea House / Tea house 52: Rasmus Rothman-Pedersen for A.C. Perch's Tea Room / Tea house 53: Mireia Avila (Comboi Creative Agency) for Wall & Keogh / Tea house 54: Helen Pugh Photography for The Royal Yacht Britannia / Tea house 55: Pages & Sips / Tea house 56: claudiodivizia, iStock / Tea house 57: travellinglight, iStock / Tea house 58: Justus Hirvi / Tea house 59: Cha'ya Moda / Tea house 60: Burak Teoman for Dem Moda / Tea house 61: Melez Tea Lab / Tea house 62: Tarihi Çinaraltı / Tea house 63: chaiiwala / Tea house 64: Olivia Lower for Housel Bay / Tea house 65: Claridge's / Tea house 66: Fortnum & Mason / Tea house 67: Andrew Montgomery for Petersham Nurseries Teahouse / Tea house 68: Postcard Teas / Tea house 69: Rob Whitrow / Tea house 70: The Langham / Tea house 71: Shangri-La / Tea house 72: krblokhin, iStock / Tea house 73: Le Luminarium / Tea house 74: Teapots Madrid / Tea house 75: Ostfriesisches Teemuseum Norden / Tea house 76: Francisco Nogueira for Sommerro / Tea house 77: Betjeman & Barton / Tea house 78: Bontemps / Tea house 79: Culturespaces, Nicolas Héron / Tea house 80: Mariage Frères / Tea house 81: Edouard Caupeil for yam'Tcha / Tea house 82: Dobrá čajovna / Tea house 83: Tejo Tea House / Tea house 84: Richard Billington / Tea house 85: Emma Shevtzoff, Svenskt Tenn / Tea house 86: Le Thé des Muses / Tea house 87: Raphaël Drommelschlager / Tea house 88: Haas&Haas / Tea house 89: Same Fusy / Tea house 90: Sprüngli / Tea house 91: Just Add Honey Tea Company / Tea house 92: Templo Té / Tea house 93: Michael Blanchard Photography for Boston Tea Party Ships & Museum / Tea house 94: Rory Martinelli / Tea house 95: SENAC / Tea house 96: Matea Aromas y Sabores / Tea house 97: Andrii Ivanchenko / Tea house 98: The Adolphus / Tea house 99: PleyadesFilms for Ty Gwyn / Tea house 100: Goofy79, iStock / Tea house 101: Steep LA / Tea house 102: Brittany Brooks, Jer Aquino, Tea at Shiloh / Tea house 103: Casa Tassel / Tea house 104: Jojo Tea / Tea house 105: Daniel Francis Haber / Tea house 106: La Brume dans mes lunettes / Tea house 107: Bottom of the Cup / Tea house 108: Dane Tashima / Tea house 109: Cha-An Teahouse, T.I.C. Restaurant Group / Tea house 110: Peter Peirce, Harney & Sons / Tea house 111: Johnny Fogg, Té Company / Tea house 112: Lauren Adams / Tea house 113: Richard W. Gretzinger / Tea house 114: Ty & Chey LLC, Steven Smith Teamaker / Tea house 115: Shot by Cerqueira, iStock / Tea house 116: Imperial Tea Court / Tea house 117: f8grapher, iStock / Tea house 118: @satginstudio (p. 197), Jeremy Kneisly (p. 198-199) / Tea house 119: Patricio Hurtado / Tea house 120: TeBella, Taylor Prater & Oxford Exchange / Tea house 121: Seven Cups Fine Chinese Teas / Tea house 122: Pia Vergara, Tamara Susa for Ski Portillo / Tea house 123: The Secret Garden Tea Company / Tea house 124: Boucan Media / Tea house 125: Inara Camp / Tea house 126: Marriott International / Tea house 127: Mahdi Albaz for Rumi Café / Tea house 128: Sofitel / Tea house 129: Groupe Saint Aubin / Tea house 130: Emily_M_Wilson, iStock / Tea house 131: Micky Hoyle for Belmond Hotel / Tea house 132: Carmien Tea / Tea house 133: Tania's Teahouse in partnership with @designcollectus taken by @gibsterg / Tea house 134: Peter Ndung'u for Kiambethu Tea Farm / Tea house 135: Café Guerrab / Tea house 136: La Mamounia / Tea house 137: Muthaiga Tea Company / Tea house 138: Tourist office / Tea house 139: Satemwa Tea Estates by Annette Kay – Malawi / 140: Stevie Mann / Tea house 141: Red Carnation Hotels / Tea house 142: Chapter Book & Tea Shop / Tea house 143: Zealong Tea Estate / Tea house 144: Oxi Tea Room / Tea house 145: The Tea Rooms 1892, Block Arcade / Tea house 146: Shot by Thom / Tea house 147: The Star Sydney / Tea house 148: Gunners Barracks – Grand Pacific Group / Tea house 149: Anson Smart / Tea house 150: David Roche, image courtesy of the White Rabbit Gallery

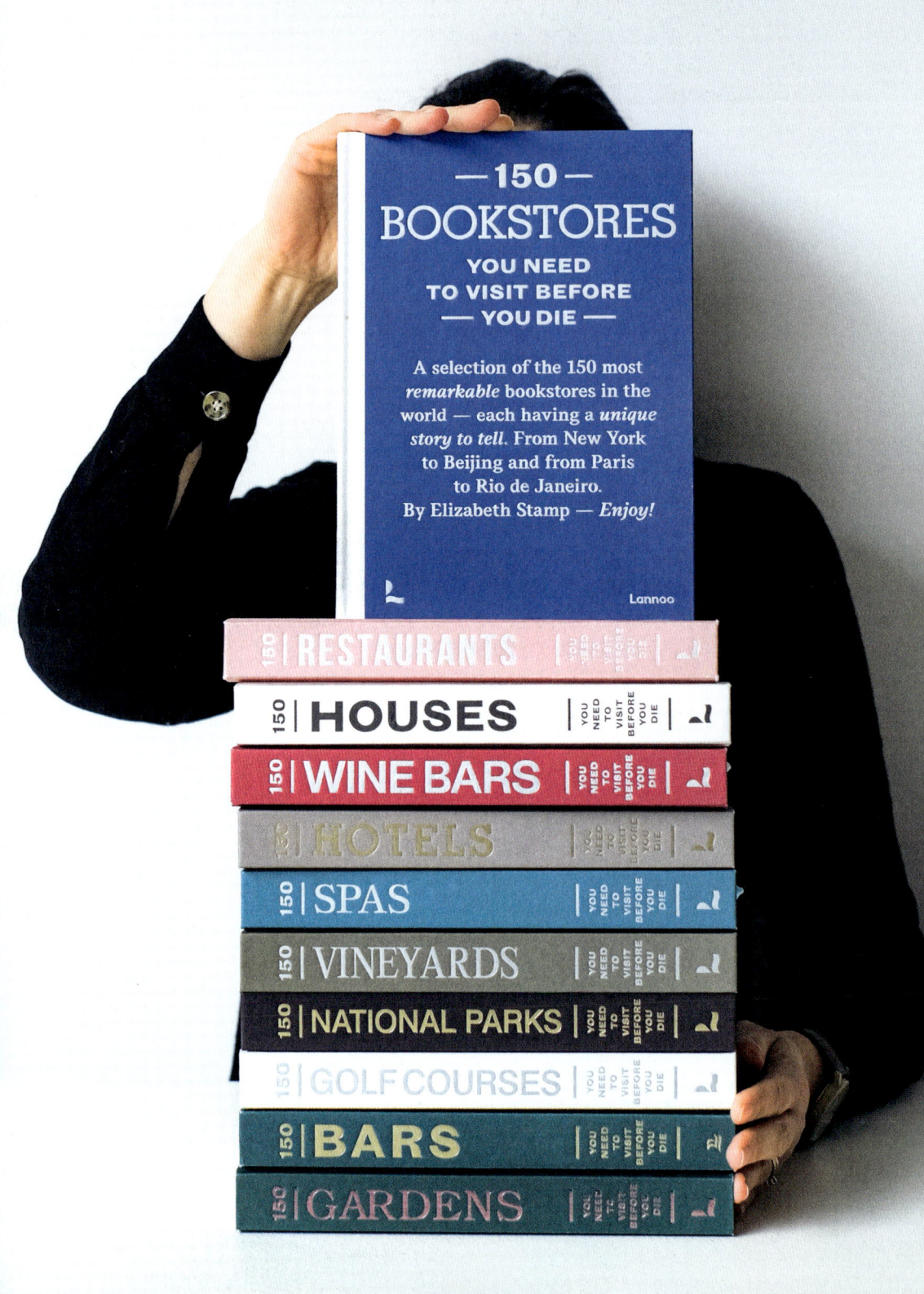

—150— BOOKSTORES

YOU NEED TO VISIT BEFORE —YOU DIE—

A selection of the 150 most *remarkable* bookstores in the world — each having a *unique story to tell*. From New York to Beijing and from Paris to Rio de Janeiro.
By Elizabeth Stamp — *Enjoy!*

Lannoo

IN THE SAME
— SERIES —

150 National Parks You Need to Visit Before You Die
ISBN 978 94 014 1970 3

—

150 Spas You Need to Visit Before You Die
ISBN 978 94 014 9747 3

—

150 Vineyards You Need to Visit Before You Die
ISBN 978 94 014 8546 3

—

150 Bookstores You Need to Visit Before You Die
ISBN 978 94 014 8935 5

—

150 Gardens You Need to Visit Before You Die
ISBN 978 94 014 7929 5

—

150 Bars You Need to Visit Before You Die
ISBN 978 94 014 4912 0

—

150 Wine Bars You Need to Visit Before You Die
ISBN 978 94 014 8622 4

—

150 Houses You Need to Visit Before You Die
ISBN 978 94 014 6204 4

—

150 Golf Courses You Need to Visit Before You Die
ISBN 978 94 014 8195 3

—

150 Hotels You Need to Visit Before You Die
ISBN 978 94 014 5806 1

—

150 Restaurants You Need to Visit Before You Die
ISBN 978 94 014 9570 7

Texts
Léa Teuscher

Editing
Amy Haagsma

Book Design
ASB (Atelier Sven Beirnaert)

Typesetting
Keppie & Keppie

Back Cover Image
© Tea Chapter

Sign up for our newsletter with news about new and forthcoming publications on art, interior design, food & travel, photography and fashion as well as exclusive offers and events. If you have any questions or comments about the material in this book, please do not hesitate to contact our editorial team: art@lannoo.com

© Lannoo Publishers, Belgium, 2025
D/2025/45/32 - NUR 450/500
ISBN 978-90-209-2661-3

www.lannoo.com

All rights reserved. No part of this publication may be reproduced or transmitted in any form or by any means, electronic or mechanical, including photocopy, recording or any other information storage and retrieval system, without prior permission in writing from the publisher.

Every effort has been made to trace copyright holders. If, however, you feel that you have inadvertently been overlooked, please contact the publishers.